Deep Soul Cleansing

Passing on the Twelve Steps...

A Study of AA's Approved Literature

Albert Einstein wrote:
"Strange is our situation here upon earth. Each of us comes for a short visit, not knowing why, yet sometimes seeming to divine a purpose. From the standpoint of daily life, however, there is one thing I do know: that we are here for the sake of each other, above all, for those upon whose smile and well-being our own happiness depends, and also for the countless unknown souls with whose fate we are connected by a bond of sympathy. Many times a day I realise how much my own outer and inner life is built upon the labours of others, both living and dead, and how earnestly I must exert myself in order to give in return as much as I have received and am still receiving."
This agrees with our sentiments—exactly...

First Edition

44+ (0)208 740 8567
www.hppublishing.com
www.hpretreats.com

This edition published in the United Kingdom
ISBN 978-0-9556930-1-4

To Kay S. "The Redhead"
without whom my entry into the programme may never have
happened.

To Kathy F.
whose hand lead me to her husband George.

To George F.
my sponsor and friend of 40 years, who taught me most of what I
have learned in this programme.

To Shannon M. (my oldest daughter)
for her consistent love, with all my warts on display over the past 41
years. And for the artwork displayed on the cover and what has now
become my primary logo.

To **all** my children
(biological and step-children) even those that don't speak to me.

To my brother Bruce
to whom I owe a deep amend I will, I trust, one day be able to make
it. Once my best friend and who I pray to find and have back in my
life once again.

To my Sponsees
without whom I never would have written this stuff down (so I
wouldn't forget it) in hopes of helping save them from my mistakes.

Finally, to Sheelagh my wife
without whom I don't feel I would have survived my insanity over
the past 23 years to become again "happy, joyous and free."

And to so many others
who have helped me along the way, and that I have neglected
mentioning. I could not possibly list you all.

Our thanks and gratitude to Alcoholics Anonymous for the gift they have given to the world of the Twelve Steps. This volume has been compiled using quotes from 13 of AA's copyrighted books and from the experience in life, both in and out of Alcoholics Anonymous, of those working the "Programme," which we recognise as the Steps. This material has been reprinted for the ease and speed of study during a Pan-Fellowship Retreat.

WE STRONGLY SUGGEST THAT EACH INDIVIDUAL WISHING TO BETTER UNDERSTAND THE 12 STEPS DO AS WE HAVE DONE AND PURCHASE AND STUDY ALL THE BOOKS OF ALCOHOLICS ANONYMOUS:

Alcoholics Anonymous
The Twelve Steps and Twelve Traditions
As Bill Sees It
The Language of the Heart
Came to Believe
The Best of the Grapevine
Dr. Bob and the Good Oldtimers
Experience, Strength, and Hope
Pass it On—Bill Wilson and the AA Message
Daily Reflections
The Home Group: Heartbeat of AA
AA Comes of Age
Living Sober

ALL THAT WE HAVE ATTEMPTED TO DO IS, TO FIND, AND "PULL OUT," THE EXPERIENCE OF THE 12 STEPS FROM THE MANY LIVES OF THOSE WHO CONTRIBUTED TO THE 13 BOOKS.

In an attempt to honour and accent the lessons and information found in these texts we have often made **bold**, ***italicized***, and <u>**underlined**</u> these 1,000 quotes from that material. In a further attempt to keep the material true to its original writing the use of these quotes often causes this written material to switch personal pronoun. Often the writing will switch from first person, to second person, to third person and back again, all within the same paragraph. The text also changes gender rather frequently. It is our intention to increase our own and the reader's depth of understanding of the 12 Steps of Alcoholics Anonymous. It really is an amazing programme.

Quotes are printed from Alcoholics Anonymous material as mentioned above.

TABLE OF CONTENTS

TABLE OF CONTENTS

TABLE OF CONTENTS

Opening Prayer*

We are here to develop and maintain a conscious contact with a *Power Greater than Ourselves*. It has been said that where two or more are gathered together in the name of Good, there this Higher Power would be in the midst. We believe that It is here with us now. We believe this is something It would have us do, and that we have It's blessing.

We pledge our honesty, open mindedness, and willingness to work these Steps, searching our hearts and minds for weaknesses and errors, that we may be free.

We believe that within each of us there is a unique connection to God and that we are real partners with It in this business of living, *accepting our full responsibilities* and certain that the rewards are freedom and growth and happiness.

For this we are grateful. We ask at all times to be guided, as we maintain conscious contact with God, finding new ways of living our gratitude.

And so it is. Amen

*This opening prayer is taken from what was called the "Al-Anon Prayer" in Southern California. It is updated in contemporary language; the gender has been removed and it specifically refers to the "Steps."

PREFACE

*A*fter Bill Wilson wrote the "Twelve Steps and Twelve Traditions" and, "coincidentally," had come out of an 11 year depression during that following year. When he finished that book, he wrote, in a letter to a close friend, *"I think that many oldsters who have put our AA 'booze cure' to severe but successful tests still find they often lack emotional sobriety. Perhaps they will be the spearhead for the next major development in AA—the development of much more real maturity and balance (which is to say, humility) in our relations with ourselves, with our fellows, and with God."* [1]

"Bill was learning, starting with the revelation of some truths about himself, that alcoholic drinking may in some people mask deeper psychological and emotional disturbances. ...Coming to Bill through the vehicle of his own depression...to find healing for sober alcoholics for whom sobriety alone...was insufficient to provide a comfortable life." [2] *"The prescription he kept returning to: 'Part of the answer lies in a constant effort to practice all of the...Twelve Steps. Persistence will cause this to sink in and affect the unconscious from where the trouble stems."* [3]

It is our belief from close investigation into the writings already provided; Bill had already made the *"next major development"*; which is a continued and powerful *"emotional sobriety."* We believe that it is NOT a coincidence that Bill came out of that debilitating depression and gained emotional sobriety while making a deeper study of the 12 Steps. He had also found that *"the 'all or nothing' attitude is a most destructive one. It is best to begin with whatever the irreducible minimums of activity are."* [4] We further believe that this small effort may assist in the reader's quest for emotional sobriety. This writer certainly has made great progress, via that work, towards no longer being run by *"grave emotional and mental disorders."* [5]

It is our desire that as many people as possible realise the power and wisdom encapsulated in the Twelve Steps. *"Never before did so many notable clergymen proclaim how the...Twelve Steps could be used for almost any human problem."* [6] We have been using these methods for many years now. They have never failed to bring about relief for those of us who have looked deep within our souls to see our part in the creation of our life's problems. Our mental, emotional, psychological, and spiritual relief has been immense. We trust the student of the programme who chooses this path will find the same. We have discovered that we *can* choose to be ***"happy, joyous and free."*** [7]

The true sign that we have *real* sobriety, of the kind defined later as: ***"a peaceful, calm, contented, serene and well-balanced life"*** (page 36.6) to be how we live our lives outside "the rooms." If we are demonstrating anger in or out of meetings we have not truly gained the *Promises*. The ability to work the Programme in meetings and with those in the fellowship is easier than in our other Relationships, Family, and Work lives. The Buddhists call this cloistered virtue. It does not create a ***"bridge to normal living."***

The "bridge" **IS** the Programme. Our experience shows that, even when sober, without a strong, powerful Programme we become as crazy as we ever were; if we don't relapse or take a sojourn into other addictions. The use of this material was originally designed for use by alcoholics but as time has gone on there seems to have been the creation of a *Pan Fellowship*.[1] Here members have found that once one addiction was "handled" with the Steps another would rear its ugly head.

Many 12 Step Programmes have sprung up from the original, with ***"Very effective answers to problems other than freedom from alcohol"*** [8]   Before there were other programmes factions ***"have always been found through special purpose groups, some of them operating within AA and some on the outside."*** [9] Even the creation of AA's General Service Organisation (formally the Alcoholic Foundation) ***"...was not an AA group. Instead, it was a group of AAs and non-AAs who devoted themselves to a special task...*** (Also) ***club managements and their dues-paying members are seen as special purpose groups, not as AA groups.***

"The same thing has happened with drying-out places and "Twelfth Step houses" managed by AAs. We never think of these activities as AA groups. They are clearly seen as the functions of interested individuals who are doing helpful and often very valuable jobs." [10]

"It was thus proven that, as individuals, we can carry AA experience and ideas into any outside field whatever, provided that we guard anonymity and refuse to use the AA name for money-raising or publicity purposes." [11]

"There seems to be no reason why several AAs cannot join, if they wish, with a group of straight addicts to solve the alcohol

---

[1] Pan Fellowship means a group where all Twelve Step Fellowships are welcome to work the Steps on multiple problems.

and drug problem together. But, obviously, such a dual purpose group should not insist that it be called an AA group nor should it use the AA name in its title." [12] This is why we call ourselves *Pan Fellowship*.

"In AA, the group has strict limitations, but the individual has scarcely any. Remembering to observe the Traditions of anonymity and non-endorsement, the AA member can carry AA's message into every troubled area of this very troubled world." [13] This *Pan Fellowship* came about by "accident." When holding a retreat using this material it gradually expanded to assist other *"troubled"* souls *"of this very troubled world."* [14] Maybe this is a fellowship and a *"book which would try to deal with the whole problem of living"* [15] through the Steps. *"I think this AA will appeal to you, because it's psychologically sound and religiously sane."* [16] We have struggled with the whole idea of this work and after long investigation find nothing "wrong" in what we are doing, either in the Traditions or anywhere in the literature. We trust if anyone has a problem they will do as exhaustive an investigation as we have. You will find much of that research on these pages.

We agree that within the programme *"our chief responsibility to the newcomer is an adequate presentation of the programme. If he does nothing or argues, we do nothing but maintain our own sobriety. If he starts to move ahead, even a little, with an open mind, we then break our necks to help in every way we can."* [17] This is what we trust this material will help us do. *"Shall we reflect that the roads to recovery are many; that any story or theory of recovery from one who has trod the highway is bound to contain much truth."* [18] We believe you'll find this book and our workbook contain just that.

This material is not so much written as it is compiled. What we have done is to compile as many quotes from 13 books of the "approved" AA literature that we believe refer to, could apply to, or imply the principle of whichever of the Twelve Steps has been singled out. These quotes are then placed in what we believe is the Step to which they apply. We agree with what was said by *"Bill W ...in a 1954 letter... 'The story section of the Big Book is far more important than most of us think."* [19] When choosing stories for the fourth Edition *"the subcommittee was mindful of Bill W's observation that 'the audience for the book is people who are coming...now. Those who are here already heard our stories.'"* [20] This material is the voice of a great many members from a great many sources. And the stories are *"most emphatically part of our common experience."* [21]

"We have also adopted procedures from a number of other sources, some very old, but all quite standard, well-known, and simple, if not easy." [22] In the *Twelve Step and Twelve Traditions* of that work it says, *"This present volume proposes to broaden and deepen the understanding of the Twelve Steps as first written in the earlier work (Alcoholics Anonymous)."* [23] Our goal is to organise all the previous works into the coherent and universally useful tool that they can be.

We don't have all the answers, *"Consequently, the full individual liberty to practice any creed or principle or therapy whatever should be a first consideration for us all. Let us not, therefore, pressure anyone with our individual or even our collective views. Let us instead accord each other the respect and love that is due to every human being as he tries to make his way toward the light. Let us always try to be inclusive rather than exclusive..."* [24]

With all the other Twelve Step Fellowships now, it is truly a wonderful thing. We no longer have to feel about those we see suffering outside the programme, *"You poor guy. I feel so sorry for you. You're not an alcoholic. You can never know the pure joy of recovering within the Fellowship..."* [25] Today there seems to be a "nut for every bolt" or maybe a programme for every nut?

When the book, "Twelve Steps and Twelve Traditions," was published for the first time *"Bill wrote: 'At first, I was dubious whether anyone would care for it, save Oldtimers who had begun to run into life's lumps in other areas."* [26] We feel much the same about this material, it takes about as deep a look at the Steps, and makes as wide an application, as we are aware of at this time. Whether many will want to make the kind of commitment, required to do this work, remains to be seen.

Though this book is often used on a kind of "crash course" type weekend, the purpose of this interpretation is to aid those working with others to quickly help them work out an acceptable daily schedule of a 12 Step way of life. This subject matter is founded on basic information from the book *Alcoholics Anonymous, Twelve Steps and Twelve Traditions* and other 12 Step and spiritual literature, where we learn that *"alcohol (or any addiction) is no respecter of economic status, social and business standing, or intelligence."* [27]

Albert Einstein once said, *"You cannot solve a problem on the level of the problem."* That is what this material and the 12 Step programme originating in Alcoholics Anonymous is trying to bring us—a solution. All other information is based on practical experience from the lives of fellow addicts. They have found peace of mind and contented sanity and sobriety by the planned way of spiritual life set forth originally in the AA literature.

Our Programmes are not accountable to any organised religion, medicine, or psychology. We have, however, drawn therapeutic practices from each of these disciplines, moulding them into a "design for living." Spiritual concepts must be embraced, but these do not involve organised religion. Although we must believe in a Higher Power, it is our privilege to interpret it according to our own understanding. The only barriers to working a successful programme are ignorance of our illness, reservations, indifference, dishonesty, self-will, and brain damage.

We must acquire honesty, humility and service and eliminate self-centredness to keep our peace and sobriety. For those who are willing to accept the 12 Step Programme as a means of recovery from Alcoholism or any other addiction, we recommend a close study of the books **"Alcoholics Anonymous (...the Big Book (...members' fond nickname for this volume))"** [28] and the *Twelve Steps and Twelve Traditions*. Don't just read them; study them *repeatedly*. These books were written by addicts for addicts and are based on the trials and experience of our members. Each Edition of the "Big Book" has updated experience of current members with contemporary problems. They have worked out a programme that has proved to be sound and effective in the lives of millions of alcoholics and others.

By using these as our textbooks, regularly attending 12 Step meetings and referring to this guide we will interpret the Twelve Steps as we progress. We will create a strong foundation upon which we can rebuild our lives.

It is our intention to use the words "our addiction" instead of alcohol whenever possible throughout this text; with the understanding that once we have quit our primary addiction we find that we have many others that pop up. Our experience shows that the programme of these Twelve Steps works no matter what the "addiction." *We also suggest the definition of addiction as, "anything that we do that we cannot seem to stop doing on our own steam."* This would include things like overeating, smoking, gambling, co-dependence, worrying, etc, not forgetting sexual behaviour, anger or rage and many other things.

The books in the "approved literature" were composed in a period when literature was written in what many see as the prejudicial style of a male dominated society. It is our intention that everything that is not quoted from those writings shall be written with a female subject in order to compensate. We hope that no one will take offence to this style of writing. However, if you do, maybe you will be able to translate those feelings to an understanding of how women have felt for centuries. It is our further intent to **bold italics** all quotes from these books so that they can be easily and immediately identified, with the exact page and paragraph at the end of this work.

"If you have decided you want what we have and are willing to go to any length to get it—then you are ready to take certain steps." [29] "Hitting bottom" is the trick. ***"One definition of a bottom is the point when the last thing you lost or the next thing you are about to lose is more important to you than booze. That point is different for everybody, and some of us die before we get there."*** [30] This cannot be taken lightly. We can decide that we have had enough and believe as did the writer of the story *"**Grounded"*** that, ***"With nothing left, I dedicated myself to learning about recovery. I fervently believed that the key to my sobriety, and hence my survival lay in the power of all I was being taught, and I spent no idle moments..."*** [31]

When you are ready to do anything suggested, going "to any lengths," then you are ready to work the Steps. *Many are not ready until they have suffered greatly. Others may never be ready.* The spiritual path laid out in the pages of *Alcoholics Anonymous* and the *Twelve Steps and Twelve Traditions* is available to all spiritual beliefs. ***"Clergyman of practically every denomination has given AA their blessing."*** [32]

The programme ***"can be achieved in any walk of life...because the achievement is not ours but God's. ...There is no situation too difficult, none too desperate, no unhappiness too great to be overcome in this great fellowship..."*** [33] and its many Twelve Step offspring.

As is said at the end of many meetings after the closing prayer, this programme *"Works if you work it. So, work it you're worth it!"* ***"With the tools and guideposts of Alcoholics Anonymous, we can learn a little of this precious gift—our gateway to human spirituality."*** [34] This swot up is an effort to express the line in the story ***"His Conscience"*** that says, ***"I am sure that I could not have in the past*** (time in the programme)*, **nor in the future enjoy my happy and contented sobriety unless I try to share it with others."*** [35]

Chapter 1

Lack of Power

Our Dilemma

LACK OF POWER IS OUR DILEMMA

" ***T****hey told me lack of power was my dilemma and that there is a solution."*[36] ***"Our human resources, as marshalled by the will, were not sufficient; they failed utterly. Lack of power, that was our dilemma. We had to find a power by which we could live, and it had to be a*** <u>***Power greater than ourselves***</u>***. Obviously. But where and how were we to find this power?"*[37] We find this "Lack of Power" in three major problem areas in our lives:

A. **LACK OF POWER—IN OUR ADDICTION** (whatever our primary, secondary (or otherwise) one is—alcohol, drugs, food, people, sex, etc.) It doesn't seem to matter what our primary addiction is as most of us find we quit one and another rears its ugly head. There have been many Groups grow out of the original Programme but there is really only one 12 Step Programme with many applications.

B. **LACK OF POWER—IN RELATIONSHIPS—**In Four Areas of Life— People, Places, Things, and most importantly, God. ***"My basic problem was a spiritual hunger."*[38]** Alcohol is called 'spirits' for a very good reason; it fills the hole where God goes. This hunger is fed by first dealing with our other relationships, which automatically heals our relationship with God. (1) ***"Nothing can be more demoralising than a clinging and abject dependence upon another human being."*[39]** (2) Then of course, ***"We have also seen men and women who go power-mad, who devote themselves to attempting to rule their fellows."*[40]** These people are just as dependent on their victims as those dependent ones. It has been said that "if one would scratch the surface of an addict we would find a co-dependant underneath." We think that before co-dependence was ever isolated as a problem it was well defined in the phrase (3) ***"a frightened human being determined to depend completely upon a stronger person for guidance and protection."*[41]** Within these three quotes one finds the co-dependent dance.

   1. People ***"It is from our twisted relations with family, friends, and society at large that many of us have suffered the most. We have been especially stupid and stubborn about them. The primary fact that we fail to recognise is our total inability to form a true partnership with another..."*[42] *"The hardest place to work this programme has been in my own home, with my children, and, finally, with*** (my wife)***.*[43]**

a. Sexual (spouses, lovers, sex, self, etc.) We seldom gave love freely; there was always a price tag. We never recognised that we can give love without expectation, **"love—which depends on the capacity of the giver, rather than the acts of the recipient..."**[44] This capacity, we found, was built through the Twelve Steps.

b. Other people—Family (children, parents, and siblings), friends, self, etc.

2. Places/Things (Cities, Countries, Cultures, etc.) **"What happens outside of me is far less important than what's happening inside. My being <u>does</u> attract my life; repeated work with each of the Twelve Steps generates changes within me that are reflected in improvements around me. Simple, but not always easy, the... programme gives me everything needed to become what I should be. ...There is no you or me or them. Everything is connected to everything else, and the salvation of each of us is linked to the salvation of all of us."**[45]

3. God (Spiritual bankruptcy) **"The words 'ye shall know the truth and the truth shall make you free' have echoed through time for two thousand years...I have only gradually come to view truth as the most beautiful and accessible aspect of Harmony, or It, or God... The world of truth is the world of what is...**

   "Truth is multifaceted, because it is reality. Your truth and mine are different, because we are different. Your beliefs are your truth, as mine are mine. When that is accepted, any cause for conflict is resolved. Neither of us is right or wrong... Today—now—is truth."[46]

In the Step Four we begin to learn how, **"We subjected each relation to this test—was it selfish or not?"**[47] **"This self-centred behaviour blocked a partnership relation with any one of those about us."**[48] We therefore begin using the tools that are essential to the healing process.

C. **LACK OF POWER—IN WORK/MONEY** (earning, debts, etc.)
"Never was there enough of what we thought we wanted. ...We lacked the perspective to see...that material satisfactions were not the purpose of living."[49]

1) *"The chief activator of our defects has been self-centred fear—primarily fears that we would lose something we already possessed or would fail to get something we demanded."*[50]

2) *"Although financial recovery is on the way for many of us, we found we could not place money first. For us, material well-being always followed spiritual progress; it never preceded."*[51] We will have more on this later in our discussion of Step 4.

What have we tried already to improve or fix these "Problem areas"? (E.g. churches, therapy, positive thinking, mind control, acupuncture, hypnosis, NLP, EST, Zen, etc.) Did any of these have lasting success? Is there anything we have left to try? Why don't they work? There certainly is nothing wrong with any of them. Many people use these techniques to great success. So, what's the problem?

Since we already know everything we know, and have tried everything we have, where do we go from here? We can't create new thoughts—stop for a moment and try to come up with a new idea to fix our dis-ease. **"Even a man with everything from the material standpoint, a man with tremendous pride and the will-power to function in all ordinary circumstances can...find himself as hopeless and helpless as the man who has a multitude of worries and troubles."**[52]

We all know how we want to be but we can't or don't, act on it. Why? Lack of Power is our dilemma. We only turn to God or a Higher Power if you prefer, when we have unbearable pain, pain over some want, weakness or failure. Only at those times when we have lost the battle of life, one more time, do we try God. The very ambition to change ourselves is in itself the problem. Where does the struggle lie? It is in our lack of acceptance of ourselves. Who or what is doing the struggling? The ego (the committee), that's who. But **we cannot trust the ego.** And what is this ego anyway? A definition that has brought relief too many of us who thought that the ego was some kind of entity, it is not, is that the ego is *simply a set of beliefs that defines the world in which we live.* These beliefs have convinced us that we need them—and not only that we *need* them, but that we **are** them.

First our ego (these beliefs) tells us to drink (or use whatever the latest manifestation of our addictive behaviour is)—we're restless irritable and discontented—so we drink or distract ourselves with our latest obsession. Just to take the edge off! But we can't stop after one and we get lost in it. The next day the committee is there with remorse, guilt and self-condemnation—our dear friend the ego. What a pal. According to Dr. Harry M. Tiebout, MD, a psychiatrist, the **"characteristic of the so-called typical alcoholic is a narcissistic, egocentric core, dominated by feelings of omnipotence..."**[53] In other words, we think we are God.

We each have to be able to see that **"I'd grown physically at the customary rate of speed, and I had acquired an average (or greater) amount of intellectual training in the intervening years, but there had been no emotional maturity at all. I realise now that this phase of my development had been arrested by my obsession with self, and my egocentricity had reached such proportions that adjusting to anything outside my personal control was impossible for me."**[54]

So, how do we change? How do we deal with our addiction, stop and stay stopped? How do we become a good spouse or mate? How can we be a good parent to our children? How do we become good employers or employees? How do we ever find and live "the good life"?

THE FOUR TRUTHS OF THE ADDICTED

It has been said that "the truth shall set us free." So what do we have to recognise about our many, varied addictions to gain this freedom?

1) Those of us practicing our disease have a life filled with **"pitiful and incomprehensible demoralisation."**[55]

2) **"Selfishness—self-centredness! That, we think, is the root of our troubles."**[56]

3) **"Above everything, we...must be rid of this selfishness. We must, or it kills us! <u>God makes this possible.</u>"**[57]

4) We must have a **"vital spiritual experience"**[58] if we hope to survive. <u>We receive God's help by working the 12 Steps.</u> We would not get this help unless we **"cleaned house so that the grace of God could enter us and expel the obsession."**[59]

Out of that first meeting between Bill and Dr. Bob we have one of the most powerful solutions to life's problems that have ever come along, **"Greater than the tread of mighty armies is an idea whose time has come"**—Victor Hugo.

The 12 Steps are certainly an **"idea whose time has come"** for it has given millions of people a solution to their addictions. Therefore, we have an answer to the first of our "three major problems." As for the second, our experience tells us that relationships are at the root of our problem, also resolved by the Steps. Finally we ask what about *money?* It seems that if we focus on our spiritual life that too is resolved within the programme.

The tools we use in our recovery are broadcast daily in 12 Step meetings. As stated earlier, it has been suggested to some of us to **"spend as much time in meetings as** (we) **had spent drinking."**[60] Going to meetings, putting our hand out to the newcomer, getting phone numbers and all the wonderful slogans are just a few of the tools of this programme. As this long time member puts it, **"I still have a sponsor and a home group today. I am a member of Alcoholics Anonymous in good standing. I learned how to be a good AA member by watching other good...members and doing what they do. I learned how to have a good marriage by watching people with good marriages and doing what they do. I learned how to be a good parent by watching good parents and doing what they do. And I finally have the freedom of believing that it is all right not to know."**[61]

So the solution to these three states of affair, the three major problems of our lives, is the Twelve Steps. This leads us to a Power greater than we are. But **"where and how were we to find this power?**

"Well, that's exactly what (the) **book** (Alcoholics Anonymous) **is about. Its main object is to enable you to find a Power greater than yourself which will solve your problem."**[62] **"Dr. Bob** (wrote)**, 'I have observed that those who follow the...programme with the greatest earnestness and zeal not only maintain sobriety but often acquire finer characteristics and attitudes as well.'"**[63] Our experience shows that we then gain Power in our lives. A connection with a Power Greater than ourselves is, not only *attained*, but *maintained* as well.

The most important question to ask ourselves at this point is "Are we willing to go to any lengths?" Because in order to follow the "Programme of Recovery" laid out on the following pages we will need all the willingness we can muster.

Chapter 2

The Twelve Steps

The Solution

THE SOLUTION

So, what is the solution to our powerlessness? *"Doctors have been notoriously unsuccessful in helping alcoholics. They have contributed fantastic amounts of time and work to our problem, but they aren't able, it seems, to arrest either your alcoholism or mine.*

"And the clergy have tried hard to help us, but we haven't been helped. And the psychiatrist has had thousands of couches and has put you and me on them many, many times, but he hasn't helped us very much, though he has tried hard; and we owe the clergy and the doctor and the psychiatrist a deep dept of gratitude, but they haven't helped our alcoholism, except in a rare few instances. But—Alcoholics Anonymous has helped.

"What is this power that AA possesses? This curative power? I don't know what it is. I suppose the doctor might say, 'This is psychosomatic medicine.' I suppose the psychiatrist might say, 'This is benevolent interpersonal relations.' I suppose others would say this is group psychotherapy.

"To me it's God."[64] We do *"not demand belief; Twelve Steps are only suggestions."*[65] However, a spiritual awakening is what the Steps are all about; the solution to our powerlessness and our addictions is in the Steps. *"I had to realise that if I did want sobriety, I had better do the Steps whether I liked them or not. Every time I ran into trouble, I ultimately found that I was resisting change."*[66]

The programme *"is not just a Project. (It) offers me an opportunity to improve the quality of my life...there is always a deeper and wider experience awaiting me."*[67] *"I cannot go back and make a brand-new start. But...I can start from now and make a brand-new end."*[68] Many of us have said, *"If I only had it all to do over again."* Well, we believe that this programme gives us that opportunity. *"Fellowship and activity kept me coming back long enough to work the Twelve Steps."*[69]

"The Twelve Steps... are not crammed down anybody's throat... Yet we powerfully unite around them because the truth they contain has saved our lives, has opened the door to a new world. Our experience tells us these universal truths work"[70] the truths that set us free. Even so, when talking with a newcomer about checking into the hospital, Dr. Bob *"told me that unless I was sincere...I would be wasting his time and mine and also money in doing this."*[71]

Most of us have been fortunate enough to experience in early sobriety the "Pink Cloud" syndrome. The pink cloud is not earned through Step work; it is a period of peace and comfort that gives us the time to work through the Steps for the first time. What we will learn is a life-long way of maintaining that, so called, Pink Cloud. Without Step work, *"sooner of later the pink cloud stage wears off and things go disappointingly dull. We begin to think that AA doesn't pay off after all. We become puzzled and discouraged."*[72] Unfortunately, unlike those in the Big Book who were pressed through the Steps for the first time in a few days, most of us don't take advantage of this time by doing the same. We begin a habit of *"resting on our laurels"* and coasting until we are suddenly, or not so suddenly, in great pain, later discussed as the *"touch stone to all spiritual growth." "There are few absolutes inherent in the Twelve Steps. Most Steps are open to interpretation, based on the experience and outlook of the individual.*

"Consequently, the individual is free to start the Steps at whatever point he can, or will"[73] whenever they want to be free. One member *"Told* (Dr. Bob) *it sounded like self-hypnotism to me and he said what of it...didn't care if it was yoga-ism, self-hypnotism, or anything else...four of them were well."*[74]

Many of us come to the programme; hear the slogan *"Don't Drink... Go to Meetings"* and think that is all there is to it. However, most of us have had to learn the hard way that meetings are not enough. It is said that *"the feeling of having shared in a common peril is* (only) *one element in the powerful cement which binds us. But that in itself would never have held us together as we are now joined."*[75] There is another slogan that brings us properly into the process. That slogan is, *"Get a Sponsor... Work the Steps."* Those of us that are *"happy, joyous and free"*[76] have learned that the path begins with *"working the Steps... I embraced them as the rungs on the ladder to salvation."*[77]

"The tools of sobriety and recovery... are there for me to use in all aspects of my life, and all I ever need is the willingness to do what is in front of me."[78] Our experience now shows that the distinction—*"there are those too, who have grave emotional, and mental disorders, but many of them do recover if they have the capacity to be honest"*[79] is profoundly true. Emotional and mental disorders are also often resolved using these powerful tools.

This Twelve Step programme *"is no success story in the ordinary sense of the word. It is a story of suffering transmuted, under grace, into spiritual progress."*[80]

THE JOURNEY OF A LIFETIME...

There are **"Twelve Steps for recovery** (from many of life's problems) **and for spiritual growth... We simply say that you will have to practice** (the) **principles because you want them for yourself— not because we insist. The choices are yours; this is your charter of freedom..."**[81] a chance for a new life. The quest for a **"Spiritual Awakening"**—the finding of a personal relationship with a **"Power greater than ourselves"** and coming in conscious contact with that Power on a daily basis. The programme has eliminated more suffering than all the drugs, alcohol and other obsessions used by all the addicts who used for that same end.

"How fortunate we...are to have a malady which compels us to seek recovery through the spiritual."[82] The elimination of our suffering has been the goal of many of us. Now we actually have a method that is tried and tested. It works. **"It took the help, understanding, and wonderful companionship that were given so freely by my ex-alkie friends—this and the programme of recovery embodied in the Twelve Steps."**[83]

"Although the world is full of suffering, it is also full of the overcoming of it."—Helen Keller.

In Neuro-Linguistic Programming (NLP), a cognitive therapeutic approach to "fixing the mind" and eliminating of suffering, there are said to be four stages in growth. In the "cognitive approach" the practitioner helps "teach" the patient a better way to think, by replacing old thought patterns with new more useful ones. They each are equally relevant to 12 Step recovery.

FOUR STAGES OF GROWTH:

1) UNCONSCIOUS INCOMPETENCE—this is the state we call denial. We are in this state when we arrive at the programme. When we walk through the doors of our first 12 Step meeting, we usually don't have any idea that we can't run our lives.

2) CONSCIOUS INCOMPETENCE—comes with the solid foundation established in the First Step. At this stage we realise we are hopelessly in trouble—without help.

3) CONSCIOUS COMPETENCE—comes with a working knowledge of the Programme of Recovery and the process of growth and change within it. Usually we reach this after completing the first Nine Steps.

4) UNCONSCIOUS COMPETENCE—finally, that area of gradual growth, for which we will continue working towards for the rest of our lives, and others, will see long before we do. When they come up to us and say, "I remember you, when... Do you have any idea how much you have changed?"

These stages fit perfectly with the unfolding progress of spiritual growth to a transformed state of *being*. This *State of Being* is living in <u>conscious contact</u> with a *Power greater than ourselves,* on a daily basis. This transformation takes place with the continuous conscious working of the Twelve Steps daily. Today, right now! ***"The Oxford Groups...threw heavy emphasis on personal work, one member with another. (The) Twelfth Step had its origin in that vital practice. The moral backbone of the 'O.G.' was absolute honesty, absolute purity, absolute unselfishness, and absolute love. They also practiced a type of confession, which they called 'sharing'; the making of amends for harms done they called 'restitution.' They believed deeply in their 'quiet time,' a meditation practiced by groups and individuals alike, in which the guidance of God was sought for every detail of living, great and small. "[84]***

Before the Big Book was written there were only Six Steps. The First Step both then and now was inspired by ***"Dr. Silkworth. It was he who was soon to contribute a very great idea without which AA could never have succeeded. For years he had been proclaiming alcoholism an illness, an obsession of the mind coupled with an allergy of the body... Held in the hands of one alcoholic talking to the next, this double-edged truth was a sledgehammer which could shatter the tough...ego at depth and lay him wide open to the grace of God."[85]*** Back then the Steps were completed for the first time in a matter of days—not weeks—not months—not years, but days. In fact most newcomers were not even allowed at a meeting till after they worked through these Steps.

"The Original Six Steps were (and current likeness is as follows)***:***

1. ***Complete deflation*** (Step 1)
2. ***Dependence and Guidance from a Higher Power*** (Steps 2, 3 & 11)
3. ***Moral Inventory*** (Step 4)
4. ***Confession*** (Step 5—which in practise also covered Step 6 & 7)
5. ***Restitution*** (Steps 8 & 9)
6. ***Continued Work with other Alcoholics"*** (Step 12) [86]

Step 10 was added as it was realised that this was not a one-time job and that we needed to enhance the first nine proposals.

Bill wrote on the history of the Twelve Steps: **"Knowing the...ability to rationalise, something airtight would have to be written... I split the word-of-mouth programme up into smaller pieces, meanwhile enlarging its scope considerably."**[87] After much deliberation with the other members at the time, we had the Steps we now use. To our relief and chagrin the **"Twelve Steps deflate ego."**[88]

What we are looking for is a spiritual experience similar to what William James had described in his book *Varieties of Religious Experience*. **"Not only, he said, could spiritual experiences make people saner, they could transform men and women so that they could do, feel, and believe what had hitherto been impossible to them... In most of the cases described,** (in his book) **those who had been transformed were hopeless people. In some controlling area of their lives they had met absolute defeat..."**[89] Something many of us could use in many areas of life! This makes our programme perfect for continued sobriety and happiness.

As we work today's first Nine Steps, it is our experience that our *Conscious Awareness* moves through these three stages: Unconscious Incompetence, which is simply not knowing that we are unable to find a solution on our own for our Addictions, our Relationship troubles and our Work/Money problems; Conscious Incompetence, which simply means knowing that we are unable to fix these things ourselves; Conscious Competence, which is finding a solution and a set of tools to life's problems via the use of the 12 Steps and the freedom within a **"dependence on a Power greater than ourselves."** By now we should all know what this member did: **"the only hope for me was the Twelve Steps."**[90]

"The more we become willing to depend upon a higher Power, the more independent we actually are. Therefore, dependence, as AA practises it, is really a means of gaining true independence of the spirit."[91] Freedom! **"I believe that the... programme is simply the will of God being put to practical, everyday use."**[92]

WHERE WE'RE GIVEN "THE PROMISES"— THE NINTH STEP.

"If we are painstaking about this phase of our development, we will be amazed before we are half way through. We are going to know a new freedom and a new happiness. We will not regret the past nor wish to shut the door on it. We will comprehend the word serenity and we will know peace. No matter how far down the scale we have gone, we will see how our experience can benefit others. That feeling of uselessness

and self-pity will disappear. We will lose interest in selfish things and gain interest in our fellows. Self-seeking will slip away. Our whole attitude and outlook upon life will change. Fear of people and of economic insecurity will leave us. We will intuitively know how to handle situations that used to baffle us. We will suddenly realise that God is doing for us what we could not do for ourselves.

"Are these extravagant promises? We think not. They are being fulfilled among us – sometimes quickly, sometimes slowly. They will always materialise if we work for them."[93]

Then, for the maintenance of these "Promises"; we spend the rest of our life working ALL the Steps through Steps Ten, Eleven and Twelve. This moves us closer to Unconscious Competence, where life gets easier and easier. We used our many addictions *"mostly to kill pain of one kind or another—physical or emotional or psychic."*[94] The following review of the Twelve Steps is meant to help in a solid understanding of the programme and bring about a "Spiritual Experience." However, before we even get to Step One our book tells us that *"The only requirement for membership is an __honest desire to stop...__"*[95] using our drug of choice. The implication is that without that honest desire to stop our addictive behaviour there will be little willingness to do the work ahead.

"Self-pity is one of the most unhappy and consuming defects that we know. It is a bar to all spiritual progress and can cut off all effective communication with our fellows because of its inordinate demands for attention and sympathy. It is a maudlin form of martyrdom, which we can ill afford.

"The remedy? Well, let's have a hard look at ourselves, and a still harder one at... (the) *Twelve Steps to recovery. When we see how many...* (Others) *have used the Steps to transcend great pain and adversity; we shall be inspired to try these life-giving principles for ourselves."*[96]

"Rarely have we seen a person fail who has thoroughly followed our path. Those who do not recover are people who cannot or will not completely give themselves to this simple programme...

"If you have decided you want what we have and are willing to go to any lengths to get it—then you are ready to take certain Steps.

"At some of these we balked. We thought we could find an easier, softer way. But we could not. With all the earnestness at our command, we beg of you to be fearless and thorough

16

from the very start. Some of us have tried to hold on to our old ideas and the result was nil until we let go absolutely."[97]

These Steps are today used for many problems and we know of little failure when they are followed diligently. *"Many people, non-alcoholics, report that as a result of the practice of...* (the) *Twelve Steps, they have been able to meet other difficulties of life. They think that the Twelve Steps can mean more than sobriety for problem drinkers. They see in them a way to happy and effective living for many, alcoholic or not."*[98] From our own experience we agree absolutely. An obsession is an obsession; and an addiction is an addiction.

We are reminded that, *"we realise we know only a little. God will constantly disclose more to you and to us."*[99] We are learning all the time. *"Whereas the Big Book...radiates Bill's joy and gratitude at having finally found a way to stay sober, the 'Twelve and Twelve' reflects an entirely different mood. ...When Bill wrote the second book, he...was forced to confront the emotional and spiritual demons that remain 'stranded' in the...psyche when the high tide of active alcoholism recedes...*

"During Bill's 15 sober years (at the time of writing)*, he had had ample opportunity to become intimately acquainted with some of the unproductive and often negative attitudes and traits that are frequently part of the disease...continuing into sobriety. By now, he knew well that...alcoholics have other problems, for which they must find solutions if they are to live comfortably...for the Steps apply precisely to the problems common to so many...after they stop..."*[100]

The more we study the Twelve Steps, written when Bill was *"barely 'dry behind the ears'...* (the more we see that they) *apply precisely to the problems common to so many."*[101] We have found few problems in life that do not benefit from the deep soul cleansing within the Twelve Step process. *"Dr. Bob...said there was the hard way and the easy way. The hard way was just by going to meetings."*[102] Living life with meetings but without the Steps is the hard way. Not that meetings aren't important; they are. But they just are not the Steps to freedom.

"For the Grapevine (Dr. Bob) *...wrote: 'As finally expressed and offered, they (the Twelve Steps) are simple in language, plain in meaning. ...It has become increasingly clear that the degree of harmonious living which we achieve is in direct ratio to our earnest attempt to follow them literally under divine guidance to the best of our ability."*[103] *"Let me try the...way of the Steps,*

the way of health and joy. The Steps are the specific medicine for the thing that's wrong (or right—it doesn't matter) with me..."[104]

"THE STEPS ARE THE PROGRAMME

"The word 'HEAL' means 'make whole.' The aim... is to help a shattered, fragmented human being find wholeness, direction, and freedom... Our use of the Twelve Steps gradually moves into growing freedom from fear, depression, anxiety, and the overwhelming self-concern that characterised life before [105] the programme.

"Failure to work all of the Steps will eventually create problems..."[106]

"I worked...in Thule, Greenland, and Barrow, Alaska. I got to know some of the Eskimos in Thule and Barrow and spent some time studying their cultures... They originally saw everything as a unity. Their families, friends, and work, the animals, the land, the sea, and God as they understood (God) *were all one."*[107]

"Each Step of the twelve is connected to every other Step, and they work as a unity... We hear that these are 'suggested' Steps. What's suggested is a programme of Twelve Steps. Used honestly and thoroughly, they provide precise results.

"Certainly it's our privilege to use part of them, none of them, or all of them."[108] Nevertheless, *"Sobriety and a plan for living that produces a personality change and a spiritual awakening are imperative. Through* (it)*, many receive the needed change and awakening just by trying to live by* (their) *principles and associating with* (the) *people. We do this by going to many...meetings with an open mind and a desire to live the good-feeling life without chemicals—liquid or otherwise.* [109]

"Through... (the programme)*, we can experience freedom from self. After all, it was self (you, me) that stood in our own way, that ran the show and ran ourselves into bankruptcy, and that hurt the ones we loved. All Twelve Steps... are designed to kill the old self (deflate the old ego) and build a new, free self."*[110] Or, as many of us now see it, uncover our free self, our Real Self.

Out of painful experience many of us have learned that *"A fragmented programme will leave me fragmented. Using part of the prescription produces inadequate results. 'Those who do not recover are people who cannot or will not completely give themselves to this simple programme..."*[111]

18

"The Twelve Steps... seemed insurmountable to me at first. But the older members... told me, 'Easy does it.'"[112]   We work the Programme one day at a time, one Step at a time.

"AN EASIER, SOFTER WAY"

The Steps **are** the easier, softer way.   *"At last, I came to the conclusion that there was 'an easier, softer way'—easier than anything I had tried for myself before AA; I came to believe."*[113] Avoidance of the process of the Steps is never found to be the 'easier, softer way.' It just seems to drag out the inevitable, though some of us will die trying to avoid them. And you might consider a definition of death as: <u>no worthwhile life</u>.

It was said earlier that the "pink cloud" that many of us experience in the early days can be and is intended to be maintained. At the end of the so called "Instruction" part of the "Big Book" it reads, *"...you will surely meet some of us as you trudge the Road of Happy Destiny."*[114] This is a very misunderstood phrase. This often seems to some of us as a drudge toward an unreachable goal. But if we dissect the phrase *"<u>trudge</u> the Road of Happy Destiny"* we find a different outcome. We looked up the word "trudge" in an American dictionary, since this was written in America by an American, and found this as one of the definitions of the word, *"trudge: to march with determination."* So instead of drudgery it's a determined march. A closer look at the words, *"the Road <u>of</u> Happy Destiny"*[115] makes it perfectly clear that it is the road that is our "Happy Destiny" not the destination. So, let us *"<u>trudge</u> the Road <u>of</u> Happy Destiny."*[116]

If the subsequent "Steps before the programme" is how life seems to be being lived today? Then maybe the *real* Twelve Steps that follow these could be a new way of life?

STEPS BEFORE THE PROGRAMME

Let's take a look at what life was like before our introduction to the power of the Steps.

1) We admitted we were powerless over nothing. We could manage our lives perfectly well thank you, and we could manage those of anyone else that would allow it.

2) Came to believe that there was no power greater than ourselves, and the rest of the world was insane.

3) Made a decision to have our loved ones and friends turn their wills and their lives over to our care.

4) Made a searching and fearless moral inventory of everyone we knew.

5) Admitted to the whole world at large the exact nature of their wrongs.

6) Were entirely ready to use our so called "character defects" at a moments notice.

7) When confronted with our "short comings"—in deep humiliation, we demanded that they be removed (until the next time we "needed" them).

8) Made a list of anyone who had ever harmed us and became willing to go to any lengths to get even with them all.

9) Got direct revenge on such people whenever possible except when to do so would cost us our own lives, or at the very least, a jail sentence.

10) Continued to take inventory of others, and when they were wrong promptly and repeatedly told them about it.

11) Sought through prayers of beseeching and negotiation to improve our unconscious desires in life; asking only for our will to be done and the power to carry that out.

12) Having had a complete physical, emotional and spiritual breakdown as a result of these Steps, we tried to blame it on others and to practice self-pity and desire sympathy in all our affairs.

(Author unknown—received over the internet)

THE REAL TWELVE STEPS

Let us try these instead... *"Here are the Steps we took, which are suggested as a programme of recovery:*

1) *We admitted we were powerless over* (our addiction)*—that our lives had become unmanageable.*

2) *Came to believe that a Power greater than ourselves could restore us to sanity.*

3) *Made a decision to turn our will and our lives over to the care of God as we understood* (God)*.*

4) *Made a searching and fearless moral inventory of ourselves.*

5) *Admitted to God, to ourselves, and to another human being the exact nature of our wrongs.*

6) *Were entirely ready to have God remove all these defects of character.*

7) *Humbly asked* (God) *to remove our shortcomings.*

8) *Made a list of all persons we had harmed, and became willing to make amends to them all.*

9) *Made direct amends to such people wherever possible, except when to do so would injure them or others.*

10) *Continued to take personal inventory and when we were wrong promptly admitted it.*

11) *Sought through prayer and meditation to improve our conscious contact with God as we understood* (God)*, praying only for knowledge of* (God's) *will for us and the power to carry that out.*

12) *Having had a spiritual awakening as the result of these Steps, we tried to carry this message to alcoholics, and to practice these principles in all our affairs."*[117]

The Twelve Steps are a *"marvellous way of life so simple in structure, so profound in practice."*[118]

Chapter 3

The Foundation

Defeat

STEP ONE

Worksheet for the First Half of Step One

"We admitted we were powerless over (our addiction)—..."[119]

This reading is to be done in preparation for our time together.

The "Big Book" *Alcoholics Anonymous*　　　Preface – Page 43

Twelve Steps and Twelve Traditions　　　Pages 21-24
(Read 21-22–daily)

Part One – Suggested work

NOTE: READ THE FOLLOWING CAREFULLY

Complete the following items giving **specific examples for each,** with dates, times and the people involved.　Please write **a paragraph rather than a sentence** for each example of your drinking/addictive behaviour.

1)　　Loss of control because of your drinking/addictive behaviour i.e. blackouts, overdoses, bingeing, ruined plans, etc.

2)　　Behaviour of a destructive nature.

3)　　Situations where you put yourself or others in danger and/or had accidents due to your addiction.

4)　　Attempts to control or stop your addiction.

5)　　Substitution of other addictive substances and/or behaviour.

6)　　Broken promises to stop or moderate your drinking/addiction made to yourself, family, friends and/or employers.

7)　　Examples of denial of addictions represented in my life.

8)　　What is the three fold nature of your dis-ease and what does that mean to you?

9)　　Do I truly feel hopeless without help?　And what does that look like?

STEP ONE

"We Admitted We Were Powerless Over (Our Addiction) **– That Our Lives Had Become Unmanageable."** [120]

"This simply means that all of us have to hit bottom and hit it hard and lastingly." [121] This is a difficult thing to do. That's why so many of us to which these Steps would be so powerful in helping with other "problems" find it so hard to admit defeat. We are all looking for freedom and we find that: **"The admission of powerlessness is the first Step in liberation."** [122] **"Only in complete acceptance of the utter defeat of my pride and ego could I begin to win."** [123]

When we first come to "the rooms" we have little or no idea that it **"is a spiritual programme and a spiritual way of life...** (We need the use of our) **full faculties as a human being to hear the message, to think about it, to review the effects of the past, to realise, to admit, and to accept. These processes are activities of the mind, which is part of the spirit."** [124]

STEP ONE—FIRST HALF

"We admitted we were powerless over (our addiction)...**"** [125]

A cry for help is an admission of "Powerlessness." Just the fact of turning up at meetings is part of that admission. However: **"We learned that we had to concede to our innermost selves that we were alcoholics. This is** (the first half of) **the first Step in recovery. The delusion that we were like other people, or presently may be, has to be smashed."** [126] **"At last, acceptance proved to be the key to my drinking problem."** [127]

The answer to our drinking problem begins with our acceptance of our disease. Then things begin to change. **"When I stopped living in the problem and began living in the answer, the problem went away. From that moment on, I have not had a single compulsion to drink...Until I could accept my alcoholism; I could not stay sober."** [128] **"I had to surrender and accept I was an alcoholic."** [129] The important attitude to start with is contained in a question asked of this member: **"My friend asked me if I really wanted to stop drinking, and if I did, would I do anything no matter what it was in order to?"** [130] The path ahead is a difficult one and without this kind of commitment we will think of a thousand excuses not to take it.

WHAT IS AN ADDICT?

"I learned the definition of a social drinker: someone who could (really) *take it or leave it."*[131] If we're alcoholics, *"that special relationship with alcohol will always be there, waiting to seduce me again. I can stay protected by continuing to be an active member..."*[132]

"It's not how much you drink; it's what drinking does to you."[133] Or one of our favourites: Can you guarantee your behaviour once you've taken a drink.

An addict is someone for whom this statement is true: that my addiction *"took me places I never meant to go."*[134] Whatever our programme however, *"The reason for a person's coming...is not important; any reason or even excuse will suffice."*[135] We can be sent by the courts, getting your spouse or a partner off your back, 'chasing a redhead,' or think someone will help get us off the streets or find us a job. Anything but believe we were alcoholics. Some of us have tried them all and somehow this wonderful programme has worked its magic.

"Despite most reports to the contrary, there is a growing recognition of certain common qualities which are regularly present in alcoholics... Characteristics of the so-called typical alcoholic is a narcissistic, egocentric core, dominated by feelings of omnipotence, intent on maintaining at all costs its inner integrity."[136]

ON STOPPING DRINKING (or any addiction)

"It's no great trick to stop drinking; the trick is to stay stopped."[137] And be happy. Use the telephone *"and call before you take a drink* (or use)*. If they don't answer, call someone else."*[138] We should never have our sobriety depend on any one person. There will always be a time when they either disappoint us or are simply unavailable.

THE THREE-FOLD NATURE OF THE PROBLEM

We must understand that this disease and any addiction has a three-fold nature,

PHYSICAL—once we have taken a drink there is an allergy, which manifests itself as craving for more*. "We are sure that our bodies were sickened... In our belief, any picture of the alcoholic which leaves out this physical factor is incomplete. It is the opinion of*

28

William D. Silkworth, MD (who wrote The Doctors Opinion) ...that **we have an allergy to alcohol.... ...As ex-problem drinkers, we can say that his explanation makes good sense. It explains many things for which we cannot otherwise account.**"[139]

The doctor further states: **"We believe...that the action of alcohol** (or other substance) **on these chronic alcoholics** (or abusers) **is a manifestation of an allergy; that the phenomenon of craving is limited to this class and never occurs in the average temperate drinker. These allergic types can never safely use alcohol in any form at all.**"[140] **"'I remember Doc** (Dr. Bob.) **emphasizing that it was an illness,'** Ernie recalled. **'He got that across to each individual he worked with.'**"[141]

Understanding this is vital. **"We have seen the truth demonstrated again and again, 'once an alcoholic always an alcoholic.'"**[142] Or, as one of the members of our retreat told us their sponsor had told them, **"Once a pickle always a pickle."** This is a good analogy because just as one can never turn a pickle back into a cucumber, we cannot be transformed back into "normal drinkers."

Now, in order to truly understand these analogies let us look at the Oxford Dictionary definition of an allergy: **"Hypersensitivity...to the action of some particular foreign material."**

"'When I asked Dr. Bob how he evolved his thinking on alcoholism,' said one member, 'he replied, 'If you're allergic to strawberries, you don't eat them, do you? Well, an alky is the same way. He's allergic to alcohol. His body just doesn't handle it....Once you get sensitised to anything; there is no way you're going to handle it from then on.'"[143]

Prior to this, in 1930's America **"all doctors...had been taught that the alcoholic was incurable and should be ignored. Doctors were advised to attend to patients who could be benefited by medicine."**[144] But what about the effect of alcohol on us?

Have we now begun to realise, as the first woman alcoholic in Chicago did, that **"a drink did something for me or to me that was different from the way it affected others... I could no longer gauge my capacity, and it might be the second or the tenth drink that would erase my consciousness."**[145] Her doctor was also taught that **"short of some miracle... Either they die of acute alcoholism or they develop wet brains and have to be put away permanently."**[146] Fortunately for that alcoholic, the doctor had read the book *Alcoholics Anonymous*. He didn't give up hope and we were there for her.

Simply put once we take a drink we are unable to guarantee our behaviour. As our friend saw, **"It's not how much you drink; it's what drinking does to you."**[147] This is what decides whether or not you are an alcoholic.

MENTAL OBSESSION

Mental knowledge is not enough to bring us relief from this disease. **"We were maladjusted to life...we were in full flight from reality, or were outright mental defectives. These things were true to some extent, in fact to a considerable extent with some of us."**[148] And what about our personality change? What is it that has the Alcoholic take another drink when all the evidence is that it will end badly?

Dr. Silkworth describes five types of alcoholics. Each of these descriptions is of a mental type. He describes (1) **"the psychopaths who are emotionally unstable** (2) **the type...who is unwilling to admit that he cannot take a drink. He plans various ways of drinking. He changes his brand or his environment** (3) **the type who always believes that after being entirely free from alcohol for a period of time he can take a drink without danger** (4) **the** (depressive or) **manic-depressive type**(s) **...about whom a whole chapter could be written** (5) **Then there are types entirely normal in every respect except in the effect alcohol has upon them. They are often able, intelligent, friendly people.**

"All of these, and many others, have one symptom (the physical) **in common: they cannot start drinking without developing the phenomenon of craving.... The only relief we have to suggest is entire abstinence."**[149]

Which brings us back to the mental aspect; **"The idea that somehow, someday he will control and enjoy his drinking is the great obsession of every abnormal drinker. The persistence of this illusion is astonishing. Many pursue it into the gates of insanity or death."**[150]

"The fact is that the alcoholic, for reasons yet obscure, has lost the power of choice in drink. Our so-called will power becomes practically non-existent. We are unable, at certain times, to bring into our consciousness with sufficient force the memory of the suffering and humiliation of even a week or a month ago. We are without defence against the first drink."[151]

"Our human resources, as marshalled by the will, were not sufficient; they failed utterly."[152] The answers for which we worked,

"These gifts of grace...were all founded on a basis of hopelessness...defeat had been absolute."[153]   *"Dr. Bob's alcoholism became more and more noticeable to the children as they grew older. He began to promise them, as well as Anne and their few remaining friends, to stop drinking. 'Promises,' he said, 'which seldom kept me sober even through the day, though I was very sincere when I made them."*[154] This is an obvious demonstration of both the mental obsession and our powerlessness over it.

The only reason a person did not succeed in working the programme, as Bill W. saw it, was they *did not succeed because they could not make the admission of hopelessness."*[155]   *"Until such an understanding is reached, little or nothing can be accomplished."*[156] We must reach a state of hopelessness, which is why when telling their story of woe: *"They grinned, which I didn't like so much, and then asked me if I thought myself an alcoholic and if I were really licked this time, I had to concede both propositions."*[157] Or at other times when we were more resistant, *"They piled on me heaps of evidence to the effect that an alcoholic* (addictive) *mentality...was a hopeless condition. They cited cases out of their own experience by the dozen. This process snuffed out the last flicker of conviction that I could do the job myself."*[158]

SPIRITUAL—in the alcoholic (or those feeling separate) a spiritual connection is missing.

Bill wrote to Dr. Carl Jung (a student of Freud) and Jung replied that the: *"craving for alcohol was the equivalent, on a low level, of the spiritual thirst of our being for wholeness, expressed in medieval language: the union with God."*[159]

In other words, the phenomenon of craving is the same craving the alcoholic has for union with God. It's not by accident that the root word for *"alcohol in Latin is 'spiritus'"*[160] and that God is Spirit. The craving for alcohol is a desire for wholeness. The craving for God is a desire to be healed, a desire to Be Whole.

The alcoholic/addict is a person who has a disintegrating personality. Wholeness is her only hope.

Remember that Albert Einstein said: *"You cannot solve a problem on the level of the problem."* Therefore you must work on the level of the solution.

This "Wholeness" mentioned above has been acquired by hundreds of thousands of alcoholics through working the *Solution;* the *"Programme;"*—the Twelve Steps of Alcoholics Anonymous. In these Steps there are principles by which we learn to live that have created the ***"Exceptions to cases such as*** (Roland H's, where) ***here and there, once in a while, alcoholics have had what are vital spiritual experiences."***[161] Those of the kind Dr. Jung said were necessary for alcoholics to live sober lives. We must ***"accept*** (this) ***programme of moral regeneration."***[162]

WE—THE FIRST WORD OF THE FIRST STEP

"We admitted we were powerless..."The first word of the First Step suggests that together we can accomplish what we have not been able to accomplish on our own. ***"It is a statistical fact that alcoholics*** (and any addict) ***almost never recovered on their own resources."***[163] Alone I can be defeated but, as stated in the Big Book, I never have to be alone again. ***"I faced the pervasive 'we' of the Twelve Steps and gradually realised that I can separate and protect my sobriety from outside hazards only inasmuch as I rely on the sober experience of other...members and share their journey through the Steps of recovery."***[164]

"We alcoholics see that we must work together and hang together, else most of us will finally die alone."[165] This is why our First Tradition states:

"Our common welfare should come first; personal recovery depends upon...unity."[166] ***"We can do together what we can't do in separation."***[167]

POWERLESS

"We were powerless..."""But the actual or potential alcoholic, with hardly an exception, will be absolutely unable to stop drinking on the basis of self-knowledge. This is a point we wish to emphasise and re-emphasise, to smash home upon our alcoholic readers as it has been revealed to us out of bitter experience."[168] ***"We learned that we had to concede to our innermost selves that we were alcoholics. This is the first Step in recovery. The delusion that we are like other people, or presently may be, has to be smashed."***[169] ***"The First Step showed me that I was powerless over alcohol and anything else that threatened my sobriety or muddled my thinking."***[170]

So what about "slips"? Many of us avoid those that have slipped, basically because of our own fear that some how slips are catching. ***"The number of times you win or lose is not important. The only thing that matters is the number of times that you try...That you try"***[171] with the help of your fellows.

It is important not to punish our sick friends—***"we prescribe no punishments for any misbehaviour, no matter how grievous. Indeed, no alcoholic can be deprived of his membership for any reason whatever.***

"Punishment never heals. Only love can heal."[172]

Bill said when asked about slips: ***"Our spiritual and emotional growth...does not depend so deeply upon success as it does upon our failures and setbacks."***[173] ***"Naturally, these episodes have brought a lot of worry to the families involved... Yet I do not know of any case but that has, in a sense, benefited. These occurrences simply serve notice on all of us that no one is ever really cured of alcoholism.*** [174]   Nor are we cured of any other addiction and obsession. So we must know that when someone slips it can be exactly what is needed for them to get back on the path. Be gentle on them and yourself.

"Slips can often be charged to rebellion; some of us are more rebellious than others. Slips may be due to the illusion that one can be 'cured' of alcoholism. Slips can also be charged to carelessness and complacency. Many of us fail to ride out these periods sober. Things go fine for two or three years—then the member is seen no more. Some of us suffer extreme guilt because of vices or practices that we can't or won't let go of. Too little self-forgiveness and too little prayer—well, this combination adds up to slips."[175]

"Only Step One, where we made the 100 per cent admission we were powerless over alcohol, can be practiced with absolute perfection."[176] This of course means that you have made a 100% admission of your powerlessness over alcohol or any addiction that is interfering with your life. Dr. Bob usually informed the newcomer: ***"'If you are perfectly sure that you want to quit...for good, if you are serious about it, if you don't merely wish to get well so that you can take up...again at some future date, you can be relieved,' he said."***[177] We had to arrest our disease first. ***"Then I was able to do something about me."***[178] ***I*** was the real unmanageable problem.

STEP ONE – SECOND HALF

Worksheet For The "Second Half" Of Step One
"...That Our Lives Had Become Unmanageable."[179]

The following is the reading to be done in preparation for our time together.

The "Big Book" of Alcoholics Anonymous	Preface to Page 43
Twelve Steps and Twelve Traditions	Pages 21-24

(Read 21-22–daily)

Part Two – Suggested work

Complete the following items giving **specific examples for each,** with dates, times and the people involved. Please write **a paragraph rather than a sentence** for each example of your ...ism*. We are talking about an ...ism not a wasm.

1) The effects of your ...ism* on family, friends and/or employers and other personal relationships.

2) Your loss, due to your ...ism*, of relationships including marriages, partnerships and/or friendships, etc.

3) Your loss, due to your ...ism*, of jobs, education, employment and other opportunities, etc.

4) Situations, which have led to breaking the law and/or convictions.

5) Physical damage; i.e. Weight gain/loss, illness, broken bones and types of treatment.

6) Loss of physical freedom and/or freedom to choose.

7) Loss of interest in hobbies, sports, people, social activities, etc.

> *...ism = trouble controlling emotions, experiencing misery, depression, trouble earning, feelings of uselessness, full of fear, unhappiness and trouble giving or receiving.

STEP ONE—SECOND HALF

"—That Our Lives Had Become Unmanageable"[180]

UNMANAGEABLE

𝕬 dictionary definition of **"unmanageable"** is: **"don't have effective control of..." "Step One requires an admission that our lives have become unmanageable."**[181] Finally, **"I saw that it was my <u>life</u> that was unmanageable—not just my drinking."**[182]

This is the so-called "Second Half" of Step One and probably the most difficult to get. Some of us think the Step means, "as a result of <u>my addiction</u> my life has become unmanageable." If you believe that, ask yourself a few simple questions. Now that you are not drinking and your life is so very manageable, can you just make a decision to never be angry again? Or become lustful? Never have your feelings hurt by anyone again? Can you say you will never be afraid again?

Or let's just take a look at life up till now. Well, **"my performance and my accomplishments in life failed to live up to my own expectations of myself."**[183] **"There were plenty of situations left in the world over which I had no personal power...if I was so ready to admit that to be the case with alcohol** (or other addictions)**... I must make the same admission with respect to much else."**[184]

So, let us ask ourselves: Is the life we are talking about inside or out? It is inside. We live in our guts, not in the world. Our ability or lack of ability to move the pieces of our life around is not the whole story. We may be able to do that quite well. **"Life had become unmanageable. I had only to reflect on the contrast between the plans I had made so many years ago for my life with what really happened to know I couldn't manage my life drunk or sober."**[185] More importantly, what were our reactions to life?

"Of myself I am nothing, the Father Doeth the works, began to carry bright promise and meaning."[186] Many of us have heard the expression, "You'll stunt your growth." That expression applies perfectly to us. Our intellect may have continued to grow, but when we found refuge in alcohol or some other substance our emotions were stunted. **"For a long time, we can endure the intellect's being ahead of the emotions... But as the years go by, the stretch becomes unbearable; and the man with the grown-up brain and the childish emotions—vanity, self-interest, false pride, jealousy, longing for social approval, to name a few—becomes a prime**

candidate for alcohol (or any number of substances). *To my way of thinking, that is the definition of ...ism; a state of being in which the emotions have failed to grow to the stature of the intellect."*[187]   Therefore we had a damaged ego, a damaged set of beliefs.

If – by some Ego inflated belief in our abilities, you still think that you are somehow strong enough, and thus have the power, to stay away from that first drink, ask yourself this: Can you have the same happy and successful life that we each looked for in the bottle and thought we found briefly (always fleetingly) while drinking, when you are not drinking? If the best we can do is live life in a miserable state of being then we are no better off than when we were drinking. The options are still the same: insanity or death.

"Our liquor was but a symptom. So we had to get down to causes and conditions."[188]

In the rooms of our meetings we hear a lot that "the first Step is the only one we have to do perfectly, to stay sober is the purpose of the programme." To them we say this is true, *if* we understand this promise of *"sobriety."*

"So we do awake, and we are sober. Then what? Is sobriety all that we are to expect of a spiritual awakening? Again, the voice of AA speaks up. No, sobriety is only a bare beginning; it is only the first gift of the first awakening. If more gifts are to be received, our awakening has to go on. And if it does go on, we find that bit by bit we can discard the old life—the one that did not work—for a new life that can and does work under any conditions whatever. Regardless of worldly success or failure, regardless of pain or joy, regardless of sickness or health or even of death itself, a new life of endless possibilities can be lived if we are willing to continue our awakening."[189]

So what does sobriety mean? Is it simply not drinking? We think not. A further dictionary definition of *"sobriety"* is: *"a peaceful, calm, contented, serene and well-balanced life."*

Furthermore, most of our numbers understand that we can *"take no sedation or narcotics, for this programme is to me one of* <u>*complete*</u> *sobriety."*[190]   Drugs have been the downfall of many alcoholics, just as alcohol has been the downfall of many drug addicts. Both seemed not to realise that ethyl alcohol <u>*is*</u> a drug. *"We have warped our minds into such an obsession for destructive drinking* (thinking or behaviour) *that only an act of Providence can remove it from us."*[191]   Our addiction(s) *"bleed*(s) *us of all self-sufficiency and all will to resist its demands. Once this stark fact is accepted, our bankruptcy as going human concerns is complete.*"[192]

The only way we know of to obtain "sobriety" as defined here is by placing our recovery first. And if you don't have that quality of sobriety, we ask: *"Are you really placing recovery first, or are you making it contingent upon other people, places, or circumstances?"*[193] Real sobriety IS **a peaceful, calm, contented, serene and well-balanced life.**

Though this is the foundation Step, it is as simple as A-B-C. In fact Step One is reduced to just the A of the ABC's in the Big Book.

> **(a)** *"That we were alcoholic and could not manage our lives."*[194]

This Step is about recognising that we are alcoholic and what a hopeless state of affairs that is. And *"that we be convinced that any life run on self-will can hardly be a success."*[195] I need help in all areas of my life. I have been defeated. *"Such is the paradox of* (our) *regeneration; strength arising out of complete defeat and weakness, the loss of one's old life as a condition for finding a new one."*[196] *"There was nothing left for us but to pick up the simple kit of spiritual tools laid at our feet."*[197]

"When we admit complete defeat and when we become entirely ready to try (our) *principles, our obsession*(s) *leave*(s) *and we enter a new dimension—freedom..."*[198] The price is defeat, *"I had to be beaten to a pulp physically, mentally, and emotionally, become bankrupt in all facets of my being, before I could give up my pride and admit defeat."*[199] But we have now seen clearly, that with the aid of the programme, we do not have to be so bull-headed—though many of us may still prefer to die than admit defeat.

"Our First Step is realistic when it declares that we are powerless to deal with the alcohol hex (or any other addictive behaviour) *on our own resources or will.*

"But even (the) *First Step asks for willingness—the willingness to admit that our willpower is not going to work head-on. But that's only a starter. All of the rest of* (the) *Twelve Steps require both willingness and willpower."*[200] Moving from one Step to the next and doing as thorough a job as possible, at this moment in time, takes an extraordinary amount of willpower; a real commitment to our choice to be free. *"When I first said at a...meeting, 'my name is Tom and I am an alcoholic* (or whatever)*...' Think of the spirituality in such a statement. My name tells me that I am a human being; the fact that I can know it, think about it, and communicate it reinforces my humanity and makes me aware*

and excited that I am!"[201] And of course the second part, identifying ourselves as an alcoholic or addict of another kind says that we are only one of many in a group. This is the beginning of a realisation that we are ALL One.

As stated earlier, the acceptance of our powerlessness and the knowledge of our *defeat* are paramount. I cannot make it on my own; "We" marks the beginning of a life-long process. Ego-deflation is the removal of our belief in our separation from each other and God. We are not alone anymore. This simple principle of self-*defeat* is implied if not stated in every one of the Twelve Steps, beginning with the word "We" in the First Step. Without the ego deflation of the addict, *"of real happiness he will know none at all."*[202]

Our *acceptance* **"That we were alcoholic and could not manage our own lives"**[203] is the beginning of our journey into the great unknown, the first in a long line of surrenders. These surrenders begin with the knowledge of our "hopelessness." To live in EGO is to live in hopelessness. Ego is relentless. **"Who cares to admit complete defeat?"**[204] Is a question well asked. We have found that **"Only through utter defeat are we able to take our first Steps toward liberation and strength. Our admissions of personal powerlessness finally turn out to be firm bedrock upon which happy and purposeful lives may be built."**[205]

Many members of Twelve Step Fellowships of all types speak of the *"Gift of desperation."* **"Many less desperate...tried...but did not succeed because they could not make the admission of hopelessness."**[206] So can **"We admit we are powerless over alcohol** (and/or X)**—that our lives had become unmanageable?"** If so*,* **"Then they outlined the spiritual answer and programme of action"**[207] when **"we discover the fatal nature of our situation. Then, and only then, do we become as open minded...and as willing to listen as the dying can be. We stand ready to do anything which will lift the merciless obsession from us."**[208]

"Step One...an amazing paradox: We found that we were totally unable to be rid of...obsession until we first admitted that we were powerless over it."[209] In this Step we've found that: **"The problem is me (ungrammatical and humiliating as this may be). I am truly grateful that there is a Fellowship—a group of warm, understanding people—to whom I could bring this 'problem of me.'"**[210] If we are truly ready to **"go to any lengths"** to correct the problem we can move forward. The solution we find is the Steps. The process continues with Step Two. Bill said **"when we admit complete defeat and when we become entirely ready to try** (the) *principles* (via the Steps)**, our obsession leaves us and we enter a new dimension—freedom under God as we understand** (God)**.** [211]

THE PRINCIPLE OF STEP ONE—

DEFEAT *"The principle that we shall find no enduring strength until we first admit complete defeat is the main taproot from which...*(our programme) *has sprung and flowered."* [212] It is the foundation of our programme. Here the acceptance of our powerlessness and the knowledge of our **defeat** are paramount, I cannot make it on my own. **"We"** begin a life-long process. **Ego deflation** is the removal of a belief in separation. We are not alone or separate. We must be clear that **"any life run on self-will can hardly be a success."** [213]

Chapter 4

The Answer

Open-Mindedness

STEP TWO

Worksheet for Step Two

"Came To Believe That A Power Greater Than Ourselves Could Restore Us To Sanity."[214]

Read in preparation:

In the "Big Book" of *Alcoholics Anonymous*   Pages 44-57

And in the **Twelve Steps and Twelve Traditions** – Step Two
                                                        Pages 25-34

Suggested work

A "Power greater than ourselves"

Please **write a paragraph** rather than a sentence for these questions. Complete all of the following items giving **specific examples** for each, with dates, times and people involved. In each suggested assignment try to come up with different examples than in Step One.

1)   What does the phrase **"a Power greater than ourselves"** mean to you?

2)   Give an example of a "Power" you have noticed working in your own or another's life. (E.g. coincidences, through other people, our programme, etc.)

3)   Would finding a "Power greater than yourself" working in your life give you hope? Why? How do you feel about the possibility of trust and lack of fear?

...could restore us to "sanity"

4)   Where and when could your behaviour—drunk or sober, **past or present**—be classified as "insane"?

5)   How has "insane" behaviour (*emotional upset*—drunk or sober) affected your relationships, your education, your work or hopes for work, your freedom?

6)   Regarding the above, why do you think we wrote in brackets "drunk or sober?"

STEP TWO

"Came To Believe That A Power Greater Than Ourselves Could Restore Us To Sanity."[215]

his seems like an innocuous Step on the surface but not when *"we had come to believe in the hopelessness and futility of life as we have been living it."*[216] Then: *"...Having reduced us to a state of absolute helplessness, you now declare that none but a Higher Power can remove our obsession..."*[217] We are condemned to *"an illness which only a spiritual experience will conquer."*[218] In other words, we now have to believe in God. But our sponsors assured us that *"it would be all right for me to doubt God, that AA was not a religious programme and, to belong, I did not have to adhere to any set of beliefs."*[219]

We were told that *"we had but two alternatives: One was to go on to the bitter end, blotting out the consciousness of our intolerable situation as best we could; and the other, to accept spiritual help."*[220] The First Step gives us defeat and hopelessness and the second gives us hope. We were *"100% hopeless, apart from divine help... For most cases, there is virtually no other solution."*[221] We had to recognise that *"willpower and self-knowledge would not help in those strange mental blank spots."*[222]

But do I *have to* believe in God? This does not seem very inviting to many of us. However the principle introduced by Step Two is not so far out of reach as we might believe. *"I learned my own version of what spirituality is. It does not mean I have to be like the saints who claimed to have direct advice and visions from God. It means I have to be concerned with my fellow man; through this alone can I receive the grace of God, my Higher Power, for, in the words of John Donne, so long before AA, 'No man is an island.'"*[223]

As Bill said: *"My intellectual heroes, the chemists, the astronomers, even the evolutionists, suggested vast laws and forces at work. Despite contrary indications, I had little doubt that a mighty purpose and rhythm underlay all. How could there be so much precise immutable law, and no intelligence? I simply had to believe in a Spirit of the Universe, who knew neither time nor limitation."*[224]

We are looking for a way to remove our *"roadblocks of indifference and prejudice* (and the) *problems of intellectuality and self-sufficiency...* (and) *self-righteousness."*[225] We find that *"defiance is an outstanding characteristic of alcoholics* (or the addictive personality). And *"self-confidence was no good whatever; in fact, it was a total liability."*[226] *Step two is a rallying point to sanity."*[227] An inquiring scientific mind is not incompatible with a spiritual quest *"the basic principle of all scientific progress: search and research, again and again, always with the open mind."*[228] One of our great scientists, Albert Einstein is quoted to say, *"Everyone who is seriously involved in the pursuit of science becomes convinced that a spirit is manifest in the laws of the Universe—a spirit vastly superior to that of man, and one in the face of which we with modest powers must feel humble.*

"Many people soberly assure me that man has no better place in the universe than that of another competing organism, fighting its way through life only to perish in the end. Hearing this, I feel that I still prefer to cling to the so-called illusion of religion, which in my own experience has meaningfully told me something very different."[229]

Where does this lead us?

A SPIRITUAL PROGRAMME AND RELIGION – THE DIFFERENCE

"I finally began to separate the religious aspects of my life from (our) *spiritual programme. Now the big difference to me is that religion is the ritual, and we all differ there, and spirituality is the way we feel about what we do. It's about my personal contact with my personal Higher Power, as I understand Him* (Her or It). *"*[230]

What Dr. Bob thought: *"Sister Ignatia said... 'There was one thing that always irritated Doctor...Some people who were on the programme for a length of time would come up to him and say, 'I don't get the spiritual angle.' I heard him say time and again, 'There is no spiritual angle. It's a spiritual programme.'"*[231]

It is often, *"stressed that* (we) *differed from churches in that members could choose their own concepts of 'God as you understand Him'"*[232] or Her, It, or whatever...

A SUGGESTED PROGRAMME. . .

*"**FIRST**, Alcoholics Anonymous does not demand that you believe anything. All of its Twelve Steps are but suggestions. **SECOND**, to get sober and stay sober, you don't have to swallow all of Step Two right now.... **THIRD**, all you really need is a truly open mind. Just resign from the debating society and quit bothering yourself with such deep questions as whether it was*

48

the hen or the egg that came first. Again I say, all you need is an open mind."[233] As a member reports: *"I did not need to find God. I only needed an open mind, and the spirit found me."*[234] We needed to realise that a complete 'psychic change' was required. And that *"something more than human power is needed to produce the essential psychic change."*[235]

"In Step Two we saw that since we could not restore ourselves to sanity, some Higher Power must necessarily do so if we were to survive."[236] As we saw in Bill's story, Ebby's suggestion was: *"Why don't you choose your own conception of God?"* Then Bill continued: *"It was only a matter of being willing to believe in a Power greater than myself. Nothing more was required of me to make a beginning."*[237] This simple statement has benefited hundreds of thousands, maybe millions, of those of us now sober from our many obsessions and addictions. Thank God this programme's opening is so very broad. That's all there is to it.

"CAME TO BELIEVE..."

What is required of us at this point in the Programme? What is the essential "belief" that we must have? *"We needed to ask ourselves but one short question. 'Do I now believe, or am I (at least) willing to believe, that there is a Power greater than myself?' As soon as a man can say that he does believe, or is willing to believe, we emphatically assure him that he is on his way. It has been repeatedly proven among us that upon this simple cornerstone a wonderfully effective spiritual structure can be built."*[238]

"We found that as soon as we were able to lay aside prejudice and express even a willingness to believe in a Power greater than ourselves, we commenced to get results, even though it was impossible for any of us to fully define or comprehend that Power, which is God."[239]

"For myself I have absolute proof of the existence of God. I was sitting in my office one time after I had operated on a woman. It had been a long four or five-hour operation, a large surgical procedure, and she was on her ninth or tenth post-operative day. She was doing fine, she was up and around, and that day her husband phoned me and said, 'Doctor, thanks very much for curing my wife,' I thanked him for his felicitations and he hung up. And then I scratched my head and said to myself, 'What a fantastic thing for a man to say that I cured his wife. Here I am down at my office behind my desk, and there she is out at the

hospital. I am not even there, and if I was there the only thing I could do, would be to give her moral support, and yet he thanks me for curing his wife.' I thought to myself—'What is curing that woman? Yes, I put in those stitches. The Great Boss has given me diagnostic and surgical talent, and He (She or It) *has loaned it to me to use... it doesn't belong to me. He* (She or It) *has loaned it to me and I did my job, but that ended nine days ago. What healed those tissues that I closed? I didn't. This to me is the proof of the existence of a Somethingness greater than I am. I couldn't practice medicine without the Great Physician. All I do in a very simple way is to help...* (God) *cures my patients."*[240]

Or as another early member recalled: *"The thought hit him that people had it all twisted up. They were trying to pour everyone into moulds, put a tag on them, tell them what they had to do and how they had to do it, for the salvation of their souls. When as a matter of fact people were through worrying about their souls, they wanted action right here and now.*

"He said, 'I came to the conclusion that there was SOMETHING, I know not what it is, but It is bigger than I. If I will acknowledge It, if I will humble myself, if I will give in and bow in submission to that SOMETHING and then try to lead a life as fully in accord with my idea of good as possible, I will be in tune.' And later the word good contracted in his mind to God...all I had to do was believe in some power greater than myself and knuckle down to It."[241]

Bill said: *"The minute I stopped arguing, I could begin to see and feel, right there, Step Two...gradually...infiltrate my life.... I came to believe in a Power greater than myself.... To acquire it, I had only to stop fighting and practice the rest of* (the) *programme as enthusiastically as I could."*[242] *"It was comforting to learn that we could commence at a simpler level."*[243]

"Most emphatically we wish to say that any alcoholic (or any addictive personality) *capable of honestly facing his problems in the light of our experience can recover, provided he does not close his mind to all spiritual concepts. He can only be defeated by an attitude of intolerance and belligerent denial."*[244]

The programme *"comes harder to those who have lost or rejected faith...Religion says the existence of God can be proved; the agnostic says it can't be proved; and the atheist claims proof of the non-existence of God. Obviously, the dilemma of the wanderer from faith is that of profound confusion."*[245] This confusion can only be eliminated with a choice to believe. *"We came to believe that alone we were powerless over alcohol* (or any addiction)*. This was surely a choice, and a most difficult one. We came to believe that a Higher Power could restore us to sanity when we became willing to practice... Twelve Steps."*[246] This was an even bigger choice. We find that this new way of life is full of choice. *"Our understanding of God grows through our willing response."*[247]

When talking about faith a member told Dr. Bob: *"I couldn't understand and I couldn't believe anything I couldn't understand. (Dr. Bob) said he supposed then that I didn't use electricity. No one actually understood where it came from or what it was. Nuts to him. He's got too many answers. What did he think the nub of the whole thing was? Subjugate self to some power above...ask for help...mean it...try to pass it on."*[248]

Then Dr. Bob was asked, *"If there was a God, why all this suffering? Wait a minute, he said, that was one of the troubles, we tried to give God some form. Make It just a Power that will help."*[249] We can make it just a Power, some kind of Universal force, available to all of us.

It doesn't *"matter how we define God's grace. We can still claim if we like that we have tapped a hidden or unused inner resource. We don't need to actually define just where that came from. Or we can believe, as most of us finally do, that we have tapped the resources of God as he exists in us and in the cosmos generally."*[250]

TOO SMART FOR THIS SPIRITUAL STUFF?

An *"Educated Agnostic,"* whose intellectual beliefs seemed to exclude a 'spiritual dimension,' said: *"I had thought much about religion and had come to rather definite conclusions. There was no God. The universe was an inexplicable phenomenon. In spite of my sorry state and outlook, there were many beautiful things in life, but no beauty. There were truths discoverable about life, but no truth. There were people who were good, kind, considerate, but no such thing as goodness. I had read rather extensively, but when people began to talk in such ultimates I was lost. I could find in life no eternal purpose or anything that might be labelled 'divine guidance.' War, illness, cruelty, stupidity, poverty and greed were not and could not be the product of any purposeful creation. The whole thing simply didn't make sense."* [251]

This was the strong intellectual belief with which he began. And when offered the solution by a bunch of addicts he thought: *"How screwy the whole thing sounded—the blind leading the blind, a union of drunks, all banded together in some kind of a spiritual belief! What could be more idiotic?!"*[252] He told himself: *"You have now too much intelligence and honesty to allow of such delusions."*[253] It has been well said that *"If we can just get a little stupid we have a chance in this programme."*

In spite of his doubts he went to a meeting. *"My wife and I attended our first gathering with former alcoholic slaves who had been made free through the rediscovery of a power for good, found through a spiritual attitude toward life...*

"I was tremendously inspired at first, but my basic thinking was not altered that evening...I felt that while the spiritual aspect of what these men had was not for me, I did believe strongly in the emphasis they put on the need to help others... But gradually, in a manner I cannot explain, I began to re-examine the beliefs I had thought beyond criticism. Almost imperceptibly my whole attitude toward life underwent a silent revolution... A belief in the basic spirituality of life has grown and with it belief in a supreme and guiding power for good."[254]

Here are the two things he claims made the difference for him. *"The first Step I took when I admitted to myself for the first time that all my previous thinking might be wrong. The second Step came when I first consciously wished to believe. As a result of this experience I am convinced that to seek is to find, to ask is to be given. The day never passes that I do not silently cry out in thankfulness, not merely for my release from alcohol, but even more for a change that has given life new meaning, dignity, and beauty."*[255]

We think that it is important to register this man's words. No-one has to take anything on "blind faith." *"I have not given up my intellect for the sake of my soul, nor have I destroyed my integrity to preserve my health and sanity. All I had feared to lose I have gained and all I feared to gain I have lost."*[256] This is a path of sanity, not delusion.

"'There is a principle which is a bar against all information, which is proof against all arguments and which cannot fail to keep a man in everlasting ignorance—that principle is contempt prior to investigation.'—HERBERT SPENCER"[257]

52

"It is only when a man has tried everything else, when in utter desperation and terrific need he turns to something bigger than himself, that he gets a glimpse of the way out. It is then that contempt is replaced by hope, and hope by fulfilment."[258]

Can we just open our eyes and see what this agnostic saw? *"I saw for the first time that those who really believed, or at least honestly tried to find a Power greater than themselves, were much more composed and contented that I had ever been, and they seemed to have a degree of happiness which I had never known."*[259]

INSANITY DISCUSSED

"The idea that somehow, someday he will control and enjoy his drinking is the great obsession of every abnormal drinker. The persistence of this illusion is astonishing. Many pursue it into the gates of insanity or death."[260] We seem to have this underlying insane belief that *"this time it will be different."* Obsession alone is a form of insanity. Insanity and ego are curiously linked together, like bacon and eggs. In our lives *"we had substituted negative for positive thinking. After we came to...* (any of the 12 Step Groups) *we had to recognise that this trait had been an ego-feeding proposition."*[261]

The insanity which Step 2 refers to is our belief that we are in control of our lives when all the evidence suggests otherwise. *"Some of us **won't** believe in God, others can't, and still others who do believe that God exists have no faith whatever He* (She or It) *will perform this miracle* [262] for us. We can't control our drinking, our relationships, our work, our children, our sex life, or anything else. We don't even seem to be able to control our own thinking. Yet we won't believe.

We all can learn, as this member did, *"that I could win my way to sobriety and sanity if I would follow a few precepts, simple in statement, but profound and far-reaching in their effect if followed. It penetrated to my inner consciousness that the mere offering of lip-service wasn't enough."*[263] The process of working these Steps is a process of becoming conscious in our lives. We have less and less bubbling up of unwanted thoughts and feelings; thoughts and feelings that have been running our lives until now. Three definitions of insanity we have heard are:

DEFINITIONS OF INSANITY –

Insanity is: *a temporary or permanent control of the conscious mind by the unconscious or subjective.*

Albert Einstein said, *"Insanity is: Doing the same thing over and over again and expecting different results"* long before we began saying it in the rooms.

Insanity is: *Thinking we can change our thinking with our same old thinking.* It is often said that a person is 'out of their mind' when they are mentally ill. But an insane person is actually entirely wrapped up, "unconscious" as they may be, in their own patterns of thought. They are actually 'in their mind.' The solution to which is "conscious" thinking.

WHAT ABOUT RATIONALISATION AND DEFIANCE?

"A dictionary definition...reads: 'Rationalisation is giving a socially acceptable reason for socially unacceptable behaviour, and socially unacceptable behaviour is a form of insanity.'"[264] *"Few indeed are the practicing alcoholics* (or whatever our addiction) *who have any idea how irrational they are, or seeing their irrationality, can bear to face it."*[265]

Defiance for the sake of it is another form of insanity. *"As psychiatrists have often observed, defiance is the outstanding characteristic of many an alcoholic. So it's not strange that lots of us have had our day at defying God."*[266] If we were to have faith at all we had to realise that, *"belief meant reliance, not defiance."*[267] It has been said that, when all else fails 'act as if.' *"It is easier to act yourself into a new way of thinking than to think yourself into a new way of acting."*[268] Therefore the expression: 'fake it till you make it."

If we can identify with any of these examples and most importantly, are open minded enough to be willing to choose our own definition of God, we have completed Step 2 enough to move on. Dr. Bob said that through the resulting tolerance we receive *"a greater freedom from the tendency to cling to preconceived ideas and stubbornly adhered-to opinions. In other words, it often promotes an open-mindedness that is vastly important—is, in fact, a prerequisite to the successful termination of any line of search, whether it be scientific or spiritual."*[269]

"As soon as we admitted the possible existence of a Creative Intelligence, a Spirit of the Universe underlying the totality of things, we began to be possessed of a new sense of Power and

direction, provided we took other simple Steps."[270] *"If we wished to grow we had to begin somewhere. So we used our own conception, however limited it was."*[271] We move on to Step Three, we don't dally.

THE PRINCIPLE OF STEP TWO

Open Mindedness

Step 2 establishes *faith* in the programme, where we first see *a power greater than ourselves* at work. **Open Mindedness** is the key.

Every 12 Step meeting is an assurance that a Power greater than ourselves **will** restore us to sanity **if** we do what's necessary. What's necessary? We go on to the next Step, and then the next, until we're working all 12 Steps as part of our daily lives.

Now we move promptly on to Step 3.

Chapter 5

The Decision

Surrender

STEP THREE

Worksheet for Step Three

"Made A <u>Decision</u> To Turn Our <u>Will</u> And Our <u>Lives</u> Over To The <u>Care</u> Of God, As We Understood (God)**"**[272]

Read in preparation, in the "Big Book" of *Alcoholics Anonymous*
Pages 58-63

Read in preparation, in *Twelve Steps and Twelve Traditions* – Step Three
Pages 35-42

SUGGESTED WORK

Complete the following items giving **specific examples for each,** with dates, times and the people involved. Please write **a paragraph rather than a sentence** for each example.

1) What evidence is there that you are willing to change your behaviour? What behaviour do you want to give up?

2) How, will you be able to change? How can you use the help available in the programme and the fellowship?

3) Define "the Programme."

4) How does your <u>will</u> relate to you carrying out your <u>thoughts</u> (beliefs)?

5) How does your <u>life</u> relate to your <u>actions</u>?

6) What are you doing today to turn over your "will and your life" to each of the following:
   a) Your Higher Power

   b) The (the Steps)

   c) Or at least listen to another idea from our Sponsors

7) In what ways are you an active or passive person? Do you get things done or put them off?

8) In what ways have you accepted or evaded responsibility in your life?

9) What does the word 'decision' mean to you? Do you think it is an active process? If so, why?

STEP THREE

"Made A Decision To Turn Our Will And Our Lives Over To The Care Of God, <u>As We Understood</u> (God)"[273]

"Practising Step Three is like the opening of a door which to all appearances is still closed and locked. All we need is a key, and the decision to swing the door open. There is only one key and it is called willingness."[274]

We've generally found that when a life event appears unmanageable, we've usually brought it on ourselves. The solution is to turn our will and our lives over to a Power greater than we are. **"If I ask for help my Higher Power will never give me anything I can't handle."**[275] While we find that *we do give ourselves* much more than we can handle, time and time again. **"I was wilful, full of will to do things I wanted to do and to get things that I wanted to have."**[276] We found that **"as long as I preferred my own will instead of God's will; the remedy simply could not be applied."**[277]

"For just as long as we were convinced that we could live exclusively by our own individual strength and intelligence; for just that long was a working faith in a higher Power impossible... As long as we placed self-reliance first, a genuine reliance upon a higher Power was out of the question. That basic ingredient of all humility, a desire to see and do God's will, was missing."[278]

We saw in Step One that we could not manage our own lives. Now in Step Three we ask a Power greater than ourselves to take over, putting ourselves in Its care. Because **"the only problems I** (and most of us) **have now are those I create when I break out in a rash of self-will."**[279] Our sponsors **"made it very plain that I had to seek God, that I had to state my case...and ask for help.**

"I've been sober for two years, kept that way by submitting my natural will to the Higher Power and that is all there is to it. That submission wasn't just a single act, however. It became a daily duty; it had to be that."[280]

"<u>We had to fearlessly face the proposition that either God is everything or else</u> (God) <u>is nothing. God either is; or</u> (God) <u>isn't. What was our choice to be?</u>"[281] Faith is a choice. What is our choice to be? The programme **"also made me very much aware, by constant repetition, of my freedom of choice, and this is the human faculty of willpower."**[282] Not wilfulness, but the will to choose.

Faith is a difficult concept to grasp. How do we find and make "conscious contact" with this *"Power greater than ourselves?" "We found the Great Reality deep down within us. In the last analysis it is only there that* (God) *may be found. It was so with us."*[283] *"I found God...had been within me at all times, just as...in all people, and I uncovered...* (this Power Greater than me) *by clearing away the wreckage of the past."*[284] Where ever we are *"God...is present at every moment in every nook and cranny of the universe."*[285] The programme *"has emphasised, God—or good—emanates from within each of us."*[286]

Unfortunately: *"Most people try to live by self-propulsion. Each person is like an actor who wants to run the whole show."*[287] The underlying belief is that *"if only people would do as he wished, the show would be great."*[288] We found this to be a *"misuse of willpower."*[289] If we can just let go, we have a chance. We now believe that *"lone courage and unaided will cannot do."*[290] We must have others to find a true relationship with a Power greater than ourselves. Our sponsors tell us: "In our struggle to find a Power greater than ourselves, you must recognise that *It is not you.* A Power greater than you are, *is you plus somebody else.*

"At first that 'somebody' is likely to be his closest AA friend."[291] This is usually their sponsor. *"He relies upon the assurance that his troubles, now made* (even) *more acute because he cannot use...to kill the pain, can be solved too. Of course the sponsor points out that our friend's life is still unmanageable even though he is sober, that after all, only a bare start on* (the) *programme has been made. ...Sobriety brought about the admission of* (our problem)*... and attendance at a few meetings is very good indeed, but it is bound to be a far cry from permanent sobriety and a contented, useful life. That is just where the remaining Steps of the programme come in. Nothing short of continuous action upon these as a way of life can bring the much-desired result"*[292] Our definition of sobriety *"a peaceful, calm, contented, serene and well-balanced life,"* absolutely requires sustained daily effort. We are turning our will over to a Power greater than ourselves, and to do this we must practice the proper use of the will. Because the *"other Steps of the...programme can be practised with success only when Step Three is given a determined and persistent trial."*[293]

Even after we have admitted our *"lives had become unmanageable"* our ego *"still cries out... 'Yes, respecting alcohol* (or whatever our drug of choice)*, I guess I have to be dependent upon AA, but in all other matters I must still maintain my independence.*

Nothing is going to turn me into a nonentity. If I keep on turning my life and will over to care of Something or Somebody else, what will become of me? I'll look like the hole in the doughnut.'

"This, of course, is the process by which instinct and logic always seek to bolster egoism, and so frustrates spiritual development."[294] We have found that in this state of self-propulsion and absorbed only with our own happiness *"human will is of no value whatever.* (Our life problems) *...will not yield to a headlong assault powered by the individual alone."*[295]

If we have a God that we believe will help us, then we will have no hesitation in turning our will and our lives over to that God—*as we understand God.*

What if we are non-believers, agnostics, or just don't think God gives a damn about us? If we trust the programme and attempt it thoroughly it will bring the desired and necessary result: a *"Spiritual Awakening"* as promised by the Twelfth Step. In our early days many of us use the meetings as our "Higher Power." Whenever we doubt the existence of a Higher Power we go to a meeting. It has been said that: "God went to the first meeting of Alcoholics Anonymous and liked it so much She's been to every one since."

What is the DECISION we have to make? We are asked to make a decision to CHANGE. HOW do we change? By studying and practising the ACTION STEPS, which include Steps Four through Twelve.

This process will bring about dramatic shifts in our WILL and our LIFE. What we are asked to do is, to turn our THOUGHTS (our will) and our ACTIONS (our life) over to the action Steps of the programme. We commit ourselves to working the rest of the Steps. As one member says in the story *"Listening to the Wind: I surrendered behind the tears of no answers and decided to do it their way."*[296] What better proof could there be of surrender than for us not to do it our way?

This is a decision that only we can make. *"Now it appears that there are certain things which only the individual can do. All by himself, and in the light of his own circumstances, he needs to develop willingness.... All of the Twelve Steps require sustained and personal exertion to conform to their principles and so, we trust, to God's will. ...Our whole trouble had been the misuse of will power."*[297]

"Being convinced, we were at Step Three, which is that we decided to turn our will and our life over to (the care of) *God as*

we understood (God). *Just what do we mean by that and just what do we do?*

"The first requirement is that any life run on self-will can hardly be a success. On that basis we are almost always in collision with something or somebody, even though our motives are good. Most people try to live by self-propulsion. Each person is like an actor who wants to run the whole show; is forever trying to arrange the lights, the ballet, the scenery and the rest of the players in his own way. If his arrangements would only stay put, if only people would do as he wished, the show would be great. Everybody, including himself, would be pleased. Life would be wonderful. In trying to make these arrangements our actor may sometimes be quite virtuous. He may be kind, considerate, patient, generous; even modest and self-sacrificing. On the other hand, he may be mean, egotistical, selfish and dishonest. But, as with most humans, he is more likely to have varied traits.

"What usually happens? The show doesn't come off very well. He begins to think life doesn't treat him right. He decides to exert himself more. He becomes, on the next occasion, still more demanding or gracious, as the case may be. Still the play does not suit him. "Admitting he may be somewhat at fault, he is sure that other people are more to blame. He becomes angry, indignant, self-pitying. What is his basic trouble? Is he not really a self-seeker even when trying to be kind? Is he not a victim of the delusion that he can wrest satisfaction and happiness out of this world if he only manages well? Is it not evident to all the rest of the players that these are the things he wants? And do not his actions make each of them wish to retaliate, snatching all they can get out of the show? Is he not, even in his best moments, a producer of confusion rather than harmony?

"Our actor is self-centred—egocentric... Whatever our protestations, are not most of us concerned with ourselves, our resentments, or our self-pity?

"Selfishness—self-centredness! That, we think, is the root of our troubles. Driven by a hundred forms of fear, self-delusion, self-seeking, and self-pity, we Step on the toes of our fellows and they retaliate. Sometimes they hurt us, seemingly without provocation, but we invariably find that at some time in the past we have made decisions based on self, which later placed us in a position to be hurt.

"So our troubles, we think, are basically of our own making. They arise out of ourselves, and the alcoholic is an extreme example of self-will run riot, though he usually doesn't think so. <u>Above everything, we alcoholics must be rid of this selfishness. We must or it kills us</u>! God makes that possible. And there often seems no way of entirely getting rid of self without (God's) *aid. Many of us had moral and philosophical convictions galore, but we could not live up to them even though we would have liked to. Neither could we reduce our self-centredness much by wishing or trying on our own power. <u>We had to have God's help.</u>"*[298] We must never forget *"that the penalty for too much self-will is death."*[299] We trust that: *"Each of us has had his own near-fatal encounter with the juggernaut of self-will, and has suffered enough under its weight to be willing to look for something better."*[300] This 'something better' is having the CARE of a loving Higher Power in our lives.

CARE

Different people approach this Step in different ways. To the man below, Dr. Bob *"submitted... the idea of God...and suggested that most, if not all, of our troubles come from being completely out of touch with the idea of God, with God himself. All my life, he said, I had been doing things of my own human will and that the only certain way for me to stop drinking was to submit my will to God and let Him* (Her or It) *handle my difficulties."*[301]

"This is the how and why of it. <u>First</u> of all, we had to quit playing God. It didn't work. <u>Next</u>, we decided that hereafter in this drama of life; God was to be our Director. (God) is the Principal; we are (God's) *agents. <u>He is the Father, and we are His children.</u>"*[302] Setting the patriarchy aside It is as our parent and we as Its children. As *"Shakespeare said, 'All the world's a stage, and all the men and women merely players.'"*[303] For fear of being redundant, we're the actors on the stage of life, NOT the directors.

Think of the CARE of a loving parent—that is the "care of God." No, not the inadequate parents we all seem to think we've had. We mean the ideal loving parent.

"I was stymied on the Third Step, with the reference to 'the care of God.' So I went around it, knowing I must return to it, and tackled the Fourth Step. Slowly and painfully, I became aware of myself. I began to see it wasn't true that I didn't believe in anything. Rather, I had believed in the wrong things:

I had believed I needed to drink for confidence

I had believed I was unattractive

I had believed I was unworthy

I had believed no one loved me

I had believed I never had a break... [304]

Many of the things, which we learned and have believed turn out not to be true. If we could choose to believe such things, surely we could choose to believe in a Power greater than ourselves. **"They told me that giving was living, and living was loving, and loving was God. And you don't have to worry about God, because He** (She or It is) **sitting right in front of your eyes."** [305]

"Most good ideas are simple, and this concept was the keystone of the new and triumphant arch through which we passed to freedom.

"When we sincerely took such a position, all sorts of remarkable things followed. We had a new Employer. Being all-powerful...provided what we needed, if we kept close...and performed (God's) **work well. Established on such a footing we became less and less interested in ourselves, our little plans and designs. More and more we became interested in seeing what we could contribute to life. As we felt power flow in, as we enjoyed peace of mind, as we discovered we could face life successfully, as we became conscious of** (God's) **presence, we began to lose our fear of today, tomorrow or the hereafter. We were reborn.**

"We were now at Step Three." [306]

We recognise that this act of surrender and thus **"the effectiveness of the whole... programme will rest upon how well and earnestly we have tried to come to 'a <u>decision</u> to turn our <u>will</u> and our <u>lives</u> over to the <u>care</u> of God, as we understood** (God)**.'"** [307]

"We thought well before taking this Step making sure we were ready; that we could at last abandon ourselves utterly to (God).

"<u>We found it very desirable to take this spiritual Step with an understanding person, such as our wife, best friend, or spiritual adviser</u>. But it is better to meet God alone than with one who might misunderstand. <u>The wording was, of course, quite optional so long as we expressed the idea, voicing it without reservation</u>. This was only a beginning, though <u>if honestly and humbly made, an effect, sometimes a very great one was felt at once</u>." [308]

Thus we surrender ourselves to a Higher Power of our own understanding. *"My situation got worse until I had to surrender completely."*[309] When the following person was on Step Three a sober member of the fellowship with *"many years of top-quality sobriety...said... 'Why don't you just do nothing for a year?' I asked him what he meant. He advised me to stay at my present job. He suggested that I simply stop worrying about whether I was making enough money or not, that I just go to work every day, enjoy the luxury of not worrying about my situation, take each day as it came, and do what seemed best that day under the circumstances—and do this for one year. Think of that! A year off from worrying! Better than a paid vacation.*

"We simply stop messing in God's business. And...when we stop messing and worrying, we <u>have</u> *turned our will and our lives over to God* (or Good) *as we understand* (or don't understand God).*"*[310] This gal relapsed and afterward tried to understand why: *"It was the realisation...of the fact that I had not fully given my problems to God.* <u>I was still trying to do my own fixing</u>.*"*[311]

"Later they went into more detail and put it to me very straight that I'd have to give over my desires and attitudes to a power higher than myself which would give me new desires and attitudes...And it worked, as long as I allowed it to do so."[312] And it will continue to work as long as we put that decision into practice via the Steps.

'To Surrender' is a verb; hence it is a conscious action. *"Though our decision was a vital and crucial Step,* <u>it could have little permanent effect unless at once followed by strenuous effort to face, and be rid of, the things in ourselves which had been blocking us</u>. *Our liquor was but a symptom. So we had to get down to causes and conditions."*[313] It is a place of serenity, though the path to that serenity is not easy. We are often dragged kicking and screaming along the road to surrender. When we finally get pushed into surrendering by the "circumstances" of our lives we then realise how wonderful and liberating surrender actually is—UNTIL NEXT TIME.

We found that there is: *"Sustained and personal exertion necessary to sustain God's will."*[314] *Part of the need for continuing, repetitive surrender."*[315] So, what is surrender? It is a state of consciousness we attain when we are finally ready to listen to our Higher Self. *"William James' Varieties of Religious Experience...gave me the realisation that most conversion experiences, whatever the variety, do have a common denominator of ego collapse at depth."*[316] It is important to remember that such an awakening is what we want and need. When we give up trying to "do it" by our willpower and ego-selves, we can then move into a higher consciousness—God Consciousness. How does this manifest itself in the programme? <u>Evidently it works through a conscious choice to work the Steps</u> to the best of our ability. When we do that, life becomes much, much easier.

In this state there is no more self-centred fear because we are in the "care" of God *as we understand God* and we are using the freely given tools of the programme to stay outside our egos as best we can.

Remember in prayer WE take the ACTION—GOD has all the RESPONSIBILITY for RESULTS! Let go and let God!

The following is a suggestion for helping in finding a Power greater than ourselves. We might add the following to our morning ***"Prayer and Meditation"***

What is God to *Me*?

What is God to me right now?

Only I can answer that question!

Is God...the promise of springtime? Is IT the glorious colours of autumn? Is IT the warm rays of the summer sun? Is IT the symphony of the winter winds? Is IT a child's laughter? Is IT the colours of the rainbow? Is IT the power of the sea? Is IT the beauty of a snow-capped mountain? Is IT Love? Is IT clarity? Is God wisdom? Is IT compassion? Is IT vitality? Is IT abundance? Is IT life itself, expressed in billions of ways? Is God the Universe? Or is IT something you've seen or felt in a Meeting?

What is IT to me? ...

God is expressed uniquely as you and as me. Therefore, IT has a very unique and personal meaning to each of us. If at this moment, you can't readily finish the phrase 'God is _____,' we urge you to take the phrase "God is" into meditation until what IT is to you, at this present time, is revealed.

Now it's your turn to fill in the blank. God is _____. Only you can answer that question! [317]

"Much to our relief, we discovered we did not need to consider another's conception of God. Our own conception, however inadequate, was sufficient to make the approach and to effect a contact."[318]

From this point forward we are living life on a different basis. **"We trust infinite God rather than our finite selves... Just to the extent that we do as we think He** (She of It) **would have us, and humbly rely on** (God)**, does He** (She or It) **enable us to match calamity with serenity."**[319]

When we take a good look at our lives today and our dependence on electricity, computers, transportation, etc. **"it is startling to discover how dependent we really are, and how unconscious of that dependence."**[320] Whereas, **"dependence, as AA practises it, is really a means of gaining true independence of the spirit."**[321] In 1958, after having finally been able to overcome his long-standing enemy, depression, a few years earlier, he had a brief episode of depression. Bill W. wrote: **"Suddenly I realised what the matter might be. My basic flaw had always been dependence on people or circumstances to supply me with prestige, security, and confidence. Failing to get these things according to my perfectionist, dreams and specifications, I had fought for them. And when defeat came, so did my depression."**[322] Turning our will and our lives over to the care of God as we understood It represents true independence, true freedom.

It is important to remember that: **"When...we speak to you of God, we mean your own conception of God."**[323] **"Once we have come into agreement with these ideas, it is really easy to begin the practice of Step Three."**[324] It says **"begin the practice of Step Three."** Many in the fellowship believe as I once did that this Step is done once. Today we believe these Steps are lived on a daily basis. If one can truly turn their will and their life over to the care of a Power greater than themselves once and never take it back as I did, is an amazing example of spirituality.

Henrietta D's wife, recalled about when he was in the hospital sobering up: **"He was there about five days before they could make him say that he couldn't control his drinking and had to leave it up to God. ...They made him get down on his knees at the side of the bed right there in the hospital and pray and say that he would turn his life over to God."**[325] This is a practice many sponsors still use today.

What about those who are not ready to surrender? For Ernie G. who eventually became the fourth member when he said he'd try. Though he said: **"'I'm not very well prepared to do that, because that's been a little out of my line...'**

"Nevertheless, they agreed to help him. They said the prayer and had him repeat it after them. 'For some reason or other, I

felt quite relieved after making this so-called surrender,' Ernie said.[326] Many of us found that we had to hit rock bottom. *"I had gotten myself into a position where I had no other place to turn; I was at a point of almost complete despair. Then, and only then, did I honestly and simply ask God to help me."*[327]

Various members describe this vital act of surrender as follows: *"That day I gave my will to God and asked to be directed. But I have never thought of that as something to do and then forget about. I very early came to see that there had to be a continual renewal of that simple deal with God; that I had perpetually to keep the bargain."*[328] *"After making this final agreement...to let God be first in my life, the whole outlook and horizon brightened up in a manner which I am unable to describe except to say that it was 'glorious.'"*[329] *"Every morning, I turn my will and my life over to the care of God as I understand Him* (Her or It). (An) *integrating power within me has gradually led me into a state of serenity and happiness which I had always considered impossible."*[330]

"Always before, I had put myself in the hands of a man and made him the sole reason for my existence and my will to live."[331]

"Instead of complete surrender, I set up forced rules for myself. I failed to ask God for help and guidance and tried to follow these self-imposed rules instead. (We often use our willpower in ways that simply don't work.) *Like so many, I do not always surrender completely; I allow the cares and worries of the day to distort my thinking...Whatever problems confront me, large or small, they can be solved wisely. Or they can be solved my way. The choice is mine.* (Life works well when) *I completely surrender my life and my thinking to my Higher Power."*[332]

Perhaps our prayer is as simple as this: *"'All right, God...I don't want to be the quarterback* (the director of the team*) any more. Tell me what You want me to do, and I will do it.'"*[333]

"Half measures availed us nothing. We stood at the turning point. We asked...protection and care with complete abandon."[334]

Before we take this Step we first recognise that, a decision without action is useless, *"Like the remaining Steps, Step Three calls for affirmative action, for it is only by action that we can cut away the self-will which has always blocked the entry of God—or, if you like, a higher Power—into our lives. Faith alone can avail nothing. We can have faith, yet keep God out of our lives."*[335]

This Step, like all the rest, is never really completed. Many of us now do this Step daily because: *"I find the times of greatest danger of self-destruction during these years were those when I, consciously or otherwise, attempted egotistically to take over the reins of my life and tried to exercise total control over my own affairs."*[336]

"The surrender was more than important; it was a must. Bob E. ... recalled that after five of six days in the hospital, 'when you had indicated that you were serious, they told you to get down on your knees by the bed and say a prayer to God...We called that the surrender. They demanded it. You couldn't go to a meeting until you did it...'The newcomers surrendered in the presence of all those people.'"[337] We can certainly see from this that surrender was a vital part of the process. *"Our motivation...is a combination of enough hurt and the grace of God."*[338]

"So when AA suggests a fearless moral inventory, it must seem to every newcomer that more is being asked...than (s)he can do."[339] But: *"Without a searching and fearless moral inventory, most of us have found that the faith which really works in daily living is still out of reach."*[340] Stopping at this stage can be fatal.

And so: *"Next we launched out on a course of vigorous action, the first Step of which is a personal housecleaning... Though our decision was a vital and crucial Step, it could have little permanent effect unless at once followed by strenuous effort to face, and to be rid of, the things in ourselves which had been blocking us. Our liquor* (whatever our addictions) *was but a symptom. So we had to get down to causes and conditions.*

"Therefore, we started upon a personal inventory. This was Step Four."[341]

THE PRINCIPLE OF STEP THREE

Surrender

When we walk through the doors of our first meeting, or first cry out for help, something begins to happen. That "something" begins to become clear by the time of our Step 3 decision. These Principles became clearer when <u>we decided to **surrender** to, and *trust* in the process of the Steps</u>, *a power greater than ourselves.* **"Dr. Bob...was wonderful at getting surrenders. You know, at first, they made all these men surrender. Out at T. Henry Williams's where they met, Dr. Bob would take them upstairs and make them say that they would surrender themselves to God.**"[342] That is the essence of Step Three.

WITH THIS KNOWLEDGE WE SAY THE THIRD STEP PRAYER –

"I finally got down on my knees and asked God for help. I couldn't go on the way I was living."[343] In this spirit many of our sponsors, took our hand and pulled us down on our knees to say the Step 3 prayer, embarrassingly for most of us.

"Many of us said to our Maker, as we understood (God)*: <u>'God I offer myself to Thee—to build with me and to do with me as Thou wilt. Relieve me of the bondage of self that I may better do Thy will. Take away my difficulties, that victory over them may bear witness to those I would help of Thy Power, Thy Love, and Thy Way of life. May I do Thy will always!*'"[344]</u>

Once our surrender has begun we are at the stage of demonstration. If we do not begin the rest of the Steps immediately, we have not surrendered at all. We remind ourselves of this surrender each morning.

Chapter 6

Cleaning House

Honesty

STEP FOUR – INTO ACTION

Worksheet for Step Four

Made A Searching And Fearless Moral Inventory Of Ourselves.[345]

Read in preparation, in the "Big Book" of *Alcoholics Anonymous* –
"Next we launched... (cont. to)...**truth about yourself.**

Pages 63-71

Read in preparation, in the *Twelve Steps and Twelve Traditions* –
Step Four   Pages 43-55

STEP FOUR –ACTION

"Made A Searching And Fearless Moral Inventory Of Ourselves"[346]

We demonstrate that we have truly turned **"our will and our lives over to the care of God as we understood Him** (Her or It)"by immediately working on Step Four. **"After the surrender, many of the Steps—involving inventory, admission of character defects, and making restitution—were taken within a matter of days.**"[347] This of course was no where near the thorough inventory that we are about to embark on.

So begins the vast "emotional re-arrangement" we discussed earlier. **"There is action and more action. Faith without works is dead."**[348] **"There is much work to be done, and none of us can do it standing still."**[349] Ideally we hit the ground running as our friend did in the story, **"Flooded with Feeling"**: **"I know that I took the Third Step (turning my will and my life over to a Higher Power) that night because I began writing a Fourth Step inventory the next day, and I continued to write until I did the Fifth Step with my sponsor."**[350]

This cannot be stressed enough: **"Though our decision** (in Step 3) **was a vital and crucial Step, it could have little permanent effect unless <u>at once</u> followed by strenuous effort to face, and be rid of, the things in ourselves which had been blocking us. Our liquor** (our addiction) **was but a symptom. So we had to get down to causes and conditions."**[351]

"Doctors have realised for a long time that some form of moral psychology was of urgent importance to alcoholics."[352] The Fourth Step **"will be the first tangible evidence of our complete willingness to move forward.**[353]

This is the point in the programme that we begin to deal with "Relationships and Work/Money" and other areas of powerlessness. **"The moral inventory is a <u>cool examination</u> of the damages that occurred to us during life and a sincere effort to look at them in a true perspective. This has the effect of taking the ground glass out of us, the emotional substance that still cuts and inhibits."**[354] **"Beginning with Step Four, we commence... to search out the things in ourselves which had brought us to physical, moral, and spiritual bankruptcy."**[355] The psychologist Carl Rogers wrote: **"We cannot change, we cannot move away from what we are, until we thoroughly accept what we are, and then change seems to come about almost unnoticed."**[356]

We want a better life. If that wasn't the case, we wouldn't be working these Steps. *"Clear vision of tomorrow comes only after a real look at yesterday. That's why we...take personal inventory."*[357] *"We thought conditions drove us to drink... It never occurred to us that we needed to change ourselves to meet conditions, whatever they were."*[358] Even though *"we tried to correct these conditions and found we couldn't to our entire satisfaction."*[359]

Once we have arrested our addiction, *"we slowly learned that something had to be done about our vengeful resentments, self-pity, and unwarranted pride."*[360]

These Steps are about acquiring faith—that of having a spiritual awakening and this Step is necessary to that end. There are many *"full of faith, but still reeking of alcohol."*[361] *"This...has to do with the quality of faith rather than the quantity."*[362] *"The fact was we really hadn't cleaned house so that the grace of God could enter us and expel the obsession."*[363]

RESENTMENTS AND FEAR – TWO STAGES

FIRST STAGE Three Columns

The first part of our inventory deals with resentments. It was found that *"as my resentment and self-pity grew, so did my alcohol problem."*[364] What is resentment? An Oxford dictionary says we resent anything that we, *"show or feel indignation at, feel injured or insulted by."* Or, we can add, are <u>disturbed</u> by.

"Next we launched out on a course of vigorous action, the first Step of which is a personal housecleaning, which many of us had never attempted...

"Therefore, we started upon a personal inventory. This was Step Four. A business, which takes no regular inventory usually, goes broke. Taking a commercial <u>inventory is a fact-finding and a fact-facing process</u>. It is an effort to discover the truth about stock-in-trade. One object is to disclose damaged or un-saleable goods, to get rid of them promptly and without regret. If the owner of the business is to be successful, he cannot fool himself about values.

"We did exactly the same thing with our lives. We took stock honestly. First, we searched out the flaws in our make-up, which caused our failure. Being convinced that self, manifested in various ways, was what had defeated us, we considered its common manifestations.

"Resentment is the 'number one' offender. It destroys more alcoholics than anything else. From it stems all forms of spiritual disease, for we have been not only mentally and physically ill, we have been spiritually sick. When the spiritual malady is overcome, we straighten out mentally and physically. In dealing with resentments, we set them on paper. We listed <u>people, institutions or principles</u> *with whom we were angry* (in column 1). *We asked ourselves why we were angry* (column 2). *In most cases it was found that our self-esteem, our pocketbooks, ambitions, our personal relationships, (including sex) were hurt or threatened* (column 3). *So we were sore. We were 'burned up.'*

"On our grudge list we set opposite each name <u>our injuries</u> (in column 3). *Was it our* <u>self-esteem</u>, *our* <u>security</u>, *our* <u>ambitions</u>, *our* <u>personal</u>, *or* <u>sex relations</u>, *which had been interfered with?*

We also added shame to our list of "Affected" areas. Shame and guilt are closely related. *"Could I suggest that you look at excessive guilt* (or shame) *for what it is? Nothing but a sort of reverse pride. A decent regret for what has happened is fine. But* (shame or) *guilt—no."*[365] *"We scarcely need to be reminded that excessive guilt or rebellion leads to spiritual poverty."*[366] *"I rebelled against everything I'd ever heard as a child, and I lived to suit myself."*[367] *"Guilt* (shame) *aims at self-destruction, and pride aims at the destruction of others."*[368]

"We were usually as definite as this example:

I'm resentful at:	The Cause	Affects my: (our injuries)
Mr. Brown	His attention to my wife.	Sex relations Self-esteem (fear)
	Told my wife of my mistress.	Sex relations Self-esteem
	Brown may get my job at the office.	Security Self-esteem (fear)
Mrs. Jones	She's a nut—she snubbed me. She committed her husband for drinking. He's my friend. She's a gossip.	Personal relationship Self-esteem (fear)

| My employer | Unreasonable—Unjust— Overbearing—Threatens to fire me for drinking and padding my expense account. | Self-esteem (fear) Security |
| My wife | Misunderstands and nags. Likes Brown. Wants house put in her name. | Pride—Personal and sex relations— Security (fear) |

Many of us will protest, "I'm not angry or resentful, I just feel hurt." But on closer inspection we will see that when we, *"fought tears,* (from that hurt) *and when* (we) *had successfully swallowed them, anger and hostility toward everyone and everything welled up in their place."*[369] This is why we tend to call them "disturbances." Keeping this in mind: *"We went back through our lives. Nothing counted but thoroughness and honesty."*[370] As we retrace our personal histories we fill in the first three columns. This can be the easy and even enjoyable part. One of our members describes this stage as *"WHO—what THEY did—and how THAT affected ME."* At this stage we really are taking other peoples' inventory, those that have done "real or imagined" harm to us throughout our lives. It's very important not to stall at this stage. *"SELF-JUSTIFICATION IS DANGEROUS."*[371]

"Dr. Silkworth...explained to me what honesty was. I always thought honesty had something to do with telling other people the truth. He explained that it had to do first with telling myself the truth."[372] When we came in to the rooms we *"instantly recognised honesty when we heard it, from the mouths of...members."*[373] But: *"If I were asked, what in my opinion was the most important factor in being successful in the programme; besides following the Twelve Steps, I would say Honesty. And the most important person to be honest with is Yourself."*[374] Without that we can not even begin the process, let alone "continue" it.

The third column reveals how intense our reaction can be and indeed *"How* (our) *instincts can exceed their proper function."*[375] *"Whenever a human being becomes a battleground for the instincts, there can be no peace."*[376] Often all that has happened is that someone made a stupid remark and we have had an extreme reaction to it. At this point we ask ourselves, *"Was it our self-esteem, our security, our ambitions, personal, or sex relations, which had been interfered with?"*[377] *"Before AA, I could not, or would not, admit I was wrong. My pride would not let me. And yet I was ashamed of me."*[378] The common theme is that the events wounded our **pride,** causing us **shame,** which we have seen are simply different sides of the same coin. Or we have become **fearful**.

The instinct for sex relations is a natural desire for companionship and the desire to reproduce. The instinct for sound personal relations is a social instinct.   After all, **"Creation gave us instincts for a purpose."**[379]   Even though our basic drives are **"surely God-given…Our desires for sex, material and emotional security and for an important place in society often tyrannise us… Nearly every serious emotional problem can be seen as a case of misdirected instinct. When that happens, our great natural assets, the instincts, have turned into physical and mental liabilities.**

"Step Four is our vigorous and painstaking effort to discover what these liabilities in each of us have been, and are."[380] What about our own contribution to our own unhappiness through the repeated misuse of these instincts?   This brings us to the "<u>Fourth Column</u>" where we take <u>our own inventory</u>.

SECOND STAGE the "Fourth Column"

"When we were finished (with the first three columns) **we considered it carefully. The first thing apparent was that this world and its people were often quite wrong. <u>To conclude that others were wrong was as far as most of us ever got</u>. The usual outcome was that people continued to wrong us and we stayed sore. Sometimes it was remorse and then we were sore at ourselves. But the more we fought and tried to have our way, the worse matters got. As in war, the victor only seemed to win. Our moments of triumph were short-lived.**

"It is plain that a life, which includes deep resentment, leads only to futility and unhappiness. To the precise extent that we permitted these, do we squander the hours that might have been worthwhile. But with the alcoholic, whose hope is the maintenance and growth of a spiritual experience, this business of resentment is infinitely grave. We found that it is fatal. For when harbouring such feelings we shut ourselves off from the sunlight of the Spirit. The insanity of alcohol returns and we drink again. And with us, to drink is to die.

"If we were to live we had to be <u>free of anger</u>. The grouch and the brainstorm were not for us. They may be the dubious luxury of normal men, but for alcoholics these things were poison.

"We turned back to our list, for it held the key to the future. <u>We were prepared to look at it, from an entirely different angle</u>. We

began to see that the world and its people really dominated us. In that state, the wrongdoing of others, fancied or real, had power to actually kill. **How could we escape? We saw that resentments must be mastered, but how? We could not wish them away any more than alcohol.**"[381]

Our goal is a fulfilling and successful life. To this end: **"we searched out the <u>flaws in our make-up</u> which caused our failure. Being convinced that self, manifested in various ways, was what had defeated us, we considered its common manifestations."**[382] Often we need help with this; **"Instincts on rampage balk at investigation. The minute we make a serious attempt to probe them, we are liable to suffer serious reactions."**[383] **"Thoroughness ought to be the watchword when taking inventory. In this connection, it is wise to write out our questions and answers."**[384] In the early days, sponsors were closely involved in the inventory process, actually pointing out our character flaws! **"Dr. Bob led me through all of these Steps. At the moral inventory, he brought up several of my bad personality traits or character defects, such as selfishness, conceit, jealousy, carelessness, intolerance, ill-temper, sarcasm, and resentment."**[385]

"In the chapter 'How It Works,' in the Big Book, I was shown some questions. The answer to these questions provided me with knowledge about my reactions to the conditions of my life. Every response, to every resentment, real or imagined, had been sick and self-destructive. I was allowing others to control my sense of well-being and behaviour. I came to understand that the behaviour, opinions, and thoughts of others were none of my business. The only business I was to be concerned with was my own!"[386]

"This was our course...

"Referring to our list again. Putting out of our minds the wrongs others had done, we resolutely looked for our mistakes. Where had we been <u>selfish, dishonest, self-seeking</u> and <u>frightened</u>? Though a situation had not been entirely our fault, we tried to disregard the other person involved entirely. <u>Where were we to blame</u>*? (responsible[2]) **The inventory was ours, not**

---

[2] **Responsible** = if we break down the word responsible, it could be broken into two words **response** and **able**. So the word could be interpreted as "What response am I able to give to any situation?" and for that I am responsible. ***Blame** is a verb and therefore with a "finger pointing" definition, this is one of the few words in the Big Book that we think could be changed for the better.

the other man's. When we saw our faults we listed them. We placed them before us in black and white. We <u>admitted our wrongs honestly</u> and were willing to set these matters straight."[387] *"Alcohol was only a symptom of much deeper problems of dishonesty and denial."*[388] The above information taken from the Big Book lays out most of the questions we ask ourselves in the Fourth Column. *"The problem of honesty touches nearly every aspect of our lives. There are, for example, the widespread and amazing phenomena of self-deception. There are those rather dreadful brands of reckless truth-telling, which are so often lacking in prudence and love. Then there are those countless life situations in which nothing less than utter honesty will do, no matter how sorely we may be tempted by the fear and pride that would reduce us to half-truths or inexcusable denials."*[389] If we look back through our lives there we will find myriad examples of these kinds of breaks with honesty. We find that *"the deception of others is almost always rooted in the deception of ourselves."*[390] Some of us say that we have never told a lie we didn't already believe.

With regard to our selfishness we remember that: *"Whatever our protestations; are not most of us concerned with ourselves?"*[391] If we wish to recover from our emotional baggage we realised that: *"Above everything, we...must be rid of this selfishness. We must, or it kills us! ... We had to have God's help."*[392] These tools make that possible.

The final two questions are inspired by this quote: *"We invariably find that some time in the past we have made <u>decisions</u> based on self which later placed us in a position to be hurt."*[393] The human mind is an interesting thing: we take a position, make a choice, or make a decision and then automatically gather evidence to support that idea. And of course: *"We are right and you are wrong."*[394] A world of people taking this position creates *"a bone-crushing juggernaut whose final achievement is ruin."*[395] For example: *"I decided that no one loved me and I didn't love them."*[396] And so we live a life without love. I'm sure we can all amass tonnes of evidence to prove that we are right about our beliefs. But weren't these decisions based on ignorance? Or worse yet weren't these beliefs established by a rash, childish state of mind? Weren't we children when we made many of them?

This is a spiritual programme and the very reason we look back through our lives for those earlier decisions. We are not talking about just a thought. It is not our thoughts but our attachment to our thoughts that causes suffering. It is being *"right"* about them. *"I had to be right all the time and only God can be that. Okay, I wanted to be God.*"[397] With our emotional growth being so far behind our intellectual development, what other result could there be?

A thought is truly harmless, unless we believe it and once we have made a decision, a choice or take a position, we tend to believe these decisions and choices. We find a good example of evidence gathering to prove the ultimate, in this chap, *"I set out to prove that there was no God, and for over twenty years, the confirmations of my opinion kept pouring in. So the first thing that I came to understand...God is...*very cooperative.*"[398] By selectively gathering evidence, real or imagined, we can and do prove or disprove absolutely anything.

In the process of going back through our lives, the question of our childhood invariably arises. *"It became necessary for me to go back to my childhood, to the time when the seeds were planted that had their noxious blooming so many years later...ignorance almost cost me my life."*[399] What, we may well ask, did a four or five year old do to deserve some of the treatment we received? Of course there is truth in this. *"The medical profession would probably tell me I was conditioned...by the things that happened to me in my childhood. And I am sure they would be right as far as they go, but AA has taught me I am* (more deeply) *the result of the way I reacted to what happened to me as a child. What is more important to me,* (it) *has taught me that through this simple programme* (in which this vital Step is of great importance) *I may experience a change in this reaction pattern that will indeed allow me to 'match calamity with serenity.'"*[400] What we need to accomplish with this Step is to obtain Power where before there was no power.

WHAT ARE WE LOOKING FOR IN "THE FOURTH COLUMN?"

"Step Four is an effort to discover our liabilities...Misguided moral inventory can result in guilt, grandiosity, or blaming (ourselves or) *others."*[401] When we can clearly see that without *"our part"* the person we resent could not have impacted us with theirs, we then are able to see that we are the engine of cause in our lives. As for our childhood we are responsible for our reactions, which have caused us much greater difficulty over the years than what was done to us. There may be others out there that are presently unknown but: *"It is important that at present we believe there is only one sure pathway to recovery."*[402] Otherwise why would we do such work? We have found *"that somehow, some way, the mental stream,*

the emotions, must be purified before the right pathway could be followed."[403]

One of the major reasons for inventory is because **"lack of power is our dilemma."** Once we see that we are not victims of other people's actions, we gain strength. Once we see that we actually put ourselves in a position to be hurt or **"made decisions that later placed us in a position to be hurt."**[404] We can see that the same power that worked so negatively in the past can now work positively. God can be in our life and lead us away from being a victim. We find **The** Power in our lives. **"The more he looks, the more astonished he becomes at the elaborate and devious excuse-making machinery by which he had been justifying himself."**[405]

This is the point at which we begin to find freedom from our resentments and fear.

FEAR

"The chief activator of our defects has been <u>self-centred</u> *fear."*[406] *"Fear is surely a bar to reason, and to love, and of course it invariably powers anger, vainglory, and aggression. It underlies maudlin guilt* (shame) *and paralysing depression...*

"The achievement of freedom from fear is a lifetime undertaking, one that can never be wholly completed...

"We shall have to try for all the freedom from fear that is possible for us to attain. Then we shall need to find both the courage and the grace to deal constructively with whatever fears remain."[407]

On the three columns earlier, *"Notice that the word "fear" is bracketed alongside the difficulties with Mr. Brown, Mrs. Jones, the employer, and the wife. This short word somehow touches about every aspect of our lives. It was an evil and corroding thread; the fabric of our existence was shot through with it. It set in motion trains of circumstances which brought us misfortune we felt we didn't deserve. But <u>did not we, ourselves, set the ball rolling</u>? Sometimes we think fear ought to be classed with stealing. It seems to cause more trouble.*

"We reviewed our fears thoroughly. <u>We put them on paper</u>, even though we had no resentment in connection with them. <u>We asked ourselves</u> <u>why we had them</u>. <u>Wasn't it because self-reliance failed us</u>? Self-reliance was good as far as it went, but it didn't go far enough. Some of us once had great self-

confidence, but it didn't fully solve the fear problem, or any other. When it made us cocky, it was worse.

"Perhaps there is a better way—we think so. For we are now on a different basis; the basis of trusting and relying upon God. <u>We trust infinite God rather than finite selves</u>. We are in the world to play the role...assign(ed). *Just to the extent that we do as <u>we think</u>* (God) <u>*would have us*</u>, *and humbly rely upon* (God)*, does He enable us to match calamity with serenity.* [408]

"Our whole treasured philosophy of self-sufficiency had to be cast aside."[409] *"So false pride became the reverse side of that ruinous coin marked 'Fear.' We simply had to be number one people to cover up our deep-lying inferiorities... At heart we had all been abnormally fearful."*[410]

"We never apologise to anyone for depending upon our Creator. We can laugh at those who think spirituality the way of weakness. Paradoxically, it is the way of strength. The verdict of the ages is that faith means courage. All men of faith have courage. They trust their God. We never apologise for God. Instead we let Him (Her or It) *demonstrate, through us, what He* (She or It) *can do. <u>We ask</u>* (God) <u>*to remove our fear and direct our attention to what He would have us be.*</u> *At once, we commence to outgrow fear."*[411]

"As faith grows, so does inner security... Therefore we...find that our basic antidote for fear is a spiritual awakening."[412]

"The practice of (the) *Twelve Steps and Twelve Traditions in our personal lives brought incredible releases from fear of every description, despite the wide prevalence of formidable personal problems* (of all kinds)*."*[413] *"Mainly these were principles designed for ego reduction, and therefore for the reduction of fear...* (Eventually) *we coined the potent and meaningful expression, 'Let us always love the best in others—and never fear their worst.'"*[414]

We found out that ego disguises itself in polar opposites. *"I realised that my feeling of inferiority was just one aspect of ego, and the arrogance I projected was the other."*[415]

OBSERVE THE STATEMENT: *"We reviewed our fears thoroughly. We put them on paper, even though we had no resentment in connection with them."*[416]

We handle these fears in much the same way as resentments. Using the same form, we write in the first column who or what we are afraid of. In the second we put down why we feel afraid. *"We asked ourselves why we had them. Wasn't it because self-reliance failed us?"*[417] And in the third column we work out how these fears affect us.

In the fourth column we look at HOW this *"self-reliance failed us."* *"Driven by a hundred forms of fear, self-delusion, self-seeking, and self-pity, we Step on the toes of our fellows and they retaliate."*[418] *"So our troubles, we think are basically of our own making. They arrive out of ourselves..."*[419]

An elder Cherokee Native American was teaching his grandchildren about life. He said to them, *"A fight is going on inside me. It is a terrible fight, and it is between two wolves.*

One wolf represents fear, anger, envy, sorrow, regret, greed, arrogance, self-pity, guilt, resentment, inferiority, lies, pride and superiority. The other wolf stands for joy, peace, love, hope, sharing, serenity, humility, kindness, benevolence, friendship, empathy, generosity, truth, compassion, and faith. This same fight is going on inside of you and every other person too."

They thought about it for a minute and then one child asked his grandfather, *"Which wolf will win?"* The old Cherokee replied *"The one I feed."*

This illustrates exactly what we are trying to understand in our inventory processes—which wolf have we fed in the past and which wolf to feed now and how.

HOW DO WE ANSWER SUCH QUESTIONS; AS?

- *"Where had we been selfish, self-centred or self-seeking?"*
- *"Where had we been dishonest?"*
- *"Where had we been frightened?"*
- *"Where had we been* (responsible) *to blame?"*
- *"What decisions did we make based on self that later placed us in a position to be hurt?"*
- *"When in the past can we remember making this decision?"*
- *"Where were we wrong? What was our part?"*

The more we work with people in these various programs the more we realise how very difficult it is to begin to look at life's situations from a whole new angle. Many of our sponsees look at us with blank stares when asked questions such as those above. These are difficult questions. Most of us think that we are anything but selfish, dishonest, and are really victims to life's deranged sense of humour. But taking them one at a time, let's see if we just might be the architects of our own life. And if we are; can we reconstruct our lives?

- **"Where had we been selfish, self-centred or self-seeking?"**

Below we find a list of attitudes that may just suggest ways in which we might possibly be "selfish, self-centred or self-seeking." The most important trait to become aware of is that consideration of others, or other opinions, is not usually our first reaction.

SELFISH / SELF-CENTRED

- Wanting special treatment
- Wanting our "needs" met
- Wanting what others have
- Wanting control
- Wanting to be the best
- Wanting others to be like me
- Wanting more than my share
- Wanting to be liked
- Not seeing others' POV
- Not seeing others' problems
- Not seeing others' "needs"
- Not being a friend
- Being dependant
- Being dominant
- Being grandiose
- Being miserly
- Being possessive
- Thinking we're better
- Thinking others are jealous
- Reacting from self-loathing

SELF-SEEKING

- Manipulating others to do our will
- Putting others down to build us up (internally or externally)
- Engaging in character assassination
- Acting superior
- Acting out to fill a void
- Engaging in gluttony
- Lusting after another
- Ignoring others' needs
- Trying to control others
- Getting revenge when I don't get my way
- Acting out to feel good
- Simply holding a resentment
- Wanting things our way
- Wanting to look good at another's expense
- Making it all about me
- Reacting self-righteously
- Too concerned about us

"Where had we been dishonest?"

Dishonesty covers much more than just "cheque book" honesty. There are many ways in which we lie to ourselves and others, both overtly and covertly. *"Life is a totality, and...it can't be compartmentalised. Dishonesty in one area creates problems in another area. Healing in one segment provides better health in another. It is all connected. Each Step blends with another in an integrated, comprehensive programme designed to transform you and me into human beings capable of willingly and joyously doing God's will."*[420]

"Doc (Dr. Bob)*...was pretty positive that God's law was the Law of Love and that all my resentful feelings which I had fed and cultivated...were the result of either conscious or unconscious, it didn't matter which, disobedience to that law...*

"Taking love as the basic command I discovered that my faithful attempt to practice a law of love led me to clear myself of certain dishonesties."[421] These dishonesties we find in ourselves as well as others. We cannot fool ourselves about honesty as this woman did during her inventory process. *"The questions he asked me that I didn't answer honestly, I thought were none of his business."*[422] We justify our lies; mainly by fooling ourselves that it is the right thing to do.

DISHONEST

- Not seeing/admitting where we were at fault
- Having a superior attitude
- Thinking we're better
- Blaming others for our problems
- Not admitting we've done the same thing
- Not expressing feelings
- Not expressing ideas
- Not being clear
- Hiding our true motives
- Lying
- Cheating
- Stealing
- Not facing facts
- Hiding from reality
- Holding on to false beliefs
- Breaking rules or laws
- Lying to ourselves
- Exaggerating
- Minimising
- Setting ourselves up to be "wronged"
- Expecting others to be what they're not
- Being a perfectionist

"Where had we been frightened?"

As it says earlier, *"fear is an evil and corroding thread"* that distorts and harms our lives. Psychology has demonstrated that humans are only born with two fears; fear of loud noises and fear of loss of physical support. Therefore all other fears are not natural. Could these fears be where our defiance comes from? *"I was as defiant as anybody could be because I was scared."*[423] Let us look at just a few of those "unnatural" fears.

FEARS

- Of peoples' opinions
- Of rejection
- Of abandonment
- Of loneliness
- Of physical injury
- Of abuse
- Of not being able to change ourselves or others
- Of not being in control
- Of our inferiority
- Of our inadequacy
- Of criticism
- Of expressing our feelings
- Of expressing our ideas
- Of getting trapped
- Of exposure
- Of embarrassment

*"**Where had we been** (responsible) **to blame?**"*

*"**All my life I had blamed everything that ever happened to me on someone else, and I usually could find someone.**"*[424] As we outlined earlier in a footnote the word *responsible* could be broken down into two words: **response** and **able**. So the word can be interpreted to mean: *"What **response** are we **able** to give to any situation?"* and for that we are responsible.

In the following exercise we will look at our response to what has happened in our lives and the results of those responses. We are looking for the lost power in our lives. By realising that it is not what has happened to us but how we reacted to those events that has defined our lives, we recognise that we can change our reactions. The goal is to have the events of our past be just that, past events and not remain decisive factors in our present. Very often we felt compelled to make these decisions or choices at an early age, when our reason was under-developed.

Most of us wouldn't ask a child for advice on how to deal with a complex emotional or spiritual dilemma. But isn't that what we have done? This has determined the very lives that we live today. All based on a child's decisions and choices? As a result we find ourselves living with emotional insecurity. The **"Common symptoms of emotional insecurity are worry, anger, self-pity and depression."**[425] Who among us would not want to rid ourselves of this emotional baggage?

Uncovering our imperfections and flaws, discovering where **we** are responsible and discarding these errors is a lifetime process. If we work the programme each day, every tomorrow gets better and better. Becoming a better human being is wonderful but it is not our final destination. It is just a Step toward the purpose for which we were born. We were not born to cry, to strive, to struggle. We have lost our way, like the prodigal son. We were born in the image and likeness of an Intelligent Universe. The purpose of our life is to return to our Creator in that intelligent image and likeness; to see this **"Great Reality"** as our presence, our soul, our very being, and let It live our life for us, as us.

Our character defects have been passed down from generation to generation. While we are not to blame for inheriting these shortcomings, we are *responsible* for their continued use. Every thought, action, word, and deed is recorded in Universal Consciousness and, like radio waves, connects with those who are receptive. From birth these defects cause us to make mistakes over and over again with every one we come in contact with. They are impersonal; logged in our memory. When a situation arises we sort through past experiences, often unconsciously, to work out how to handle it. It's all we know. If in our past experiences we became angry, violent and yelled; or became passive and weak then that's how we react now. If it was to lie, we lie; if we were grovelling, we grovel. It is impersonal. We are not to blame.

The most important thing for us to get from this question is that we are responsible for:

1. ***Our emotions***—our feelings

2. ***Our actions,*** reactions and inactions

3. ***Our beliefs,*** stemming from our thinking—decisions and choices

Blame (Responsible)

- For harsh judgement
- For ignoring the facts
- Being careless
- Bringing the past into the present
- Blaming others for our feelings
- Not working our programme
- For our own upset
- For our ignorance
- Not dealing with emotions

"What decisions did we make based on self that later placed us in a position to be hurt?"

"When in the past can we remember making this decision?"

In order to understand the decisions we have made in these situations, we should understand how the human mind works. What follows is an over-simplified explanation of the mental process involved. The human mind makes a decision (usually unconsciously) based on what it perceives as necessary for its survival. Once this judgment has been made, our mind then gathers evidence to prove to itself that it has made the right decision. Our mind never gathers evidence to prove it's wrong or even take into account facts that may suggest it's not right. Unless of course by proving that we are wrong again, is evidence of us being right about always being wrong. This is where everything could get very complicated. For this work let's "Keep it Simple": **Our ego-mind never thinks it's wrong.** We call our data, "our experience."

The ultimate aim of our continuing inventory is to recognise and transform these past choices and decisions and replace them with reasonable ones. These choices and decisions are what have created our beliefs in life; not what actually happened to us, but what we made "what happened" mean. Regaining "Power" in our lives is accomplished by this recognition and the changing of these old decisions and choices; and therefore our beliefs. Then we find those beliefs are supported by the Universe just as our past beliefs have always been. As she looked back on her life, this woman said, **"Slowly, my life seemed to unfold before me, shedding insights on childhood resentments, jealousies, and fears that had mushroomed in adulthood."**[426]

On this subject of decisions or choices let us look at a few other things that can assist us in our quest for freedom. In early childhood we tend to watch our parents very closely, it doesn't seem to matter much whether we like who they are or not. Our choices as to who we emulate are usually based on who seemed to get their way. Who appeared to get what they wanted? This is why those of us who have had a bullying parent, even though we hated the way they were, end up being bullies ourselves. Or, when we have had what seemed to be a weak and whiney victim as one of our parents who in the end seems to get their way, we adopt the role of victim in life. Often our personalities are parts of both personality traits.

"When taking the kind of look at our lives that this programme requires, we see that when establishing the very foundation of our lives we were given choice over our response to everything. This is what mystics (men who have walked in enlightenment) have been trying to tell us for millennia. At this stage of the Steps we resemble the Prodigal Son in the biblical story, who returned home and was presented with a ring and a cloak, symbols of maturity and responsibility. Likewise, when we make conscious connection to the presence of a Higher Power and take full responsibility for our own lives and actions, we become responsible, and therefore really free, adults.

"Whatever we trusted and believed in yesterday we have become today. Whatever we trust and believe in today becomes our tomorrow. This is the miracle of the programme. We are no longer shackled by our past unconscious beliefs and behaviour patterns. Through exercising free choice today, we reshape our tomorrows. One day at a time." – George F.

The beliefs that we have held onto that do not serve us well we can, through inventory, discard. If we do not inventory them, and therefore find that they have no value, we are doomed to repeat these past beliefs again and again. We are surely free to do so, we are not automatons. If we truly desire a new life we *must* see that the things that we thought were good for us are not always so. The reason is that we are using the same old information locked in the memory banks of our minds. A human mind, that is weighing and measuring what is best for its destiny, is waging a losing proposition. We only have to look at our lives up till now to see that our unaided judgement is flawed. Uncovering our past mistakes, discovering where **we** made the decisions and choices that **truly** harmed us, and discarding these errors is a lifetime practice.

What about our "geographic cures" for our problems? When things got too bad **"I moved away. I never thought about changing myself, I always thought about changing people, or changing places."**[427]

We are all trying to win at this game of life. What we learn in the programme is that we can only truly win when we create positive, loving attitudes towards life itself. Napoleon Hill once wrote: **"what ever the mind... can conceive and believe it can achieve."**[428] We lay particular emphasis on this part of the process acknowledged recently by us, as part of the inventory process. Yet it has always been there: **"we invariably find that in the past we have made decisions based on self which later placed us in a position to be hurt."**[429] Finally, the decisions that most affect us are those generalised ones that colour our overall beliefs about people, places, things and God.

So, what is the underlying personality characteristic of those of us with addictive personalities? Well **"a number of eminent psychologists and doctors made an exhaustive study of a good-sized group... The doctors weren't trying to find out how different we were from one another; they sought to find whatever personality traits, if any, this group...had in common. These distinguished men had the nerve to say that most...under investigation were still childish, emotionally sensitive, and grandiose."**[430] This implies that up till now our most defining decisions were made by **"childish, emotionally sensitive, and grandiose"** sides of ourselves. What a kettle of fish that is, no wonder our lives are such a mess.

94

DECISIONS

- People are stupid
- Women are weak
- Women are dangerous
- Women are ...
- Men are better off
- Men are liars
- Men are ...
- We can't trust women
- We can't trust men
- I am stupid
- I am always right
- I am always wrong
- Nobody loves me
- I'm unlovable
- I'm ugly
- I have a bad temper
- My nose is too big
- Sex is dirty
- Marriage is ...
- Life is ...
- Heights are...
- Bugs are ...
- Pets are ...
- Whites are ...
- Blacks are ...
- Spanish are ...
- Germans are ...
- Americans are ...
- British are ...
- French are ... Etc. etc. etc.

"Where were we wrong? What was our part?"

Admitting that we are wrong is very difficult for many of us. But we have all made mistakes, a lot of them. Besides for our purposes wrong simply means mistaken. Our part is often found after reviewing the answers to the above questions. What we are looking for here is that part for which we are responsible. That part that if we had not perpetrated, the damage to our present lives could not have happened.

OUR PART

- Gathering evidence to prove ourselves right
- Making sweeping generalisations
- The rest of our part will be a distillation of the answers to the preceding questions

Some of us use what we have learned in the programme to look at what others aren't doing; this is *"known as 'taking someone else's inventory,' a practice at which...* (we) *can be expert."*[431] But we find this practice to be a fruitless one.

The way to reach God and freedom is through a thorough self-survey. This is done by taking every disturbing defect, resentment, fear, financial and sex problem of our memory, and seeing where the problem and disinformation started. Finding out what decisions or choices we made and where we deceived and deluded ourselves. This is our chosen path of freedom.

STEP 4 –RESENTMENT AND FEAR

"Resentment is the 'number one' offender.... (1) *I'm resentful at...* We listed people places and institutions or principles with whom we were angry or afraid... (2) *The Cause*... On our grudge list we set opposite each name our injuries... (3) *Affects my*...On our list we set opposite each name what was affected in us. Was it our **self-esteem,** our **security,** our **ambitions,** our **personal,** or **sex relations**, which had been interfered with?" **Fear, Pride**/Shame etc. [432]

FEAR – "*We reviewed our fears thoroughly. We put them on paper, even though we had no resentment in connection with them."*[433] We write our fears right after or intermingled with our resentments.

*The Deep Soul Cleansing Workbook is available with all the following forms presented in it. You'll find all the additional material available and how to acquire it at the back of this publication. Included you'll also find a website where you can download these forms for free.

I'm Resentful at Or I Fear: (1)	The Cause (2)	Affects my: (Check below) (3)
Person, Place or Thing		o Self-Esteem o Security o Ambitions o Personal Relations o Sex Relations o Pride/Shame o Fear

STEPS 6 & 7 Preparation - List Major "Character Defects"

Step 9 Amends	Step 8
	o **Now** o **Later** o **Never**

I'm Resentful at Or I Fear: (1)	The Cause (2)	Affects my: (Check below) (3)
Person, Place or Thing		o Self-Esteem o Security o Ambitions o Personal Relations o Sex Relations o Pride/Shame o Fear

STEPS 6 & 7 Preparation - List Major "Character Defects"

Step 9 Amends	Step 8
	o **Now** o **Later** o **Never**

I'm Resentful at Or I Fear: (1)	The Cause (2)	Affects my: (Check below) (3)
Person, Place or Thing		o Self-Esteem o Security o Ambitions o Personal Relations o Sex Relations o Pride/Shame o Fear

STEPS 6 & 7 Preparation - List Major "Character Defects"

Step 9 Amends	Step 8
	o **Now** o **Later** o **Never**

CLEANING HOUSE—HONESTY

Ask yourself: ** (AA 67.3) * (AA 62.2)	Putting out of our minds the wrong others have done, we resolutely looked for our own mistakes... We admitted our wrongs honestly...** Col (4)
Where and how have (I) been selfish, self-centred or self-seeking?**	
Where and how have (I) been dishonest?**	
Where and how have (I) been frightened?**	
For what am (I) (responsible) to blame?**	
What decisions did I make based on self that later placed me in a position to be hurt?*	
When in the past can I remember making this kind of decision?*	
Where was I wrong** and what was my part?	
Ask yourself: ** (AA 67.3) * (AA 62.2)	Putting out of our minds the wrong others have done, we resolutely looked for our own mistakes... We admitted our wrongs honestly...** Col (4)
Where and how have (I) been selfish, self-centred or self-seeking?**	
Where and how have (I) been dishonest?**	
Where and how have (I) been frightened?**	
For what am (I) (responsible) to blame?**	
What decisions did I make based on self that later placed me in a position to be hurt?*	
When in the past can I remember making this kind of decision?*	
Where was I wrong** and what was my part?	
Ask yourself: ** (AA 67.3) * (AA 62.2)	Putting out of our minds the wrong others have done, we resolutely looked for our own mistakes... We admitted our wrongs honestly...** Col (4)
Where and how have (I) been selfish, self-centred or self-seeking?**	
Where and how have (I) been dishonest?**	
Where and how have (I) been frightened?**	
For what am (I) (responsible) to blame?**	
What decisions did I make based on self that later placed me in a position to be hurt?*	
When in the past can I remember making this kind of decision?*	
Where was I wrong** and what was my part?	

NOW ABOUT SEX...

"Perhaps we are mixed up with women (or men) *in a fashion we wouldn't want advertised. We doubt if, in this respect,* (we) *are fundamentally much worse than other people. But drinking* (or any addiction) *does complicate sex relations in the home."*[434] Now we move on to look at our sex conduct and harm done others where we may not have had resentment involved.

"Now about sex, many of us needed an overhauling there. But above all, we tried to be sensible on this question. It's so easy to get way off track. Here we find human opinions running to extremes—absurd extremes perhaps. One set of voices cry that sex is a lust of our lower nature, a base necessity of procreation. Then we have the voices, who cry for sex and more sex; who bewail the institution of marriage; who think that most of the troubles of the race are traceable to sex causes. They think we do not have enough of it, or that it isn't the right kind. They see its significance everywhere. One school would allow man no flavour for his fare and the other would have us on a straight pepper diet. We want to stay out of this controversy. We do not want to be the arbiter of anyone's sex conduct. We all have sex problems. We'd hardly be human if we didn't. What can we do about them?

"We reviewed our own conduct over the years past. Where had we been selfish, dishonest, or inconsiderate? Whom had we hurt? Did we unjustifiably arouse jealousy, suspicion or bitterness? Where were we at fault, what should we have done instead? We got this all down on paper and looked at it.

"In this way we tried to shape a sane and sound ideal for our future sex life. We subjected each relationship to this test—was it selfish or not? We asked God to mould our ideals and help us to live up to them. We remembered always that our sex powers were God-given and therefore good, neither to be used lightly or selfishly nor to be despised and loathed.

"Whatever our ideal turns out to be, we must be willing to grow toward it. We must be willing to make amends where we have done harm, provided that we do not bring about still more in so doing. In other words, we treat sex as we would any other problem. In meditation, we ask God what we should do about each specific matter. The right answer will come, if we want it.

"God alone can judge our sex situations. Counsel with persons is often desirable, but we let God be the final judge. We realise

100

that some people are as fanatical about sex as others are loose. We avoid hysterical thinking or advice.

"Suppose we fall short of the chosen ideal and stumble? Does this mean we are going to get drunk? Some people tell us so. But this is only a half-truth. It depends on us and on our motives. If we are sorry for what we have done, and have the honest desire to let God take us to better things, we believe we will be forgiven and will have learned a lesson. If we are not sorry, and our conduct continues to harm others, we are quite sure to drink. We are not theorising. These are facts out of our experience.

"To sum up about sex: We earnestly pray for the right ideal, for guidance in each questionable situation, for sanity, and for the strength to do the right thing. If sex is very troublesome, we throw ourselves the harder into helping others. We think of their needs and work for them. This takes us out of ourselves. It quiets the imperious urge, when to yield would mean heartache."[435]

Above, it asks if our sex conduct has been selfish or not? *"If our sex conduct is selfish, we may excite jealousy, misery, and a strong desire to retaliate in kind."*[436] Of course this doesn't justify their actions either, but it certainly makes us complicit. Sex, if troublesome, can and should be treated with the same processes as our other addictions. Daily prayers asking for help in living up to our new ideals is not unreasonable. Whether we are alcoholics, drug addicts, spendaholics, food addicts or anything else, sex can be a good thing to monitor. Some of us slip from one addiction to another, anything but do the necessary daily work! Anything we can use to excess may become a problem for those of us with the "MORE" dis-eases of addiction. *"In other words, we treat sex like we would any other problem."*[437] After having completed our "sex inventory"(which follows), *"We asked God to mould our* (sex) *ideals and help us to live up to them."*[438]

*The Deep Soul Cleansing Workbook is available with all the forms presented in it. You'll find all the additional material available and how to acquire it at the back of this publication. Included you'll also find a website where you can download these forms for free.

Step 4 – NOW ABOUT SEX

SEX – Looking at both the past and present, what sex situations have caused me anxiety, bitterness, frustration, or depression? We reviewed our (sex) conduct over the years past. Answer yes or no questions with how or why.

Who: _____ **My conduct:** _____

_____

(Questions are culled from both "Big Book" of Alcoholics Anonymous [439] and the 12 & 12 [440].)

Where and how was I selfish or self-seeking?

Where and how was I dishonest?

Where and how was I inconsiderate?

Whom had I hurt and how badly?

Did I unjustifiably arouse jealousy, suspicion or bitterness?

Where and how was I responsible? What should I have done instead?

Did I spoil my marriage (relationship) *and/or injure my children? How?*

Did I jeopardise my standing in the community? How?

Did I burn with guilt that nothing could extinguish? Did I insist that I was the pursued—not the pursuer, and thus absolve myself? Explain.

How have I reacted to frustration in sexual matters? When denied did I become vengeful or depressed? Did I take it out on other people? How?

If there was rejection or coldness at home, did I use this as a reason for promiscuity? Explain.

What decisions did I make based on this experience that has affected my relationships?

What is the earliest time I can remember making this decision?

STEPS 6 & 7 Preparation - List Major "Character Defects"					

Step 9 Amends	Step 8
	○ **Now**
	○ **Later**
	○ **Never**

Make as many copies of this form that you need to complete your inventory.

Step 4 –HARM TO OTHERS (of any kind)

"We might...ask ourselves what we mean when we say that we have 'harmed' other people. What kinds of 'harm' do people do one another, anyway? To define that word 'harm' in a practical way, we might call it the result of instincts in collision, which cause physical, mental, emotional, or spiritual damage to people... If we lie or cheat, we deprive others not only of their worldly goods, but of their emotional security and peace of mind."[441] There are many subtler forms of harm we do. There is often harm we have done to others that has not been found in our resentments and other disturbances. Maybe there is unprovoked vandalism, keying a car just because we're envious. Stealing and shoplifting could very easily fall into this category unless we have dealt with them in resentments against ourselves.

We search our memories to find any of these kinds of offences. We don't want to miss anything consciously. And of course the more we can deal with now the less we will have to deal with later. If they're there, we deal with them; if not, we move on.

*The Deep Soul Cleansing Workbook is available with all the forms presented in it. You'll find all the additional material available and how to acquire it at the back of this publication. Included you'll also find a website where you can download these forms for free.

Step 4 –HARM TO OTHERS (of any kind)

HARMS TO OTHERS – This is where you put those acts of stealing, or violence, any harm done to others that was not covered in your resentments etc.

Who: _____ **My conduct:** _____

_____

(The following questions are culled from both the "Big Book" Alcoholics Anonymous [442] and the Twelve Steps and Twelve Traditions.[443])

Where and how was I selfish or self-seeking?

Where and how was I dishonest?

Where and how was I inconsiderate?

Where and for what was I to blame (responsible)*?*

What should I have done instead?

What people were hurt and how badly?

Did I spoil my marriage (relationship) *and/or injure my children? How?*

Did I jeopardise my standing in the community? How?

What decisions did I make based on this experience that has affected my relationships?

What's the earliest time I remember making this sort of decision?

STEPS 6 & 7 Preparation - List Major "Character Defects"					

Step 9 Amends	Step 8
	○ **Now**
	○ **Later**
	○ **Never**

Make as many copies of this form that you need to complete your inventory.

Step 4 – ABOUT MONEY and/or WORK

Money can be an immense cause of disturbance. *"Most...have said they had no troubles that money would not cure."*[444] This has quite often been an illusion. Buying our way out of trouble usually caused even more trouble. *"We believe that* (the) *Steps are for the whole of life."*[445] *"Worst of all, we forgot God. In money matters we had faith only in ourselves, and not too much of that.*

"This all meant of course that we were still far off-balance. When a job still looked like a mere means of getting money rather than an opportunity for service, when the acquisition of money for financial independence looked more important than right dependence on God, we were still victims of unreasonable fears. And these were fears which would make a serene and useful existence, at any financial level, quite impossible.

"But as time passed we found that with the help of (the) *Twelve Steps we could lose those fears, no matter what our material prospects were. ...It did not matter too much what our material condition was. Money gradually became our servant and not our master. It became a means of exchanging love and service with those about us... We found that freedom from fear was more important than freedom from want."*[446]

Money problems are not a separate issue; *"anytime I see a... member climbing the walls about money, I see a person in real trouble."*[447] Whether it is regarding our own finances or the meeting treasury about which we are disturbed, there is something amiss. For example one member who was passing the basket asked: *"'How can we trust the beginners not to take some of the money for themselves?'*

"'Listen,' I told him, 'you can't get uptight about money, or you're in real trouble. We'll just have to trust them. The money is incidental.'"[448] Most of the attendees at our retreats here in England find it difficult to believe us when we tell them that in the groups we started out in many years ago we use to announce "Put what you can afford in, and if you are desperate take some out."

"Still more wonderful is the feeling that we do not have to be especially distinguished among our fellows in order to be useful and profoundly happy... in God's sight all human beings are important ...we are no longer isolated and alone in self-constructed prisons... True ambition is the deep desire to live usefully and walk humbly under the grace of God."[449] Life becomes worthwhile <u>because of who we **really** are</u>, not in spite of who

we thought we were. *"Temptations rarely come only once, to be vanquished and disappear. Whether the attraction is that of money or alcohol, it is likely to surface again and again over the years."*[450]

"We decided it was time we took another kind of inventory. We came to the conclusion that we were powerless over money and that our lives were very, very unmanageable, still."[451] Most of us find that when we work the process and use good records-keeping (an inventory of its own) life got better even in this area. *"My every need was being met as long as I accepted and acknowledged the Divine Help which was so generously given."*[452]

"Also of importance for most... are the questions they must ask about their behaviour respecting financial and emotional security. In these areas fear, greed, possessiveness, and pride have too often done their worst. Surveying (our) *business or employment record, almost any alcoholic* (or other addict) *can ask questions like:* (those found on the form ahead)*."*[453] So let us make this a start and continue to look at this and other areas in later Steps.

After completing this stage: *"A tremendous change took place in my work, in my relationship with my employers, in my association with my co-workers and in my dealings with our customers. Crazy as the idea seemed when broached to me by these men who had found it worked, God did come right into my work when permitted, as He* (She or It) *had come into the other activities connected with my life."*[454]

*The Deep Soul Cleansing Workbook is available with all the forms presented in it. You'll find all the additional material available and how to acquire it at the back of this publication. Included you'll also find a website where you can download these forms for free.

Step 4 – ABOUT MONEY and/or WORK

Employer or Business Deal: _____

My Conduct: _____

(Questions are culled from the *Twelve Steps and Twelve Traditions*.[455])

Did fear and inferiority about my fitness for my job destroy my confidence and fill me with conflict? How?

Did I try to cover up those feelings of inadequacy by bluffing, cheating, lying, or evading responsibility? How?

Did I gripe that others failed to recognise my truly exceptional abilities? To whom did I grumble and how?

Did I overvalue myself and play the "big shot"? Give examples.

Did I have such unprincipled ambition that I double-crossed and/or undercut my associates? Who and how?

Was I irresponsible, wasteful and extravagant? Give examples.

Did I recklessly borrow money, caring little whether it was repaid? Give examples.

Was I a pinchpenny, refusing to support my family properly? How?

Did I try to cut corners financially? Give examples.

What about the "quick money" deals, the stock market, and the races? How about gambling? Give examples.

Did I juggle credit accounts ("robbing Peter to pay Paul")? How?

Did I manipulate the food budget or other spending allowances? How?

What Character defects contributed to my financial instability?
(Enter Below)

STEPS 6 & 7 Preparation - List Major "Character Defects"					

Step 9 Amends	Step 8
	○ **Now**
	○ **Later**
	○ **Never**

Make as many copies of this form that you need to complete your inventory.

ARE WE COMPLETE WITH STEP FOUR?

"If we have been thorough about our personal inventory, we have written down a lot. We have listed and analysed our resentments. We have begun to comprehend their futility and their fatality. We have commenced to see their terrible destructiveness. We have begun to learn tolerance, patience and good will toward all men, even our enemies, for we look on them as sick people...

"In this book (Alcoholics Anonymous) *you read again and again that faith did for us what we could not do for ourselves. We hope you are convinced now that God can remove whatever self-will has blocked you off from* (God)*. If you have already made a decision, and an inventory of your grosser handicaps, you have made a good beginning. That being so, you have swallowed and digested some big chunks of truth about yourself."*[456]

It was wisely said that *"the truth shall set you free." "How truth makes us free is something that we... can well understand... It continues to release us from conflicts and miseries beyond reckoning; it banishes fear and isolation... May we...quicken our search for still more genuine honesty, and deepen its practice in all our affairs."*[457]

Let us recognise right here that: *"**Step Four is beginning of lifelong practice.**"*[458] *"Once we have a complete willingness to take inventory, and exert ourselves to do the job thoroughly, a wonderful light falls upon this foggy scene. As we persist, a brand new kind of confidence is born, and the sense of relief at finally facing ourselves is indescribable. These are the first fruits of Step Four."*[459] The knowledge sets in that if we continue this work through out our lives we shall remain free; free to live life happily in God's grace.

THE PRINCIPLE OF STEP FOUR—

Honesty

It can be argued that each of these "Principles" is buried in all the Steps; *"Honesty"* is the key. However, with Step 4 we begin a lifetime of taking responsibility for our lives with *honest self-survey*. *"...Absolute honesty...each of us has to conceive what this great ideal may be—to the best of our ability."*[460]

Chapter 7

The Admission

Confession

STEP FIVE

"Admitted To God, To Ourselves and To Another Human Being The Exact Nature Of Our Wrongs"[461]

Read in preparation, in the "Big Book" of *Alcoholics Anonymous* –
Pages 72-75

Read in preparation, in the *Twelve Steps and Twelve Traditions* –
Step Five   Pages 56-63

- -

STEP FIVE

"Admitted To God, To Ourselves and To Another Human Being The Exact Nature Of Our Wrongs"[462]

" *L ooking at Step Five, we decided that an inventory, taken alone, wouldn't be enough. We knew we would have to quit the deadly business of living alone with our conflicts, and in honesty confide these to God and another human being."*[463] Why do we have to tell **"another human being the exact nature of our defects?"**[464] Let's face it; we sure wouldn't lay ourselves open to anyone if it wasn't absolutely necessary. **"All of** (the) **Twelve Steps ask us to go contrary to our natural desires...they deflate our egos. When it comes to ego deflation, few Steps are harder to take than Five. But scarcely any Step is more necessary to long-time** (comfortable) **sobriety and peace of mind than this one.**

"If we have swept the searchlight of Step Four back and forth over our careers, and it has revealed in stark relief those experiences we'd rather not remember, if we have come to know how wrong thinking and action have hurt us and others, then the need to stop living by ourselves with those tormenting ghosts of yesterday gets more urgent than ever. We have to talk to somebody about them.

"So intense, though, is our fear and reluctance to do this, that many...at first try to by-pass Step Five. We search for an easier way—which usually consists of the general and fairly painless admission that when drinking (or whatever our drug of choice) **we were sometimes bad actors...**

"But of the things which really bother and burn us, we say nothing. Certain distressing and humiliating memories, we tell ourselves, ought not be shared with anyone. These will remain our secret. Not a soul must ever know. We hope they will go to the grave with us."[465] Besides that, the thought of admitting **we** may have had a part in each situation that possibly harmed us even more than *their* behaviour, was unthinkable.

"We have been trying to get a new attitude, a new relationship with our Creator, and to discover the obstacles in our path."[466] This Step moves us closer to that goal; **"you ought to make a beginning as soon as you can."**[467]

"This is perhaps difficult—especially discussing our defects with another person. We think we have done well enough in admitting these things to ourselves. There is doubt about that.

In actual practice, we usually find a solitary self-appraisal insufficient."[468]

There *"are ...good reasons why we should do so. The best reason first: If we skip this vital Step, we may not overcome drinking. Time after time newcomers* (and not-so-newcomers) *have tried to keep to themselves certain facts about their lives. Trying to avoid this humbling experience, they have turned to easier methods. Almost invariably they got drunk. Having persevered with the rest of the programme, they wondered why they fell. We think the reason is that they never completed their housecleaning. They took inventory all right, but hung on to some of the worst items in stock. They only thought they had lost their egoism and fear; they only thought they had humbled themselves. But they had not learned enough of humility, fearlessness and honesty, in the sense we find it necessary, until they told someone else their entire life story....* (If we don't we don't reap the full benefit of the process).

"Psychologists are inclined to agree with us. We have spent thousands of dollars for examinations. We know but few instances where we have given these doctors a fair break. We have seldom told them the whole truth nor have we followed their advice. Unwilling to be honest with these sympathetic men, we were honest with no one else."[469]

"Few muddled attitudes have caused us more trouble than holding back on Step Five. Some people are unable to stay sober at all, others will relapse periodically until they really clean house. Even... old-timers, sober for years, often pay dearly for skimping on this Step (or future Tenth Steps). *They will tell how they tried to carry the load alone* (doing inventory in their heads); *how much they suffered..."*[470] But if we have someone else to help keep us on track we find that: *"As we took inventory, we began to suspect how much trouble self-delusion had been causing us."*[471] *"What comes to us alone may be garbled by our rationalisation and wishful thinking. The benefit of talking to another person is that we can get...direct comment and counsel on our situation, and there can be no doubt in our minds what that advice is."*[472]

WITH WHOM DO WE SHARE OUR INVENTORY?

"We must be entirely honest with somebody if we expect to live long or happily in this world. Rightly and naturally, we think well before we choose the person or persons with whom to take

this intimate and confidential Step."[473] It is important to do this as quickly as possible. *"Only by discussing ourselves, holding back nothing, only by being willing to take advice and accept direction could we set foot on the road to straight thinking, solid honesty, and genuine humility."*[474]

"Until we actually sit down and talk aloud about what we have so long hidden, our willingness to clean house is still largely theoretical."[475] We must make a decision, with whom will we share our work? The following are some possible suggestions.

PRIEST, MINISTER OR RABBI

"Those of us belonging to a religious denomination which requires confession must, and of course, will want to go to the properly appointed authority whose duty it is to receive it. Though we have no religious connection, we may still do well to talk with someone ordained by an established religion. We often find such a person quick to see and understand our problem."[476]

PSYCHOLOGIST OR DOCTOR

"We search our acquaintances for a close-mouthed, understanding friend. Perhaps our doctor or psychologist will be the person."[477] A doctor or psychologist may be amazed at our inventory. We should be careful that they don't encourage our beliefs that everything is "THEIR" (other people in our inventories) fault. The *incident* may well be entirely "their fault" but we must always take responsibility for how we reacted.

"It is important that he be able to keep a confidence; that he fully understand and approve what we are driving at..."[478]

OUR SPONSORS

We suggest that we put to good use the experience of our sponsors when going through our Fifth Step. *"We shall want to speak with someone who is experienced, who not only has stayed dry but has been able to surmount other serious difficulties."*[479] We must always remember our definition of real sobriety. *"Our sponsors...are the carriers of...tested experience with Step Four."*[480] If we have been working with our sponsors through the first four proposals then she already has a relationship with us and that relationship can only get stronger. Of course, this is based on the assumption that our sponsor has done a thorough **"searching and fearless moral inventory"** of herself. The sponsor will share back where others would not and therefore provide assurance **"that his case is not strange or different...probably not...worse than those of anyone else... This the sponsor promptly proves by talking freely and easily, and without exhibitionism, about his own defects, past and present."**[481]

There is another advantage to having our sponsors hear our Fifth Step: by the time we are done she will know us just about as well as any human being can. This means that in the future relationship there is a lot of background that it becomes totally unnecessary to re-tell. It will make it much easier to talk to our sponsor. She also won't be able to be manipulated easily and will help us with the **"Danger of rationalisation."**[482] We find that for one person to know so much about us, warts and all, and still be our friend and sponsor is very liberating. As mentioned above, when we are sharing our Fifth Step; our sponsor usually shares back in areas where she identifies with us. This brings us even closer together. You may find, as we have, that she becomes your closest friend.

When deciding who to confide in we should remember that **"it is important that he be able to keep a confidence; that he fully understand and approve of what we are driving at; that he will not try to change our plan."**[483] So, if we chose someone other than our sponsor (who should understand) we must be clear about our intentions. We are attempting to understand our part, not trying to find an ally in blaming everyone else.

"When we decide who is to hear our story, we waste no time. We have a written inventory and we are prepared for a long talk... We are engaged upon a life-and-death errand....

"We pocket our pride and go to it, illuminating every twist of character, every dark cranny of the past."[484]

We may well find that like most people with problems **"Too much of my life has been spent in dwelling upon the faults of others. This is a most subtle and perverse form of self-satisfaction, which permits us to remain comfortably unaware of our own defects. Too often we are heard to say, 'If it weren't for him (or her), how happy I'd be!'"**[485]

It is time we looked only at ourselves. We are damaged. **"We reacted more strongly to frustrations than normal people. By reliving these episodes and discussing them in strict confidence with somebody else, we can reduce their size and therefore their potency in the unconscious."**[486] **"The damned-up emotions**

118

of years break out of confinement, and miraculously vanish as soon as they are exposed. As the pain subsides, a healing tranquillity takes its place."[487] This is the beginning of the real freedom we failed to find through our many different addictions. This is a form of deep soul cleansing.

"The practice of admitting one's defects to another person is, of course, very ancient. It has been validated in every century, and it characterises the lives of all spiritually centred...people.[488] In a different form the same result is strived for on the psychiatrist's couch and by the psychologist where the therapist listens and helps the patient become aware of, and unload, their unhealthy thinking.

Remembering what our definition of sobriety is: *"a peaceful, calm, contented, serene and well-balanced life." "Most of us would declare that without a fearless admission of our defects to another human being we could not stay sober."*[489] Like this woman, one of the first 100 members, wrote: *"I dragged out all my sins of commission and omission, I told everything I could think of that might be the cause of creating a fear situation, a remorse situation, or a shame situation."*[490]

"What are we likely to receive from Step Five? For one thing, we shall get rid of that terrible sense of isolation we've always had."[491] *"Until we had talked with complete candour of our conflicts, and had listened to someone else do the same thing, we still didn't belong. Step Five was the answer. It was the beginning of true kinship with man and God."*[492] Often the *"results are tranquillity and consciousness of God."*[493] This however does not always result at this early stage; remember the "promises" come during the process of completing Step Nine.

For many of us, the effect is that we see ourselves differently. We saw that in life, *"I hated myself worse and worse, and as I hated myself I became more defiant towards everything and everybody."*[494] This would continue to be our legacy if we didn't continue through the Steps.

ARE WE COMPLETE WITH STEP FIVE?

When we have finished sharing our inventory *"Returning home we find a place where we can be quiet for an hour, carefully reviewing what we have done. We thank God from the bottom of our heart that we know Him* (Her or It) *better. Taking this book* (Alcoholics Anonymous) *down from the shelf we turn to the page, which contains the Twelve Steps* (page 59). *Carefully reading the first five proposals we ask if we have omitted anything, for we are building an arch through which we shall walk a free man at last. Is our work solid so far? Are the stones properly in place? Have we skimped on the cement put in the foundation? Have we tried to make mortar without sand?"*[495]

The point is: Have we done everything we know to do and exposed all that we are aware of up until now? *"We must be entirely honest with somebody if we expect to live long or happily in this world."*[496] If so we come to see that: *"Sometimes I have failed, but I am not a failure; I have made mistakes, but I am not a mistake."*[497] Our sponsors help us realise that we are each an individualised expression of God. We are all on the same path toward that very truth.

"Once we have taken this Step, withholding nothing... We can look the world in the eye. We can be alone at perfect peace and ease. Our fears fall from us."[498] *"The Fifth Step enabled me to see my part in my resentments and fears."*[499] When this has been completed thoroughly *"you have swallowed and digested some big chunks of truth about yourself."*[500] We begin to understand the meaning of the phrase "the Truth, shall set you free." *"If you have already made a decision, and an inventory of your grosser handicaps, you have made a good beginning."*[501] We come to terms with ourselves. *"By the grace of God, I have admitted my powerlessness over people, places and things...*

"I have given up believing that any human power can relieve me of that empty feeling. ...it is only a loving God who can give me inner peace and emotional stability."[502] We continually remind ourselves that this is only the *"beginning of a lifelong process."* WE WILL NEVER COMPLETE A "PERFECT INVENTORY." We do the best we can. By the end of Step Five we have the confidence that comes with learning that: *"All of my horrible <u>suffering was self-induced.</u>"*[503]

Over the years there have been as many different ways of completing the Steps as there are groups. Today *"a number of 'modern,' AA-oriented treatment facilities were encouraging patients to go through the first five Steps of the...programme before they were released—a procedure not much different from what the first group was doing in 1935."*[504] This inventory though is as thorough as we know to make it. It is more than likely that it won't be done in a few days as were early ones. But this approach has deeper rewards. We move quickly on to Steps 6, 7, 8, and 9, but we continue our inventory, in Step 10 on a daily and yearly basis.

THE PRINCIPLE OF STEP FIVE

Confession

Our journey begins with the *courage* to come to meetings and ask for help. For some of us our recovery starts with our first meeting. For others it comes when we ask for help from a sponsor. But certainly for all of us that *courage* is there by the time we begin the **confession** of our "short comings" in Step Five. This is the, ***"beginning of true kinship with man and God.*** (We) ***lose*** (a) ***sense of isolation, receive forgiveness and give it; learn humility; gain honesty and realism about ourselves."***[505]

Chapter 8

Getting Ready

Willingness

STEP SIX

"Were Entirely Ready To Have God Remove All These Defects of Character."[506]

STEP SIX PREPARATION

Read in preparation, in the "Big Book" of *Alcoholics Anonymous* –
Page 76.1

Read in preparation, in the *Twelve Steps and Twelve Traditions* – Step Six
Pages 64-70

STEPS 6 & 7 Preparation - List Major "Character Defects"					

STEP SIX – SEE OUR DEFECTS

"Were Entirely Ready To Have God Remove All These Defects of Character"[507]

here is not much said about Step Six in the "Big Book" of *Alcoholics Anonymous*. There is only this beginning right after Step Five and the self-inquiry as to whether our work so far is solid, the "Big Book" tells us in so many words that more will be revealed when it says: *"Our book is meant to be suggestive only. We realise we know only a little. God will disclose more to you and to us."*[508] We find that the first words, in the *"Twelve Steps and Twelve Traditions"* about Step Six read: *"This is the Step that separates the men from the boys."* And, it continues, *"any person capable of enough willingness and honesty to try repeatedly Step Six on all his faults—without any reservations whatever—has indeed come a long way spiritually."*[509]

"Since most of us are born with an abundance of natural desires, it isn't strange that we often let these far exceed their intended purpose. When they drive us blindly, or we wilfully demand that they supply us with more satisfactions or pleasures than are possible or due us, that is the point at which we depart from the degree of perfection that God wishes for us here on earth. That is the measure of our character defects."[510]

In order to realise the full impact of this Step we must first understand why we have *"character defects"* and how they have damaged our relationships. We recognise that *"we are set in conflict not only with ourselves, but with other people who have instincts, too."*[511] *"Since our blindness is caused by our own defects, we must first deeply realise what they are."*[512] Character defects are the weapons that we as *"self-reliant"* and rebellious people use, to one degree or another, to fulfil our instinctual desires. And so: *"At Step Six, many of us baulked—for the practical reason that we did not wish to have all* (these weapons) *our defects of character removed"*[513] from our arsenal. At this point hopefully we begin to realise *"that to be relieved of alcoholism* (or any ism) *I would have to be different."*[514] We must let go of our old ways of being.

At this point we start to realise that *"Rebellion may be fatal."*[515] *"But that is not all of the danger. Every time a person imposes his instincts unreasonably upon others, unhappiness follows."*[516] And that is true for all concerned. To completely give up the "weapons" we have used to get what we want and survive life's big and little disappointments is to have NO *"self-reliance"* whatsoever. *"We have admitted certain defects; we have ascertained in a rough way what the trouble is; we have put our finger on the weak items in our personal inventory. Now these are about to be cast out...the exact nature of our defects."*[517]

What does this mean? We believe that in order to be **"entirely ready to have God remove all these defects of character"**[518] we would have to be *entirely ready* to depend on God alone, for our defences, to be completely ready to dump the weapons with which we've defended ourselves all our lives. This would be the **"point at which we abandon limited objectives and move toward God's will for us."**[519]

"Experience has taught us we cannot live alone with our pressing problems and the character defects which cause or aggravate them."[520] In the process of these Steps we have agreed that lack of power is our dilemma. We are looking for a Power greater than ourselves to replace our will and care for our lives. But how many of us have such a degree of faith that we could completely surrender to the will of a Power Greater than these defects of character or, as we see them, weapons for getting what we want? This would be to truly understand that self-reliance is to separate oneself from God. This separation is the cause of powerlessness. We work Step Six to the best of our ability—recognising that it is clearly the beginning of a lifelong endeavour.

At the end of this chapter is a list of **"Character Defects"** to make note of, adding them to your inventory as you re-read your inventory, including; sex relations, resentments, harm to others and/or fears on each Person, Place or Thing. **"Now let's ponder the need for a list of the more glaring personality defects all of us have in varying degrees."**[521]

You will find the so-called **"SEVEN DEADLY SINS of PRIDE, GREED, LUST, ANGER, GLUTTONY, ENVY, and SLOTH."**[522] On the form they are in caps and bolded. We prefer to call them the 'seven deadly mistakes' or the 'seven prime character defects.' It can be argued that the others on the list are simply reactions to, variations of or degrees of these seven. For this exercise we don't think it much matters; the point is to see that OUR LIVES HAVE BEEN RUN BY BEHAVIOURS THAT DON'T WORK to get us what we truly want. Peace. **"All these failings generate fear, a soul-sickness in its own right. Then fear generates more character defects. Unreasonable fear that our instincts will not be satisfied drives us to covet the possession of others, to lust for sex and power, to become angry when our instinctive demands are threatened, to be envious when the ambitions of others seem to be realised while ours are not. We eat, drink, and grab for more of everything** *than we need, fearing we shall never have enough. And with genuine alarm at the prospect of work, we stay lazy. We loaf and procrastinate, or at best work grudgingly and under half-steam. These...are the termites that ceaselessly devour the foundations of whatever sort of life we try to build."*[523] It's no wonder we need the help of a Power greater than ourselves to be relieved of these *"shortcomings."* Our hope is to gradually (if not immediately) be relieved of their use, first through our recognition that they no longer serve us, if indeed they ever have. Then the humility to admit our helplessness to do this task on our own, and to have our defects removed through prayer in the Seventh Step. Obviously, this is not a one time thing either.

This would require a complete and perfect humility in Step Seven. In Step Six we see how *"This is the Step that separates the men from the boys."*[524]   *"Perfect humility would be a state of complete freedom from myself, freedom from all the claims that my defects of character now lay so heavily upon me. Perfect humility would be full willingness, in all times and places, to find and do the will of God."*[525] Once we have seen these defects and have agreed that they do not bring us the happiness we desire, we are willing to let go of them. *"Our first practical move towards humility must consist of recognising our deficiencies. No defect can be corrected unless we clearly see what it is."*[526] Then *"we shall need to make a brand new venture into open-mindedness."*[527]

"We then look at Step Six. We have emphasised willingness as being indispensable. Are we now ready to have God remove from us all the things, which we have admitted are objectionable? Can (God) *now take them all—every one? If we still cling to something we will not let go, we ask God to help us be willing."*[528] We trust, at this point, that we are ready to humbly ask for their removal in Step Seven.

THE PRINCIPLE OF STEP SIX

Willingness

All our answers will be found deep inside. *Willingness* is the key. We must be *willing* to resist our own will-power and the demand of our self-will to keep acting out with our defects of character. Once we have found these weapons to be defective, (in fact they usually backfire) our *willingness* to let go of them becomes simpler. We do find that it is not easy to change our habitual defensive behaviour, making this Step much more difficult than it may seem.

LIST OF CHARACTER DEFECTS—OUR WEAPONS

Abandonment

Abusive

Addictions

Aggravation

Agitation

Airhead

Alcoholism

Attention seeking

ANGER

Annoyance

Arrogance

Belligerent

Blame

Bigotry

Bored

Caretaking

Co-dependence

Competing

Coldness

Compulsions

Condescending

Confusion

Controlling

Cowardice

Cynicism

Deceit

Dependence

Depression

Devious

Disbelief

Dishonesty

Dislike

Dismay

Drug addiction

Dissatisfaction

Doubt

Egocentricity

ENVY

Evasiveness

False Humility

False Pride

Fear

Frustration

GLUTTONY

Gossip

Grandiosity

GREED

Hate

Hero-Worship

Hypersensitivity

Hypocrisy

Impatience

Inconsiderate

Indignation

Insecurity

Insincere

Intolerance

Irritation

Jealousy

Judgement

Lazy

Lying

LUST

Manipulative

Martyrdom

Mind-Reading

Negativity

Obsession

Offensive

Over-eating

Over-reactive

Over-sensitive

Panicky

Passivity

Patronising

Paranoia

People-pleasing

Perfectionism

Phoney

Playing dumb

Possessiveness

Prejudice

PRIDE

Procrastination

Rage

Rebellious

Rejection

Resentment

Resistant

Righteousness

Self-Centred

Self-Condemnation

Self-Hate

Self-Importance

Self-Indulgence

Selfishness

Self-Justification

Self-Obsession

Self-Pity

Self-Righteous

Self-Seeking

Shame

SLOTH

Sensitivity

Spite

Stoic

Suspicion

Touchy

Two-faced

Ungrateful

Unwillingness

Vanity

Vengeful

Victim

Vindictiveness

Violent

Withdrawn

Chapter 9

Asking for Removal

Humility

STEP SEVEN – RELEASING SELF-DEFENCE

*"**Humbly Asked** (God) **To Remove Our Shortcomings.**"*[529]

STEP SEVEN PREPARATION
Read in preparation, in the book *Twelve Steps and Twelve Traditions* – Step Seven   Pages 71-78

STEPS 6 & 7 Preparation - List Major "Character Defects"					

STEP SEVEN – RELEASING SELF-DEFENCE

*"**Humbly Asked** (God) **To Remove Our Shortcomings.**"*[530]

𝕿here is a lot we could say about this Step. Though it is greatly neglected in the *Big Book*, it is covered well in the *Twelve Steps and Twelve Traditions.*

What does it mean to be at Step Seven? At the beginning of our journey together we admitted our powerlessness. This has had disastrous consequences on our life, the result being total unmanageability. Therefore it was understood that the only solution was to find a ***"Power Greater than ourselves"*** that could, and would, resolve our problems. Each of the Steps so far has been a gradual movement towards that end. ***"Humility means 'to show submissive respect,' and by being humble I realise I am not the centre of the universe... Daily communion with God demonstrates my humility and provides me with the realisation that an entity more powerful than I is willing to help me if I cease trying to play God myself."***[531]

*"**SINCE this Step so specifically concerns itself with humility, we should pause here to consider what humility is and what the practice of it can mean to us.**"*

*"**Indeed, the attainment of greater humility is the foundation principle of each of** (the) **Twelve Steps. For without some degree of humility, no alcoholic** (or addict of any kind for that matter) **can stay sober** (or abstinent) **at all. Nearly all...have found, too, that unless they develop much more of this precious quality than may be required just for sobriety, they still haven't much chance of becoming truly happy. Without it, they cannot live to much useful purpose, or, in adversity, be able to summon the faith that can meet any emergency.**"*

*"**Humility, as a word and as an ideal, has a very bad time of it in our world. Not only is the idea misunderstood; the word itself is often intensely disliked. Many people haven't even a nodding acquaintance with humility as a way of life...**"*[532]

*"**Never was there enough of what we thought we wanted... We had lacked the perspective to see that character-building and spiritual values had to come first, and that material satisfactions were not the purpose of living.**"*[533] We are therefore looking to make humility a way of life. Why? In the past *"**whenever we had to choose between character and comfort, the character-building was lost in the dust of our chase after what we thought was happiness. Seldom did we look at character-building as**"*

something desirable in itself, something we would like to strive for whether our instinctual needs were met or not. We never thought of making honesty, tolerance, and true love of man and God the daily basis of living."[534]

Just how has that served us until now? Did it cost us more than we knew? Why did some have faith that seemed to work and we did not? Bill said: **"For just so long as we were convinced that we could live exclusively by our own individual strength and intelligence, for just that long was a working faith in a Higher Power impossible... As long as we placed self-reliance first, a genuine reliance upon a higher Power was out of the question. That basic ingredient of all humility, a desire to see and do God's will, was missing."[535]**

Until we came into the rooms the only solution to life problems was to drink or use. **"Step Seven is change in attitude which permits us to move out of ourselves towards God."[536]** How do we become willing to change our thinking and surrender to God? We put self-reliance aside in this Step.

"For us, the process of gaining a new perspective was unbelievably painful. It was only by repeated humiliations that we were forced to learn something about humility. It was only at the end of a long road, marked by successive defeats and humiliations, and the final crushing of our self-sufficiency, that we began to feel humility as something more than a condition of grovelling despair...

"So it is that we first see humility as a necessity. But this is the barest beginning. To get completely away from our aversion to the idea of being humble, to gain a vision of humility as the avenue to true freedom of the human spirit, to be willing to work for humility as something to be desired for itself, takes most of us a long, long time. A whole lifetime geared to self-centredness cannot be set in reverse all at once. Rebellion dogs our every step at first."[537]

Our humiliations are actually proof of a lack of humility. One cannot be humiliated if they are humble. We ought to recognise that humiliation is the LACK of Humility; they are not the same thing at all. Humiliation is actually the opposite of Humility. How can we judge our progress so far? How do we know that we are ready to move on from here?

"When we have taken a square look at some of these defects, have discussed them with another, and have become willing to have them removed, our thinking about humility commences to have wider meaning... We enjoy moments in which there is

something like real peace of mind... Where humility had formerly stood for a forced feeding of humble pie, it now begins to mean the nourishing ingredient which can give us serenity."[538]

Yes, it is humility itself that has provided what are very possibly our first experiences with peace of mind and serenity. *"There can be no absolute humility for us humans. At best, we can only glimpse the meaning and splendour of such a perfect ideal... Only God...can manifest in the absolute; we human beings must live and grow in the domain of the relative. We seek humility for today."*[539]

"Our eyes begin to open to the immense values which have come straight out of painful ego-puncturing. Until now, our lives have been largely devoted to running from pain and problems. We fled from them as from the plague. We never wanted to deal with the fact of suffering. Escape via the bottle (or another addiction) *was our solution. Character-building through suffering might be all right for saints, but certainly didn't appeal to us."*[540]

Let us stop for a moment and take a look back at our time in the Programme so far. Since we have been sober we have not done the things we use to do to avoid pain, such as drink. *"But in the longer run we clearly realise that these are only pains of growing up, and that nothing but good can come from them if we turn more and more to the entire Twelve Steps for the answers."*[541] We have now experienced to some measure serenity and peace of mind: *"I learned that there was satisfaction in the accomplishment of even menial tasks and that humility—applied as teach-ability and the search for truth—could be a higher Power in disguise."*[542] Now, with the benefit of 20/20 hindsight, we can see how much progress we have made in reaching this point.

"In every case, pain had been the price of admission into a new life. But this admission price had purchased more than we expected. It bought a measure of humility, which we soon discovered to be a healer of pain. We began to fear pain less, and desire humility more than ever.

"During this process of learning more about humility, the most profound result of all was the change in our attitude towards God... We began to get over the idea that the higher Power was a sort of lifesaver, to be called upon only in an emergency. The notion that we would still live our own lives, God helping a little

now and then, began to evaporate... Refusing to place God first, we had deprived ourselves of his help."[543]

PAIN IS GOOD

Pain is not to be avoided but to be recognised for what it is—NOTIFICATION. One of the things discovered by some of us is that the very thing we have been shunning all our lives—PAIN, is actually a good thing. Not something to steer clear of but truly a thing to be seen as warning that we are off track. When we are in alignment with our Higher Power there is no pain. When we find ourselves in pain we simply are out of line with God.

The biggest discovery for many of us was that there is no pain in the present. We have discovered that pain comes from memories of past traumas or projections into possible events of the future. So, our simplistic slogan, "One Day at a Time" is actually a brilliant possibility of happiness, right here and right now. God lives in the **present,** which must be why **present** and **gift** are synonymous?

THREE POINTS STAND OUT

We are reminded here that there are three points that stand out as we embark on Step Seven:

1. *"A great turning point in our lives came when we sought for humility as something we really wanted, rather than as something we <u>must</u> have."*[544]

2. *"The chief activator of our defects has been self-centred fear—primarily fear we would lose something we already possessed or would fail to get something we demanded."*[545]

3. *"The Seventh Step is where we make the change in our attitude which permits us, with humility as our guide, to move out from ourselves towards others and towards God."*[546]

We have no humility, when we instruct another person, what they should do, or not do, without being asked for our help. A close personal friend and I have an expression: *"God save us from helpful people!"* Offering advice or "help" without first being asked doesn't work for either party, ever!

By now *"We have admitted certain defects; we have ascertained in a rough way what the trouble is; we have put our finger on the weak items in our personal inventory. Now these are about to be cast out."*[547] With prayer we release *"the exact nature of our defects"*[548] to the care of God.

PLAQUE ON THE DESK OF DR. BOB

"On his desk, Dr. Bob had a plaque defining humility:

'Perpetual quietness of heart. It is to have no trouble. It is never to be fretted or vexed, irritable or sore; to wonder at nothing that is done to me, to feel nothing done against me. It is to be at rest when nobody praises me, and when I am blamed or despised, it is to have a blessed home in myself where I can go in and shut the door and kneel to my Father in secret and be at peace, as in a deep sea of calmness, when all around and about is seeming trouble.'"[549]

"Let yourself go and let God be God in you," wrote Meister Eckhart. An intellectual knowledge of this Higher Power as the presence, power, and intelligence is only a beginning. It is not sufficient to prevent our acting out by using the former weapons of our "survival"—our character defects—or to give us health and freedom from lack and limitation. We find that when we use these "weapons" we may win the battle but lose the war. And *"the more we fought and tried to have our own way, the worse matters got. As in war, the victor only <u>seemed</u> to win."*[550]

The truth regarding this Universal Spirit must be realised; not mentally stated and intellectually understood or simply agreed with, but *realised*. Since time in memoriam only a handful of mystics have recognised and truly embraced this realisation enough to make a profound and lasting change in human affairs. So we pray daily for the removal of all our shortcomings.

"Then comes the day when, finally freed in large degree from rebellion, we practice humility because we deeply want it as a way of life."[551] *"In Step Seven, we humbly ask... God to remove our shortcomings such as* (God) *could or would under the conditions of the day we asked."*[552] If they have not been removed, it is because we still believe they have some value, and that they don't *"stand in the way of my usefulness to* (God) *and my fellows."*[553] But *"We well know that our defects...have been and still are very great. And we hope that we shall never cease to rededicate ourselves to their correction."*[554]

"Recalling the afternoon he spent with Dr. Bob in his office, Earl said, 'He very carefully helped me through my moral inventory,

suggesting many, many bad personality traits and character defects. When this was finished, he asked me if I would like to have these defects removed.'

"Without much thought, I said, 'Yes, I would.' And then he asked me to get down on my knees at the desk with him, and we both prayed audibly to have these defects of character removed."[555]

THE PRINCIPLE OF STEP SEVEN

Humility

Step 7 reminds us to give up our attempts at fixing ourselves and turn it over to God, an act of **humility** and open-mindedness that most of us never understood. **Humility** is in the acceptance of who we are. This is the spiritual opposite of living in our character defects. **"The curious paradox is that when I accept myself as I am, then I change."**[556] **Humility** shines forth when I accept myself (the egos) warts and all.

WITH THIS KNOWLEDGE WE SAY THE SEVENTH STEP PRAYER

"My creator, I am now willing that you should have all of me good and bad. I pray that you now remove from me every single defect of character, (including _____) *which stand(s) in the way of my usefulness to you and my fellows. Grant me strength as I go out from here to do your bidding.*

Amen"[557]

Chapter 10

Becoming Willing

Forgiveness

STEPS EIGHT – PREPARING TO MEND

"Made A List Of All People We Have Harmed, and Became Willing To Make Amends To Them All."[558]

Read in preparation, in the "Big Book" of *Alcoholics Anonymous* –
Page 76-84

Read in preparation, in the *Twelve Steps and Twelve Traditions* – Step Eight
Pages 79-84

Note that we have embedded the Amends in the Inventory sections. This should make it simpler to do and stop us conveniently "forgetting" anyone. But there are extra pages of Amends, here and in the Personal Inventory Workbook, for any additional amends necessary.

Step 9 Amends	Step 8
(Person, Place or Thing)	o Now o Later o Never
Step 9 Amends	Step 8
(Person, Place or Thing)	o Now o Later o Never
Step 9 Amends	Step 8
(Person, Place or Thing)	o Now o Later o Never
Step 9 Amends	Step 8
(Person, Place or Thing)	o Now o Later o Never
Step 9 Amends	Step 8
(Person, Place or Thing)	o Now o Later o Never
Step 9 Amends	Step 8
(Person, Place or Thing)	o Now o Later o Never
Step 9 Amends	Step 8
(Person, Place or Thing)	o Now o Later o Never

STEP EIGHT – PREPARING TO MEND

"Made A List Of All People We Have Harmed, And Became Willing To Make Amends To Them All."[559]

" In Step Eight, we continued our house cleaning, for we saw that we were not only in conflict with ourselves, but also with people and situations in the world in which we lived. We had to begin to make our peace, and so we listed the people we had harmed and became willing to set things right."[560] Taking out our inventory again, making a list of all the relationships we have damaged. We have already listed who or what we harmed in Column One and we outlined the part we played in Column Four. **We do this whether or not they "deserved what they got."**

Alcoholism and other addictions are never defeated once and for all. We do not recover by merely agreeing with the principles of our philosophy—we must live by them. Steps Eight and Nine work in conjunction with each other. *"Now we need more action, without which we find that 'Faith without works is dead.' Let's look at Steps Eight and Nine."*[561]

Through Steps 1-7 we have learned a lot about ourselves and it is now time for us to repair the damage we have done to ourselves and others—regardless of whether we feel they did more harm to us—and learn to forgive. *"Learning to live with others is a fascinating adventure."*[562] As stated earlier, in each of the 12 Steps we surrender a little more. In Steps Eight and Nine we surrender more of our Egos than ever before.

"Steps Eight and Nine are concerned with personal relations. FIRST, we take a look backwards and try to discover where we have been at fault; NEXT we make a vigorous attempt to repair the damage we have done; and THIRD, having thus cleaned away the debris of the past, we consider how, with our new-found knowledge of ourselves, we may develop the best possible relations with every human being we know.

"This is a very large order. It is a task which we may perform with increasing skill, but never really finish. Learning how to live in the greatest peace, partnership, and brotherhood with ALL men and women, of whatever description, is a moving and fascinating adventure... To a degree, he has already done this when taking personal inventory, but now the time has come when he ought to redouble his efforts to see how many people he has hurt, and in what ways. This re-opening of emotional wounds, some old, some still painfully festering, will first look

like a purposeless and pointless piece of surgery. But if a willing start is made, then the great advantages of doing this will so quickly reveal themselves that the pain will be lessoned as one obstacle after another melts away.

"These obstacles, however, are very real. The first, and one of the most difficult, has to do with forgiveness."[563] Forgiveness is the key here. As our sponsors point out, with some humour, how are we going to mend what we "think" is *our* one percent damage in the relationship if we don't first forgive *their* 99 percent? *"The idea that we can be possessively loving of a few, can ignore the many, and can continue to fear or hate anybody, has to be abandoned."*[564]

This is the particular role of this Step in our recovery. It *"entails forgiveness... Before I placed the first name on my list, I said a little prayer: 'I forgive anyone and everyone who has ever harmed me at any time and under any circumstances."*[565] *"This grace that overcomes death by forgiveness is the truth that has set me free to regard myself and you as acceptable."*[566] Maybe what has been done truly **IS** unacceptable but **the person who has done it *is NOT* unacceptable**. *"Somehow, I believed that there could be no forgiveness for any failure...my distorted sense of justice told me there was no reason for God to forgive me."*[567] So we became unacceptable to ourselves. This inability to forgive ourselves is a major problem. The solution lies in first forgiving others, which is what this Step is all about.

WHERE DO WE GO FOR OUR LIST?

In several places in the literature it tells us, as did Bill: *"We made a list of people I had hurt or toward whom I felt resentment."*[568] And later it says: *"We have a list of all the persons we have harmed and to whom we are willing to make amends. We made it when we took our inventory... (where) we subjected ourselves to a drastic self-appraisal... Probably there are still some misgivings. As we look over the list of business acquaintances and friends we have hurt, we may feel diffident about going to some of them on a spiritual basis."*[569]

In Step Eight we become willing to make amends to all the people we have harmed. *"We realised that the people who wronged us were perhaps spiritually sick. Though we did not like their symptoms and the way these disturbed us, they, like ourselves, were sick too. We asked God for the same tolerance, pity, and patience that we would cheerfully grant a sick friend... God will*

146

show us how to take a kindly and tolerant view of each and every one."[570]

It may not be difficult to list the people who suffered because we drank, used or became obsessed, or add to it those from whom we stole or those we simply owe money. The hard part is the dawning realisations that it's not only us, our sponsors and God that get to hear about it. But the very people we are disturbed by.

"When listing the people we have harmed, most of us hit another solid obstacle. We got a pretty severe shock when we realised that we were preparing to make a face-to-face admission of <u>our</u> wretched conduct to those we had hurt. It had been embarrassing enough when in confidence we had admitted these things to God, to ourselves, and to another human being. But the prospect of actually visiting or even writing the people concerned now overwhelmed us, especially when we remembered in what poor favour we stood with most of them. There were cases, too, where we had damaged others who were still happily unaware of being hurt. Why, we cried, shouldn't bygones be bygones? Why do we have to think of these people at all? These were some of the ways in which fear conspired with pride to hinder our making a list of all the people we had harmed."[571] Our real problem is to arrive at a state of mind that *"concedes to our innermost selves"* the damage we have done, and to embrace a sincere willingness to make amends for our part, <u>**without the mention of their part**</u>.

Step Eight is the process of removing from within us the following *"Obstacles: (of) reluctance to forgive; non-admission of wrongs to others; purposeful forgetting.* (Requiring the) *"necessity of* (an) *exhaustive survey of* (the) *past. Deepening insight results from thoroughness... Step Eight is the beginning of the end of isolation."*[572] Here we let go of self-justification: *"For most of us, self-justification was the maker of excuses; excuses, of course, for drinking* (or other addictive behaviour)*, and for all kinds of crazy and damaging conduct. We had made the invention of alibis a fine art."*[573] Hesitation on this Step often leads to dangerous lapses into self-justification. *"Some of us...clung to the claim that...we never hurt anybody but ourselves... This attitude, of course, is the end result of purposeful forgetting. It is an attitude which can only be changed by a deep and honest search of our motives and actions."*[574]

When this is complete, we then discuss with our sponsors appropriate Step Nine amends relating to each incident. We believe that where two or more are gathered together in the name of good, a *"Power greater than ourselves"* will be present and the right answers as to what we need to do emerges in that meeting. Don't be confused at what we are doing; we are on a spiritual journey. And **"going it alone in spiritual matters is dangerous. How many times have we heard well-intentioned people claim the guidance of God when it was all too plain that they were sorely mistaken? ...They had deluded themselves and were able to justify the most arrant nonsense on the ground that this was what God had told them."**[575] This is why it is so important that we work with our sponsors in the process of agreeing whether or not amends are called for in each case, and if so what form they will take.

In the book *Alcoholics Anonymous* we find a lot of discussion about how and when to make a particular type of amend. We are reminded that we wait for a discussion with our Sponsors before making any final decisions. Painful experience has shown that we should check out our "inspirations" before we rush out and make amends. Inappropriate amends can cause even more damage. **"It is worth noting that people of very high spiritual development almost always insist on checking with friends or spiritual advisors the guidance they feel they have received from God. Surely, then, a novice ought not lay himself open to the chance of making foolish, perhaps tragic, blunders in this fashion. While the comment or advice of others may by no means be infallible, it is likely to be far more specific than any direct guidance we may receive while we are still so inexperienced in establishing contact with a Power greater than ourselves."**[576] That is what we truly want, an answer from a Power greater than we are, not our own answer. Not because our ideas are necessarily wrong, but because they don't or haven't worked to bring us and others the peace we all desire.

"We must be willing to make amends where we have done harm, provided that we do not bring about still more harm in so doing."[577] Now this may sound like a way out, but we can and should discuss our concerns with our sponsors.

In Step Eight (1) we **"made a list"** and (2) become **"willing to make amends."** These are the two basic premises of this Step. **"As year by year we walk back through our lives as far as memory will reach, we shall be bound to construct a long list of people who have, to some extent or other, been affected."**[578] The bottom line is our *willingness to forgive* those wrongs, *"real or imagined,"* that have been done to us and to make amends for our part. **<u>Never do we mention their part</u>.** It is only logical that we cannot **"make amends"** if we are not willing to forgive them. Let us be clear that <u>forgiveness is NOT justification</u>; don't try to justify other people's

148

actions in order to forgive them. It doesn't seem to work. ***"If we are now about to ask forgiveness for ourselves, why shouldn't we start out by forgiving them, one and all?"***[579]

How can we look for forgiveness if we are withholding our forgiveness? ***"Probably there are still some misgivings. As we look over the list of business acquaintances and friends we have hurt, we feel diffident about going to some of them... If we haven't the will to do this, we ask until it comes. Remember it was agreed at the beginning we would go to any lengths for victory over alcohol*** (or whatever addiction)***."***[580]

"The moment we ponder a twisted or broken relationship with another person, our emotions go on the defensive. To escape looking at the wrongs we have done another, we resentfully focus on the wrong he has done us. This is especially true if he has, in fact, behaved badly at all. Triumphantly we seize upon his behaviour as the perfect excuse for minimising or forgetting our own."[581] Note that on our form there are three possible boxes to tick. They are ***"now, later, and never."*** We are obviously looking for our level of willingness to make each amend. Though remember ***"we admitted our wrongs honestly and were willing to set these matters straight."***[582]

When we find that we have ticked later or never, and we want to be free ***"In meditation, we ask God what we should do about each specific matter. The right answer will come, if we want it."***[583] Or we may try this: ***"If you have a resentment you want to be free of, if you will pray for the person or the thing that you resent, you will be free. If you will ask in prayer for <u>everything you want for yourself to be given to them</u>, you will be free. Ask for their health, their prosperity, their happiness, and you will be free. <u>Even when you don't really want it for them and your prayers are only words and you don't mean it, go ahead and do it anyway</u>. Do it every day for two weeks, and you will find you have come to mean it and to want it for them, and you will realise that where you use to feel bitterness and resentment and hatred, you will feel compassionate understanding and love.***

"It worked for me...and it will work for me every time I am willing to work it."[584]

So liberating is this process that we may find it becomes a habit. ***"We shall want to hold ourselves to the course of admitting the things <u>we</u> have done, meanwhile forgiving the wrongs done us, real or fancied."***[585] Abraham Maslow said: ***"Ninety-eight percent of us die before we taste the nectar of our magnificence."*** Nothing stands in the way of that magnificence more than our lack of forgiveness for ourselves and others—"Seek not for whom our unforgiveness tolls, it takes toll on thee!" There is no greater release from the **"bondage of self"** than forgiveness.

Those people we have taken offence to are merely symbols of our inner mistakes. They bear witness to the times wherein we have failed to remember God in our fellows. Spiritual wisdom demonstrates that others can never hurt the truly spiritual person, so when we can claim that we are "truly spiritual" there is no forgiveness necessary. We must look at others differently and find God where we formerly believed error existed. Searching for where and how my behaviour has affected others **"I expressed my entire willingness to approach these individuals, admitting my wrong."**[586]

There is a useful analogy that makes a lot of sense about letting go of past hurts, "real or imagined." Imagine I am holding my arm straight out with a weight in my hand clearly marked "ONE POUND" I then asked you, "How heavy is this weight?" In all probability you would promptly say: "one pound."

Strictly speaking, you would be absolutely right. But the objective weight is not the whole story. How heavy it is to me would depend on how long I try to hold on to it. If I hold it for a minute, that is no problem. After all it only weighs a pound. However, if I hold on to it for an hour, my arm will ache something fierce. If I hold on to it for a day, someone would have to call an ambulance for me. In each case, it is the same weight. But the longer I hold it, the heavier it becomes.

That's how it is with Resentments, Dishonesty, Sex Problems, Harm Done to Others, and Fear. The longer we carry these disturbances, the heavier the psychological burden becomes. It may express itself as increasingly damaging outbursts of anger, rage and other hurtful behaviour toward others and/or ourselves. Just as with the one pound weight—we have to put it down for our comfort. This is what this process is concerning, relieving ourselves of these past burdens. Later in Step Ten we will discover how to find relief from our disturbances on a daily basis but for now: **"We have listed the people we have hurt by our conduct, and are <u>willing</u> to straighten out the past if we can."**[587]

"We should...make an accurate and really exhaustive survey of our past life as it has affected other people... Since <u>defective relations with other human beings have nearly always been the immediate cause of our woes, including our alcoholism,</u> (or other addictions) no field of investigation could yield more satisfying

and valuable rewards than this one... Thoroughness, we have found, will pay—and pay handsomely."[588]

Before we go on to a discussion of Step Nine there is one further point that we wish to make clear. Few of us realise that <u>our own names</u> belong at the top of the list of people we have wronged. By working and living this programme we are, first and foremost, making amends to *ourselves*. ***"Though the harm done others has not been great, the emotional harm we have done ourselves has*** (been enormous)*...*

"While the purpose of making restitution to others is paramount, it is equally necessary that we extricate from an examination of our personal relations every bit of information about ourselves and our fundamental difficulties that we can."[589] We are making amends to our physical health, our mental health, and to our troubled spirits. No matter how it looks to us, the bottom line is that we are doing these Steps for our own good. However much our amends do for those we make them to, *we* benefit much more ourselves. We are then ready for Step Nine.

THE PRINCIPLE OF STEP EIGHT

Forgiveness

Forgiveness begins when we release our resentments and hurts "real or imagined" and become ready to make our amends. ***Forgiveness*** is the first Step in "Mending" our relationships with people, places and things. But more importantly we mend our relationship with ourselves and God.

Chapter 11

Mending Relationships

Restitution

STEP NINE

"Made Direct Amends To Such People Wherever Possible, Except When To Do So Would Injure Them Or Others."[590]

Read in preparation, in the "Big Book" of *Alcoholics Anonymous* –
Page 76-84

Read in preparation, in the *Twelve Steps and Twelve Traditions* – Step Nine
Pages 85-89

For Step Nine we discuss with our Sponsors those direct amends we understand that we need to make around the "People, Places or Things."

Step 9 Amends	Step 8
(Person, Place or Thing)	○ Now ○ Later ○ Never
(Person, Place or Thing)	○ Now ○ Later ○ Never
(Person, Place or Thing)	○ Now ○ Later ○ Never
(Person, Place or Thing)	○ Now ○ Later ○ Never
(Person, Place or Thing)	○ Now ○ Later ○ Never
(Person, Place or Thing)	○ Now ○ Later ○ Never
(Person, Place or Thing)	○ Now ○ Later ○ Never

STEP NINE

"Made Direct Amends To Such People Wherever Possible, Except When To Do So Would Injure Them Or Others."[591]

" S *teps Eight and Nine are concerned with personal relations. First, we take a look backward and try to discover where we have been at fault; next we make a vigorous attempt to repair the damage we have done; and third, having thus cleaned away the debris of the past, we consider how, with our new found knowledge of ourselves, we may develop the best possible relations with every human being we know.*

"This is a very large order. It is a task which we may perform with increased skill, but never really finish. Learning how to live in the greatest peace, partnership, and brotherhood with all men and women, of whatever description, is a moving and fascinating adventure."[592] If (as stated earlier) deep inside is where we will find God, then the same is true of other people. Deep inside them is a God centre also. That means that God is in me and in you. So if we open our eyes we can surely see God in ALL we meet. With some people it may be more difficult than with others but **it is our responsibility to look for that presence in one another.** This will bring us a tranquil mind, and *"A tranquil mind is the first requisite for good judgement."*[593] This is something most of us have found to be lacking in our lives.

In Step Eight we found forgiveness for ourselves in forgiving others. *"God is all-loving and all-forgiving. The memories of my past are being dimmed by the life I now aspire to"*[594] a life made real by our work on Step Nine. Most of us have *"learned that going back and facing something unpleasant, regardless of how tough it is at the time, is a lot easier than running away."*[595] Geographic cures don't work.

Many of us say, *"I want to do this, but I can't. This is too much. I could never go and make up to all the people I've done wrong to."*[596] The very thought of working this Step has kept many people from working the programme. But we are aware that, in life *"The real fault is to have faults and NOT to AMEND them"* said Confucius. This is where the next huge shift takes place in our lives. It is the final Step in the process of *"emotional re-arrangement."* Here we will have our awakening. *"Don't give up until the miracle happens."*[597]

THE RULE OF STEP NINE

There are some simple rules that we must follow on this road to freedom. For we have learned that **"we cannot buy our own peace of mind at the expense of others."**[598]

"<u>The rule is we must be hard on ourselves, but always considerate of others</u>."[599] **"Amends...should always be forthright and generous."**[600]

"First we will wish to be reasonably certain that we are on the...beam. Then we are ready to go to these people, to tell them what AA is, and what we are trying to do."[601] **"We admitted our wrongs honestly and were willing to set these matters straight."**[602]

"Never was I to be critical of them. I was to right all such matters to the utmost of my ability."[603]

"GENERAL PRINCIPLES WHICH WE FIND GUIDING."[604]

"Reminding ourselves (again) **that we have decided to go to any lengths to find a spiritual experience, we ask that we be given strength and direction to do the right thing, no matter what the personal consequences may be. We may lose our position or reputation or face jail, but we are willing. We have to be. We must not shrink at anything.**

"Usually, however, other people are involved. Therefore, we are not to be the hasty and foolish martyr who would needlessly sacrifice others to save himself."[605]

"Before taking drastic action, which might implicate other people, we secure their consent. If we have obtained permission, have consulted others, asked God to help and the drastic Step is indicated we must not shrink."[606]

As is seen in the story **"Grounded", "I was found guilty and sentenced to sixteen months in federal prison. My two co-defendants received twelve-month sentences and chose to remain free pending appeals, while I chose to go to prison and get it over. I had learned how to live life on life's terms and not my own."**[607] The outcome of this man's willingness to amend his behaviour is amazing and shouldn't be missed. We don't have the space here to relay the story again. It is very important that we face these amends regardless of personal consequences. **"Readiness to take** (the) **consequences of our past and to take responsibility for** (the) **wellbeing of others is** (the) **spirit of Step Nine."**[608]

"Belief in the power of God, plus enough willingness, honesty and humility to establish and maintain the new order of things, were the essential requirements."[609] To find the right answers *"I was to sit quietly when in doubt, asking only for direction and strength to meet my problems as* (God) *would have me."*[610]

"Now we go out to our fellows and repair the damage done in the past. We attempt to sweep away the debris that has accumulated out of our effort to live on self-will and run the show ourselves."[611] *"We should be sensible, tactful, considerate and humble without being servile or scraping. As God's people we stand on our feet; we don't crawl before anyone."*[612]

"<u>Under no condition do we criticise such a person or argue</u>. Simply we tell him that we will never get over drinking until we have done our utmost to straighten out the past. We are there to sweep our side of the street, realising that nothing worthwhile can be accomplished until we do so, <u>never trying to tell him what to do. His faults are not discussed.</u> We stick to our own. If our manner is calm, frank, and open, we will be gratified with the result."[613]

This idea is so important it is repeated later in the *Big Book*, with an additional twist. *"Being very careful not to criticise them. Their defects may be glaring, but the chances are that our actions are partly responsible."*[614]

"There can only be one consideration which should qualify our desire for a complete disclosure of the damage we have done. That will arise in the occasional situation where to make a full revelation would seriously harm the one to whom we are making amends. Or—quite as important—other people... It does not lighten our burden when we recklessly make the crosses of others heavier."[615]

"There may be some wrongs we can never fully right. We don't worry about them <u>if</u> we can honestly say to ourselves that we would right them if we could. Some people cannot be seen—we send them an honest letter. And there may be a valid reason for postponement in some cases. <u>But</u> we don't delay if it can be avoided."[616]

ON A SPIRITUAL/RELIGIOUS APPROACH

"It is seldom wise to approach an individual, who still smarts from our injustice to him, and announce that we have gone religious. In the prize ring this would be called leading with the

chin.   Why lay ourselves open to be branded fanatics or religious bores?   We may kill a future opportunity to carry a beneficial message.... He is going to be more interested in a demonstration of good will than in our talk of spiritual discoveries.

(However) *"We don't use this as an excuse for shying away from the subject of God. When it will serve any good purpose, we are willing to announce our convictions with tact and common sense."*[617]

Before we rush out and zealously make amends willy-nilly it is strongly suggested that *"we lay the matter before our sponsor or spiritual advisor, earnestly asking God's help and guidance—meanwhile resolving to do the right thing when it comes clear, cost what it may."*[618]

RELATIONSHIPS

By Step Nine we have begun to see that this programme is about healing relationships; our relationship with others, our relationship with God, and also our relationship with ourselves. I was one of those who said, "I'm not hurting anyone but myself." But that wasn't true. For example, *"I had 'dropped out'—never sending cards, returning calls, being there for people, or taking part in their lives."*[619] Yes, I had had an effect on others. If we have been thorough in our work, we will begin to realise what our Alcoholic friend here did: *"I came to see that we all are really one, and I no longer feel alone."*[620] Relationships, we now find, are what a good life is all about.

LIES

"In the very moment of acknowledging myself to be a liar, I turned out not to be one (in that instance, anyhow)."[621] A history of habitual lying and deceit is sometimes very hard to face up to and deal with. But we can turn the corner through diligent effort. Realising that telling the truth is truly easier than lying and it is a life changing experience.

FAMILY

"My family members suffer from the effects of my disease. Loving and accepting them as they are—just as I love and accept AA members—fosters a return of love, tolerance and harmony to my life."[622]

160

"We ought to sit down with the family and frankly analyse the past as we now see it, <u>being very careful not to criticise them</u>... So, we clean house with the family asking each morning in our meditation that our Creator show us the way of patience, tolerance, kindliness and love."[623]

"The chances are that we have domestic troubles... After a few years with an alcoholic, a wife (or husband) *gets worn out, resentful and uncommunicative. How could* (s)*he be anything else?"*[624] The most powerful thing that most of us learn in our personal relationship with our spouse is: *"She works her programme...and I work mine, both of us living in today, one day at a time."*[625] Even if they have not chosen the Twelve Steps as their path, they still have their own "programme."

"We cannot disclose anything to our wives or our parents which will hurt them and make them unhappy. We have no right to save our own skin at another's expense."[626] However, by working this programme we *"have seen hundreds of families set their feet in the path that really goes somewhere; have seen the most impossible domestic situations righted; feuds and bitterness of all sorts wiped out."*[627] *"There is scarcely any form of trouble and misery which has not been overcome among us."*[628]

"Maybe we are divorced, and have remarried but haven't kept up the alimony to number one. She is indignant about it, and has a warrant out for our arrest. That's a common form of trouble too... we are willing"[629] to make amends, no matter what the outcome is to us.

SOMEONE WE HATED?

"The question of how to approach the man we hated will arise.... With a person we dislike, we take the bit in our teeth. It is harder to go to an enemy than a friend, but we find it much more beneficial to us. We go to him in a helpful and forgiving spirit, confessing our former ill feeling and expressing our regret."[630]

"In nine cases out of ten the unexpected happens. <u>Sometimes the man we are calling upon admits his own fault, so feuds of years' standing melt away in an hour. Rarely do we fail to make satisfactory progress. Our former enemies <u>sometimes</u> praise what we are doing and wish us well. Occasionally, they will offer assistance. <u>It should not matter, however, if someone does throw us out of his office</u>. We have made our demonstration, done our part. It's water under the dam."[631]

WORK/MONEY

"Most...owe money. We do not dodge our creditors. Telling them what we are trying to do, we make no bones about our drinking (or whatever our problem has been)*... Arranging the best deal we can we let these people know we are sorry... We must lose our fear of creditors no matter how far we have to go."*[632]

At work *"We may be short in our accounts and unable to make good... we are sure we would...lose our job if it were known. Maybe it's a petty offence such as padding the expense account. Most of us have done that sort of thing... We may lose our position...but we are willing."*[633] And so we act, after discussing it with our sponsor and anyone else it may affect.

WHAT ABOUT A CRIMINAL OFFENCE

"Perhaps we have committed a criminal offence which might land us in jail if it were known to the authorities... we are sure we would be imprisoned...if it were known. Reminding ourselves that we have decided to go to any lengths to find a spiritual experience we ask that we be given the strength and direction to do the right thing, no matter what the personal consequences may be. We may...face jail, but we are willing. We have to be. We must not shrink at anything."[634]

"Yes, there is a long period of reconstruction ahead. We must take the lead. A remorseful mumbling that we are sorry won't fill the bill at all... (again) *being careful not to criticise them.* (The other person's) *defects may be glaring, but the chances are that our actions are partly responsible... we clean house."*[635]

Up to now *"If we have carefully followed directions, we have begun to sense the flow of...Spirit into us. To some extent we have become God-conscious. We have begun to develop this vital sixth sense. But we must go further and that means more action."*[636] Before we have finished we will begin to feel better and, *"We will want to rest on our laurels. The temptation to skip the more humiliating and dreaded meetings that still remain may be great. We will often manufacture plausible excuses for dodging these issues entirely. Or we may just procrastinate, telling ourselves the time is not yet."*[637] Believing the time will come and the right opportunity to make the amend will present itself is sometimes a way of avoiding making amends at all. *"At some point we will want to summon all our courage, head straight for the person concerned, and lay our cards on the table."*[638] This, of course, is on the condition that we are willing to become even freer and happier than we find ourselves presently. Most of us with these "more" diseases, have never had what we thought was enough of anything. Yet we avoid pressing forward when we get to a stage where we are merely OK; another paradox.

Remember: *"It is easy to let up on the spiritual programme of action and rest on our laurels. We are headed for trouble if we do."*[639] Once the Promises begin to be fulfilled we tend to relax. This is a very dangerous thing to do. We are warned over and over in the *Big Book* not to let this happen and through our own hard earned experience we agree. *"Simple, but not easy; a price had to be paid. It meant the destruction of self-centredness."*[640] Be sure you not only finish this Step but move on to the "Maintenance Steps" promptly.

TRUSTING THOSE WHO HARMED US

"I trusted no one, for others were but a reflection of my own self, and I could not trust me."[641] If this is the case how can we learn to trust ourselves and others? *"Most surely, there can be no trust where there is no love, nor can there be real love where distrust holds its malign sway.*

"But does trust require that we be blind to other people's motives or, indeed, to our own? Not at all; this would be folly. Most certainly, we should assess the capacity for harm as well as the capability for good in every person that we would trust. Such a private inventory can reveal the degree of confidence we should extend in any given situation.

"However, this inventory needs to be taken in a spirit of understanding and love. Nothing can so much bias our judgment as the negative emotions of suspicion, jealousy, or anger.

"Having vested our confidence in another person, we ought to let him know of our full support. Because of this, more often than not he will respond magnificently; and far beyond our first expectations."[642]

"For my recovery to be thorough, I believed it was NOT important for those who had legitimately harmed me to make amends to me. What is important in my relationship with God is that I stand before (God)*, knowing I have done what I can to repair the damage I have done.* [643] We now know that, *"...they, like ourselves, were sick too. We asked God to help us show them the same tolerance, pity, and patience that we would*

cheerfully grant a sick friend. When a person offended we said to ourselves, "This is a sick man. How can I be helpful to him? God save me from being angry. Thy will be done."[644]

"Above all, we should try to be absolutely sure that we are not delaying because we are afraid. For the readiness to take the full consequences of our past acts, and to take responsibility for the well-being of others at the same time, is the very spirit of Step Nine.[645] After all, this is a major Step towards our main objective, *"a spiritual awakening"* and the fulfilment of the promises.

In the programme *"I have had to be torn down and then put back together differently. No one could live such an irresponsible, immature life as I had without consequences.* (It) *made it possible for me to face the consequences of my actions.*

"Most importantly, (It) *has enabled me to go back and start growing up all over again in all areas of my life. Truth and sincerity do not come easily for me. Admitting that I am wrong or that I do not know is difficult for me."*[646] But if we want the Promises to come true, we do it anyway.

Those of us who are sound in our thinking realise, as the woman in *"A Feminine Victory"* did, she said: *"I know that my victory is none of my human doing... The glorious thing is this: I am free, I am happy, and perhaps I am going to have the blessed opportunity of 'passing it on."*[647] These constitute a small portion of "The Promises."

The Promises

"If we are painstaking about this phase of our development, we will be amazed before we are half way through. We are going to know a new freedom and a new happiness. We will not regret the past nor wish to shut the door on it. We will comprehend the word serenity and we will know peace. No matter how far down the scale we have gone, we will see how our experience can benefit others. That feeling of uselessness and self-pity will disappear. We will lose interest in selfish things and gain interest in our fellows. Self-seeking will slip away. Our whole attitude and outlook upon life will change. Fear of people and of economic insecurity will leave us. We will intuitively know how to handle situations that used to baffle us. We will suddenly realise that God is doing for us what we could not do for ourselves.

"Are these extravagant promises? We think not. They are being fulfilled among us – sometimes quickly, sometimes slowly. They will always materialise if we work for them."[648]

The Twelve Steps remove mental, emotional and spiritual suffering, both past and present. *"As we work the first nine Steps, we prepare ourselves for the adventure of a new life."*[649] With these tools we find that while pain is still inevitable, suffering is optional. We have discovered that when we no longer see any value in suffering and/or self-righteousness—healing is instantaneous. As a direct result of these Steps *"I have had come true for me the old wish, 'If I could live my life over, knowing what I know'... I know: the joy of living, the irresistible power of Divine Love and its healing strength, and the fact that we, as sentient beings, have the knowledge to choose...and, choosing good, are made happy."*[650]

THE PRINCIPLE OF STEP NINE

Restitution

'Making amends' means "to mend" the affects of our past behaviour, it is *"restitution, the restoration of good personal relations by making amends for harms done."*[651] Our new-found and life long experience of "mending" and making *restitution* for our actions, past and present, begins on Step Nine. This is where the "promises" are fulfilled, giving us an understanding of *freedom* never before experienced.

Chapter 12

Maintaining
Our Awakening

Continue—Improve—Practice
(CIP)

THE MAINTENANCE STEPS

hat happens if we *"let up on the spiritual programme of recovery and rest on our laurels?"*[652] The definition of resting on our laurels is: "Resting on past success—which won't hold up in the present."

Here is a twist on the promises that seems to apply:

NEGATIVE PROMISES

If we are careless about this phase of our development, we will be lost before we are halfway through. We will renew our obsession with our addictions and sacrifice ALL true happiness. We will forget the word serenity, and have NO peace. No matter how far down the scale we have already gone, we will fall even lower. We will resent the past and then repeat it, over and over again. That feeling of uselessness and self-pity will return, and more. We will focus on selfish things and hide from our fellows. Sanity will slip away. Our whole attitude and outlook upon life will change for the worse. Fear and hatred of people and of economic insecurity will consume us. We will again be baffled by even the most normal of situations. We will suddenly believe that the programme is useless and that God will do nothing for us.

Are these exaggerated consequences? WE THINK NOT!! They have been fulfilled among us, sometimes quickly, sometimes slowly. They have always materialised when we have ceased working this programme of recovery—the Twelve Steps.

Though this is obviously a light-hearted answer to the above question, we found this was the actual result for us—**USING OR NOT.**

So, let us stay on course. Having worked the previous nine Steps we have uncovered a new self. *"A whole new world of happiness and love began to unfold before my eyes, a truly new way of living."*[653] *"There are Steps of recovery, of maintenance. Each one has its own place."*[654] The main question that the last three Steps ask, and answer, is: *"Can we stay sober and keep emotional balance under all conditions?"*[655] Remembering that our definition of sobriety includes emotional balance, we are grateful to say the answer is in the affirmative. *"We ought not to settle...for half-measures in taking the Steps, or for too much of the stale and flat in our sober days.*

"No...we have to keep looking for something better than dullness, better than average living, better than mediocre spirituality."[656] When we first came into the programme *"we took a look at* (the) *Twelve Steps for recovery but many of us promptly*

forgot ten of them, as perhaps not needed. We bought only the concept that we were alcoholics (had addictions or obsessions)*; that attendance at meetings and a helping hand to the newcomers would be sufficient to solve the...problem, and probably all problems."*[657] Or unfortunately, as often happens, we go through the Steps once, declare ourselves 'cured' or think that a few meetings is all we need to maintain what we gained, and fail to work the programme on a daily basis.

"But by degrees certain dissatisfactions set in, even with our own group; it was not as wonderful as we had first supposed... There were people we simply did not like, and the ones we did admire failed to give us the attention we thought we deserved. At home we were also shocked. After the pink cloud had departed from the household, things seemed as bad as ever. The old wounds weren't healing at all.

"So each of us looked up his sponsor and regaled him with these woes. Our resentments, anxieties, and depressions were definitely caused, we claimed, by our unfortunate circumstances and by the inconsiderate behaviour of other people. To our consternation, our sponsors didn't seem impressed either. They had just grinned and said, 'Why don't we sit down and take a hard look at all*...Twelve Steps? Maybe you have been missing a lot—in fact, nearly everything.'*

"Then we began to take our own inventories, rather than the other fellow's. Getting into the swing of self-examination, we finally began to discover our real responsibilities toward ourselves and toward those around us... Little by little, we found that all progress, material or spiritual, consisted of finding out what our responsibilities actually were and then proceeding to do something about them. These activities began to payoff. We found that we didn't always have to be driven by our own discomforts as, more willingly; we picked up the burdens of living and growing.

"Then, most surprisingly, we discovered that full acceptance and action upon any clear-cut responsibility almost invariably made for true happiness and peace of mind."[658] Please don't do as so many of us have done and *"rest on our laurels."* We have not found a way to keep *"it"* without continual effort. *"In this programme there aren't any half measures. In here you must go all the way."*[659]

Some of us will remember, if we're lucky enough to survive, hearing what we <u>wanted to hear</u> instead of what was <u>really being said</u>: *"the older members...told me, 'Easy does it.' In the light of subsequent events it became evident that I took their advice far too literally, for, after some months of happy sobriety I drank again. Had I tried honestly and sincerely to practice the Twelve Steps I would have seen from my continuous moral inventory that I was getting off beam—I would have found that there were some active resentments in my life, a terrific amount of self-pity. But more important, I would have found that once again I was sitting in the driver's seat—I was running the show.*

"The Higher Power to whom I had turned, and who had sustained me, had once again been thrust into the background, while my emotions were running my life."[660] *"In the programme...we can have this new way of life...if we are willing to change our way of thinking and be honest, first with ourselves, then with others. We are told to practice the Twelve Steps...to the best of our ability every day, one day at a time. It is suggested that we do not try to do a lifetime of repairs in one day."*[661]

Even with spiritual experiences of the "flash of light" variety, some *"have been given this experience and then have thrown their wings away, because they mistakenly thought that the Absolute would sustain them automatically."*[662] This is what our continued review of the Steps, both with others and on our own, is all about: maintaining the effect of this wonderful experience, whether it is sudden or gradual. It matters little what kind of experience we have. *"I took to the programme with enthusiasm, minded the slogans, went to meetings, made friends, and carried the message as I understood it then.*

"Shortly after...I underwent a religious conversion. I had been...about as ill-informed on spiritual matters in general as one can imagine. Upon truly discovering...I studied theology in its many branches, became a lay member of religious order, and was a daily communicant. I felt secure, so I drifted away from the Fellowship, no longer participating in meetings, lost track of my (programme) *friends, and became extremely 'busy'... I took a drink, after thirteen years of sobriety...*

"The deterioration of my spiritual life was slow; the physical and mental effects were not especially noticeable for quite a while. Inevitably, the time came when I faced the fact that (again my addiction had me) *I could neither cut down...nor could I stop... "When I returned...its precepts seemed entirely new to me... Instead of taking the Steps and forgetting them, this time I began living them daily, finding new meaning in each one.*

"My...way of life now demands constant action—an active self-honesty and recognition of the necessity for living in day-tight compartments... Each day, I must surrender and rededicate my life, or I shall lose all that I have gained...

(The programme) *"succeeds because, one and all, we have a common goal toward which we are working: mental, emotional, and spiritual growth, through love and service...*

"For me, coming to believe is not a one-time experience, it is an action to be performed daily as long as I live and grow."[663] This is exactly what the 'Maintenance Steps' are all about.

If we've worked through the Steps, we have been *"catapulted into... the fourth dimension of existence...* (knowing) *happiness, peace, and usefulness, in a way of life that is incredibly more wonderful as time passes."*[664] We certainly want to keep hold of this. But: *"No one among us has been able to maintain anything like perfect adherence to these principles. We are not saints. The point is that we are willing to grow along spiritual lines. The principles we have set down are guides to progress. We claim spiritual progress NOT spiritual perfection."*[665] We need to be aware that: *"In God's economy, nothing is wasted. Through failure, we learn a lesson in humility which is probably needed, painful as it is."*[666] This leads us to the conclusion that we must continue doing what we have done in the first Nine Steps (only more-so), as well as learning and practicing more prayer and meditation, passing on all we have learned to others.

The last three Steps of the programme help us not only to maintain our spiritual awakening but to keep growing. We find that there is a powerful *"Connection between self-examination and meditation and prayer. (This builds) an unshakeable foundation for life...* (Where the) *First result is emotional balance."*[667] If we devote just a few minutes each morning, to begin with, to prayer and meditation and another few minutes every night to a review of our day, acknowledging those reactions to our day that didn't please us much, we shall gain an even greater knowledge of ourselves. We can note our growth, or lack of it, and make adjustments accordingly.

We do this by praying and meditating for the relief of those recurring shortcomings (as in Step 6 and 7) that cause pain both to us and others. This daily inventory is no easier to swallow than our original inventory, where we had to go through the Surrender process of Steps 1, 2, and 3. Prayer and meditation also helps to raise our consciousness. Of course, there is also our daily practice of helping others and we *"practice these principles in all our affairs."*[668]

Ernie G. said: ***"On Saturday, we'd go...see Dr. Bob...if we were having problems, he'd pray about it. 'Keep it on a spiritual basis,' he'd say. 'If you keep principles ahead of personalities and you're active and sharing your programme with other people, it will work out.' He said, 'Alcohol*** (or any addiction) ***is a great leveller of people, and AA is, too.'"***[669]

In other words, to practice Steps 10, 11, and 12 is to practice all of the Steps on a daily basis, along with additional prayer and meditation and the passing on of this message to others. ***"We note with high interest how so many of us are trying to practice*** (these) ***principles in all of our affairs, how the quest for emotional and spiritual growth is quickening and is being reflected at home, at work, and in the world at large. Our families, too, have adopted*** (the) ***Twelve Steps as their own."***[670] We find today, that many other groups of people have instituted these Steps for the purpose of some transformation in their lives.

The trick seems to be in knowing that we don't know everything. It has been well said: ***"Let NOT the wise man glory in his wisdom."***[671] We need to continue this life long work, every day, no matter how difficult it is. ***"We can exercise our will power along this line all we wish. It is the proper use of the will."***[672] ***"We know that if we rebel against doing that which is reasonably possible for us, then we will be penalised. And we will be equally penalised if we presume in ourselves a perfection that simply is not there.***

"In our slow progress away from rebellion, true perfection is doubtless several millennia away."[673] So Easy Does It! Wear your humility lightly; regard your instincts with caution. ***"Spiritual growth through the practice of*** (the) ***Twelve Steps, plus the aid of a good sponsor, can usually reveal most of the deeper reasons for our character defects, at least to a degree that meets our practical needs. Nevertheless, we should be grateful that our friends in psychiatry have so strongly emphasised the necessity to search for false and often unconscious motivations."***[674] Working the Steps on a daily basis is what these last three Steps embody. ***"I now see that awakening and growing is something that never need stop and that growing pains are never to be feared, provided I am willing to learn the truth about myself from them."***[675] We discover that pain is good; it reveals the areas where we are out of touch with God.

"For most of us, the first few years...are something of a honeymoon. There is a new and potent reason to stay alive, joyful activity aplenty. For a time, we are diverted from the main life problems. That is all to the good.

"But when the honeymoon has worn off... Maybe difficulties have intensified at home, or in the world outside. Then the old behaviour patterns reappear. How well we recognise and deal with them reveals the extent of our progress."[676] Working the programme doesn't stop life's problems from arising, no matter how much we pray. *"I've had more problems but, thank God, I have had the teachings of* (the programme) *with which to face them."*[677] These teachings are the tools we use to maintain and improve the gifts we have received so far. As this gal from Texas said: *"I know that if I do daily what I have done for these last thirteen and a half years, I will stay sober."*[678] Which we believe also maintains our emotional sobriety.

"God willing, we...may never again have to deal with drinking, but we have to deal with sobriety every day."[679] And that, we assure you, is more than enough to handle. Bill wrote: *"Sometimes we become depressed. I ought to know; I have been a champion dry-bender case myself. While the surface causes were a part of the picture—trigger-events that precipitated depression—the underlying causes, I am satisfied, ran much deeper.*

"Intellectually, I could accept my situation. Emotionally, I could not.

"To these problems, there are certainly no pat answers. But part of the answer surely lies in the constant effort to practice all of (the) *Twelve Steps."*[680]

The programme *"does not teach us how to handle our* (addictions)*...It teaches us how to handle sobriety."*[681] *"Faith has to work twenty-four hours a day in and through us, or we perish."*[682] Bill said: *"We have found much of heaven and we have been rocketed into a fourth dimension of existence of which we had not even dreamed."*[683]

"The great fact is just this, and nothing less: That we have had deep and effective spiritual experiences which have revolutionised our whole attitude toward life, toward our fellows and toward God's Universe. The central fact of our lives today is the absolute certainty that our Creator has entered into our hearts and lives in a way which is indeed miraculous. (God) *has commenced to accomplish those things for us which we could never do for ourselves."*[684] Why would we let it die? *"Faced with...destruction, we soon became as open minded on spiritual matters as we had tried to be on other questions."*[685]

174

"I never bargained for this programme's changing the course of my life or showing me the way to freedom and happiness."[686] *"True happiness is found in the journey, not the destination."*[687] And we *"owe it to the grace of God and to three words in the Twelve Steps: <u>continue, improve, and practice.</u>"*[688] That is what these *"Maintenance Steps"* are all about, those three little words. *"A new life has been given us or, if you prefer, 'a design for living' that really works."*[689] <u>**Continue**</u>—to work all the Steps, daily, <u>**Improve**</u>—our spiritual life, today and <u>**Practice**</u>—all the principles of all of the Steps, all the time.

The *Big Book* tells us: *"We, of Alcoholics Anonymous, are more than one hundred men and women who have <u>recovered</u> from a seemingly hopeless state of mind and body. To show other alcoholics* (and now many other afflictions) *precisely how we have recovered is the main purpose of this book."*[690]

What is the difference between *"recovered"* and *"recovering"?* The difference <u>**as we see it**</u> is: **Recovered** alcoholics have completed the Twelve Steps and therefore have acquired the Promises. A *recovering* alcoholic is one that has either not worked the Twelve Steps and therefore has not received the Promises; or one who has worked the Steps, received the Promises, but then *"rested on their laurels"* by not working the *"Maintenance Steps"* of 10, 11, and 12 on a daily basis. As one of us said so well: *"I was finally accountable for my own recovery. I was responsible for taking (or not taking) the action."*[691] However, let us be clear, recovered does not mean cured.

This is where we learn to live life in small daily doses. *"We cast off the burdens of the past and the anxieties of the future, as we begin to live in the present, one day at a time.*

"Above all we reject fantasizing and accept reality."[692] *"I remember I complained that I didn't have a job, and Paul said, 'You do have a job. Your job is staying sober and working at this programme. That's a full-time job by itself.'"*[693]

At the start of this material we explained that we were at the beginning of a life long journey. In practicing Step 10, we actually are working Steps 4 through 9; practicing Step 11 we are actually working Steps 1, 2, 3, 6 and 7; and Step 12 reminds us to *"Practice* (all) *these principles in all our affairs"* and to pass on everything we have learned, to others, in order to keep it ourselves. Basically the message is: *"Work All the Steps, All the Time."* We cannot work Step 10 without first surrendering. This surrender comes about through the same process as defined in Steps 1, 2, and 3.

"One of the worst bits of advice I ever got was to work the first nine Steps once and then try to subsist on the last three for the rest of my life. That is simply another fragmentation. Redoing every one of the Steps provides results I never experienced with the other method. The demands of the programme are simple, precise, and specific. Viewing each of us as a totality, rather than a collection of slightly related parts, the programme speaks to our conditions wherever we are in sobriety. The Steps enable us to move from where we are within ourselves toward the place we belong.

"(It) *works, but does not work on my terms. A fragmented, 'individual' programme is destined to bring only partial recovery and leave me...bewildered and lost.*"[694] This is why we have tried to make it clear above that, Steps 10, 11, and 12 embody all the Twelve Steps. Our retreats allow us to review all the Steps at least once a year. If, *"We still can't handle life, as life is. There must be a serious flaw somewhere in our spiritual practice and development."*[695] Even though we have obtained a *"welcome surcease* [3](see footnote)*..."*[696] from our previous insanity, we must be vigilant and maintain our effort.

This programme *"is not just a project.* (It) *offers me an opportunity to improve the quality of my life... there is always a deeper and wider experience awaiting me."*[697] "(It) *is not a plan for recovery that can be finished and done with. It is a way of life, and the challenge contained in its principles is great enough to keep any human being striving for as long as he lives. We do not and cannot, outgrow this plan."*[698]

As a "recovering" alcoholic what we are recovering from is alcoholism. Which is the use of *"deeper seated"* problems, discussed in the Big Book, without cleaning them up as we go along. As we "Continue, improve, and practice a daily programme, we are convinced that we can maintain the Promises gained from working the first Nine Steps on a daily basis if we work the 10th, 11th, and 12th Steps of this simple programme. *"Character-building and spiritual values had to come first."*[699]

"We are not cured of alcoholism. What we really have is a daily reprieve contingent on the maintenance of our spiritual condition."[700] However, we find *"clear-cut directions are given showing how we recovered."*[701] Is this a lot of work? Yes! Though *"we find that we are compensated for a consistent effort by the countless dividends we receive."*[702] If we have thoroughly worked

---

[3] A temporary cessation

the programme up to this point we have found a life **"beyond our wildest dreams."** You would think we would recognise that: **"I wouldn't give it up or trade it for anything. And the only one who can take it away from me is me."**[703]

Nonetheless, the danger is great: **"It is easy to let up on the spiritual programme of action and rest on our laurels. We are headed for trouble if we do, for alcohol** (or any addiction) **is a subtle foe."**[704] **"As if to illustrate the danger, Jud O. noted that in 1969 he picked up a drink one week before he was to have his 30th anniversary. 'I had retired...and taken a European tour. I had been fairly active in AA for a number of years, but then I got busy with my work and wasn't going to meetings. My wife was in the hospital, and I was feeling sorry for myself....'**[705] Our obsessions of the mind and addictions are subtle foes. Don't rest on your laurels.

Whatever gifts we have received from the programme there are those of us that have still **"rested on our laurels."** We paid the price in many ways: **First** by getting more and more out of touch with our once proud spiritual connection; **second,** by behaving as we once did under the influence of alcohol, or another drug of choice; we now did these things without a drink or drug; and **finally,** after many, many years of spiritual decline, resorting yet again to drink or drugs and hitting an even lower bottom.

"Every time I ran into trouble, I ultimately found that I was resisting change."[706] **"All of my sobriety and growth, mentally, emotionally, and spiritually, are dependent upon my willingness to listen, understand, and change."**[707]

We think we are *so* different, that we are somehow "special." **"Slips may also occur after ...**(one) **has been a member...for many months or even several years, it is in this kind** (of slip)**, above all, that one finds a marked similarity...** (with) **the...behaviour...of 'normal' victims of other diseases.**

"It happens this way: When the tubercular patient recovers sufficiently to be released from the sanatorium, the doctor gives him careful instructions for the way he is to live when he gets home...

"For the first several months, perhaps for several years, the patient follows directions. But as his strength increases and he feels fully recovered, he becomes slack... When he does this, nothing untoward happens. Soon, he is disregarding the directions given him when he left the sanatorium. Eventually, he has a relapse!

"The same tragedy can be found in cardiac cases... In both...cases, the acts which led to the relapses were preceded by wrong thinking. The patient in each case rationalised himself out of a sense of his own reality. He deliberately turned away from his knowledge of the fact that he had been the victim of a serious disease. He grew overconfident. He decided he didn't have to follow directions.

"Now that is precisely what happens with... (one of us) *who has a slip... He starts thinking wrong before he actually embarks on the course that leads to a slip.*

"There is no reason to charge the slip to alcoholic behaviour or a second heart attack to cardiac behaviour. The alcoholic slip is not a symptom of a psychotic condition. There's nothing screwy about it at all. The patient simply didn't follow directions."[708]
The writer has had precisely that experience, regarding my heart, even though I had some five angina attacks. After a few years of taking my medication and doing what was prescribed, I felt I would have no more problems so I stopped taking my heart medication, at the chagrin of my heart specialist. Fortunately, I came across this quote about three months after that and decided to begin taking it again and follow the instructions of the experienced.

So, heed the warning of others before you. **"With all the earnestness at our command, we beg of you to be fearless and thorough from the very start. Some of us have tried to hold on to our old ideas and the result was nil until we let go absolutely... With** (the programme)**, I could stay sober under any and all conditions."**[709] And remember our definition of real sobriety is: **"a peaceful, calm, contented and well-balanced life."** Can you imagine maintaining that under *any* conditions? To do so we must work the programme daily because **"bitter experience has shown... that continuous sobriety requires continuous effort."**[710]

CONSISTENT EFFORT = CONSISTENT RESULTS i.e. the Promises delivered today and every day. It is our hard-earned experience that if we are not getting consistent results it is because we are not making consistent effort. We have **"rested on our laurels."** **"It was a very long time before we knew we could go even more broke on spiritual pride. When we...got our first glimmer of how spiritually prideful we could be, we coined this expression: 'Don't try to get too damned good by Thursday!' That old-time admonition may look like another of those handy alibis that can excuse us from trying for our best. Yet a closer view reveals just the contrary. This is our...way of warning against pride-**

blindness, and the imaginary perfections that we do not possess."[711]

"In its deeper sense AA is a quest for freedom—freedom under God...

"Paradoxically, though, we can achieve no liberation from the...obsession until we become willing to deal with those character defects which have landed us in that helpless condition. Even to gain sobriety only, we must attain some freedom from fear, anger, and pride; from rebellion and self-righteousness; from laziness and irresponsibility; from foolish rationalisation and outright dishonesty; from wrong dependencies and destructive power-driving.

"In this freedom quest, we are always given three choices. (1) *A rebellious refusal to work upon our glaring defects can be a ticket to destruction.* (2) *Or, for a time, we can stay sober with a minimum of self-improvement and settle ourselves into a comfortable but often dangerous mediocrity.* (3) *Or we can continuously try hard for those sterling qualities which can add up to greatness of spirit and action—true and lasting freedom under God, the freedom to find and do his will.*

"For most of us this last choice is really ours; we must never be blinded by the futile philosophy that we are just the hapless victims of our inheritance, our life experience, and our surroundings—that these are the sole forces that make our decisions for us. This is not the road to freedom. We have to believe that we can really choose.

"Shall we try only for the temporary comforts of a complacent mediocrity? Or shall we consistently face the disciplines, make the sacrifices, and endure the discomforts that will qualify us to walk the path that invariably leads toward true greatness of spirit and action? ...

"We shall always have to deal with the fearful forces which are released when the human ego runs amuck—the same forces that are shattering the world of our time.

"Vigilance will always be the price of survival."[712] And we gain not just an everyday survival, but a life of continued peace and joy and happiness. *"The essence of growth is a willingness to change for the better and then an unremitting willingness to shoulder whatever the responsibility."*[713] Let us keep growing and not allow ourselves to stagnate. *"Hence genuine peace will always be a chief ingredient of...freedom."*[714]

"Faith without works is dead—action is the magic word!"[715] *"I trust that if I continue to work the Steps, practice the...principles in my life, and share my story, I will be guided lovingly toward a deep and mature spirituality in which more will be revealed to me."*[716] Let's keep the action going. However, it has become very clear to many of us that: *"The more I learn, the less I know—a humbling fact—but I sincerely want to keep growing."*[717] Most of us find that, *"Growing spiritually is the answer to our problems...* (accomplished by) *placing spiritual growth first."*[718] *"A spiritual awakening is what a man does through his willingness to have his life transformed by following a proven programme of spiritual growth, and this is a never-ending venture."*[719] So let's maintain what we have gained, and grow to even greater spiritual heights.

It is often repeated that: *"We are not saints. The point is that we are willing to grow along spiritual lines. The principles we have set down are guides to progress. We claim spiritual progress rather than spiritual perfection."*[720] Somehow, we feel that this gives us an excuse for all kinds of bad behaviour. Yes, it is true that: *"We shall look for progress, not perfection."*[721] But that does not mean that we shouldn't <u>strive</u> for perfection. If we don't hold up perfection as an ideal we will not make progress towards it. We monitor where we have fallen short of our desired goal. There is continuous effort require in the "Maintenance Steps." *"Spirituality happens to be extremely practical. Prayer, reading the...literature, going to meetings, using the Steps, and helping another...all combine to <u>make my life easier</u> and more comfortable, hour to hour, day to day."*[722]

One of the first hundred members described the rewards of continued effort: *"Come into my home and see what a happy one it is. Look into my office; it is a happy human beehive of activity. Look into any phase of my life and you will see joy and happiness, a sense of usefulness in the scheme of things, where formerly there was fear, sorrow and utter futility."*[723] Doesn't it sound like the effort to continue working the process just might be worth it? Someone mentioned the other day that they were not willing to just throw themselves into the programme like some kind of unquestioning follower. Can they, I wonder, say the same of their life as the member quoted above?

In the programme *"I've learned...that the more I worry about me loving you, and the less I worry about you loving me, the happier I'll be.*

"I have learned that the more I give, the more I will have; the more I learn to give, the more I learn to live."[724] In the story titled *"Texas Flower"* it says: ***"I know that I must work at it as long as I live; I know that it is only by working at it that I can stay sober and have a happy life. It is an endless career.***

"It has changed not simply one department of my life—it has changed my whole life...It is a way of life that pays as it goes, every Step of the way, in compensations that have been wonderfully rich and rewarding... It pays daily in more harmonious relations with my fellow men, in ever clearer insight into the meaning of life, and in the answering love and gratitude wherever and whenever I have been the instrument of God's will in the lives of others. In all these ways I've experienced, in ever growing measure and beyond all expectations and rewards, a joy which I had never before imagined."[725] Why would we give this up to "rest on our laurels?" It is truly hard to understand, but we do. It's a choice we must each make for ourselves. When we choose one way we maintain the "Promises," the other we find ourselves on a "Dry Drunk."

"A dry drunk is an emotional storm."[726] *"I believe a dry drunk is a period of temporary insanity... A dry drunk is a self-imposed separation from others and from God."*[727]

"Perhaps, in the last analysis, a dry drunk is mostly a childish tantrum, an interval of immaturity, a regression to those frantic...days of self-will run riot."[728]

A BRIDGE TO NORMAL LIVING

This is the Step where we begin to create and maintain the bridge to normal living. My sponsor George F., a life long friend and my spiritual guide wrote:

> "If we choose to be happy, we must determine what is important in our life. When we are young we spend our time trying to figure out how to behave with others in authority, our peers and those older or younger than ourselves. That there is a pecking order becomes apparent very quickly. Soon we decide that there are others above us who are stronger and smarter as we search for our niche in life.
>
> "Fortunate is she that sooner or later discovers her talents and accepts them as her individual path. Unfortunate is she that follows the path suggested by another or wishes to be different because another path seems more prestigious, lucrative or

easier. The fortunate person that puts her talents to good use in the work-place has one third of her life in order. Now she must determine what is really important in life. Is it **Spiritual life** as a member of a Twelve Step Fellowship? Is it our **Relationships** as a family and community member? Or, is it her **Work/Money** as a breadwinner so that she may be "self-supporting through her own contributions?" There must be balance between all three areas of life or her life will be one of ups and downs—sorrow and suffering. Too much attention in any one area—work, relationships or recovery—can cause real problems. We can find balance in the *Golden Triangle* or Triangle of Balance.

TRIANGLE OF BALANCE

Work/Money   **Relationships**

Spiritual life

"It is important to create balance in our lives—with our programme as the foundation—if we wish to stay centred, comfortable and content. Once we have completed the first nine Steps, it's time to actively work towards such balance. Too often we hear people in the programme preach that this is the "bridge to normal living," and find them really talking about abandoning their programme and meetings once life has improved. The programme *is* the bridge, and without it we fall back into our old patterns of behaviour. This is where balance comes in."

Up until the "Maintenance Steps" we have probably put our recovery first. We may even have spent far more time on our programme work than anything else. This is certainly appropriate in the beginning. But now it's time for balance and *stewardship* in our lives. Too much time at work and we're in trouble. The same is true for the programme and our relationships. It is fairly normal for us to switch from one to the other. For example, we may find ourselves concentrating all our energy on an ailing relationship. This rarely works, neither saving the

182

relationship nor maintaining a balanced life. Too much focus in any single area and life begins to fall apart.

From our triangle we can see that our **Spiritual Life**, our programme, is the foundation. And we keep that focus via the Maintenance Steps. With our daily balance sheet we can see where we stand each day. We correct our course and move forward poised for a new day.

Chapter 13

Disturbance Control

Stewardship

STEP TEN

"*<u>Continued</u> To Take Personal Inventory And When We Were Wrong Promptly Admitted It.*"[729]

Read in preparation, in the "Big Book" of *Alcoholics Anonymous* –
Pages 84-85

Twelve Steps and Twelve Traditions – Step Ten – Pages 90-97

STEP TEN

"<u>Continued</u> To Take Personal Inventory and When We Were Wrong Promptly Admitted It."[730]

We must remember what we have learned from the previous Nine Steps: gaining power in our lives means taking responsibility for our own emotions, comfort, feelings and conduct. Then we can find our Higher Power. **"When we approach Step Ten we commence to put our...way of living to practical use, day by day, in fair weather or foul. Then comes the acid test: can we stay sober, keep in emotional balance, and live, to good purpose, under all conditions?"[731]** Always we keep at the forefront of our minds the collective knowledge that sobriety, defined as just not drinking or using is in itself not enough: **"at Step Ten, we had begun to get a basis for daily living, and we keenly realised that we would need to continue taking personal inventory."[732]**

Often as we go through our day the only thing that has happened is someone has made a stupid remark. After which, our emotions have been affected to the extreme and we fume. This is where Step 10 comes in.

"Step Ten...suggests we continue to take personal inventory and continue to set right any new mistakes as we go along. We vigorously commenced this way of living as we cleaned up the past. We have entered the world of the Spirit. Our next function is to grow in understanding and effectiveness. This is not an overnight matter. It should continue for a lifetime."[733]
"'Resentment is (still) **the Number One offender.' It is a primary cause of relapses."[734]**

"We react sanely and normally, and we find that this has happened automatically. We will see that our new attitude...has been given us without any thought or effort on our part. It just comes! That is the miracle of it. We are not fighting it, neither are we avoiding temptation. We feel as though we had been placed in a position of neutrality—safe and protected...the problem has been removed. It does not exist for us. We are neither cocky nor are we afraid. That is our experience. That is how we react so long as we keep in fit spiritual condition. (We find this to be true with any problem on which we thoroughly work the 12 Step process.)

"It is easy to let up on the spiritual programme of action and rest on our laurels. We are headed for trouble if we do."[735] But we can maintain our **"emotional sobriety. <u>If we examine every disturbance we have, great or small, we will find at the root of it</u>**

some unhealthy dependency and its consequence unhealthy demand. Let us, with God's help, continually surrender these hobbling demands. Then we can be set free to live and love; we may then be able to Twelve Step others into emotional sobriety."[736]

WE MUST NOT **"REST ON OUR LAURELS"** NO MATTER HOW MUCH WE ARE TEMPTED TO DO SO. If we do we risk losing what we have gained. **"We learned that if we were seriously disturbed, our first need was to quiet that disturbance, regardless of whom or what we thought caused it."**[737] We are no longer victims of other people's behaviour. We're free and we are going to remain that way. We can and will maintain the Promises we have now gained by working all of the types of Tenth Steps suggested below. We have **"to continue to take inventory every day if** (we) **expect to get well and stay well."**[738]

"A business which takes no regular inventory usually goes broke."[739] Our new found "business of living" is no different. Our inventories often contain errors: **"Of course, my self-analysis has frequently been faulty. Sometimes I've failed to share my defects with the right people; at other times, I've confessed their defects, rather than my own; and at still other times, my confession of defects has been more in the nature of loud complaints about my circumstances and my problems.** [740] This is the reason why written inventory always works better than doing it in our heads.

"Long ago I was lucky enough to see that I'd have to keep up my self-analysis or else blow my top completely. Though driven by stark necessity, this continuous self-revelation—to myself and others—was rough medicine to take. But years of repetition has made this job far easier."[741] **"If we go on growing, our attitudes and actions toward security—emotional security and financial security—commence to change profoundly. Our demand for emotional security, for our own way, had constantly thrown us into unworkable relations with other people."**[742] This we find to be the absolute foundation of all relationship problems.

We must always keep in mind that **"the first requirement is that we be convinced that any life run on self-will can hardly be a success."**[743] Therefore any inventory involves a similar surrender to that in the first three Steps. We at least acknowledge that we must write inventory at the end of each day. It is amazing that no matter how long we are around: **"Some of us have tried to hold on to our old ideas and the result was nil until we let go absolutely."**[744]

188

Eventually most of us learn that **"the more we fought and tried to have our own way, the worse matters got."**[745]

This process is about gaining a measure of control over our life. As another member put it: **"I have no control over some of the things that happen in my life, but with the help of God I can now choose how I will respond."**[746] The best way of understanding Step Ten and Eleven, is to see them as a daily practice of all the previous Steps, One to Nine, simultaneously. All the processes used in those Steps will be duplicated in Step Ten at some point. Remember that our Step Four Inventory was **"but the beginning of a life long practice."**[747] A practice where, **"I place the principles of spirituality ahead of judging, fault-finding, and criticism."**[748]

"Perhaps life, as it has a way of doing, suddenly hands us a great big lump that we can't begin to swallow, let alone digest."[749] **"Mental and emotional difficulties are sometimes very hard to take while we are trying to maintain sobriety... Adversity gives us more opportunity to grow than does comfort or success."**[750]

Earlier in Step Four, we talked about the "ONE POUND WEIGHT," (130.4-6) our task now is to practice letting go of it more quickly, before there is damage to ourselves or our relationships. Whatever disturbing burdens we pick up today, let's release them as soon as possible. We must not get unduly emotional about this work. We only desire the truth that will set us free. Remember that **"inventory is a fact-finding and fact-facing process. It is an effort to discover the truth... We took stock honestly."**[751] That is what this Step is all about, facts not emotions.

The cry of the "self-satisfied" is often, **"'Well, I'm sober and I'm happy. What more can I want or do? I'm fine the way I am.' We know** (from our own experience) **that the price of such self-satisfaction is an inevitable backslide, punctuated at some point by a very rude awakening. We have to grow or else deteriorate. For us, the 'status quo' can only be for today, never tomorrow. Change we must; we cannot stand still...**

"We have come to believe that (the) **recovery Steps and Traditions do represent the approximate truths which we need for our particular purpose. The more we practice them, the more we like them.**

"While we need not alter our truths, we surely improve their application to ourselves...and to our relation with the world around us. We can constantly Step up 'the practice of these principles in all our affairs.

"Let us continue to take our inventory... searching out our flaws and confessing them freely. Let us devote ourselves to the repair of all faulty relations that may exist, whether within or without."[752]

THREE TYPES OF TENTH STEPS

FIRST IS THE *"'SPOT-CHECK' INVENTORY"*[753]

"Although all inventories are alike in principle, the time factor does distinguish one from another. There's the "spot-check" inventory, taken at any time of the day, whenever we find ourselves <u>tangled up</u>."[754]

"Before we ask what a "spot-check" inventory is, let's look at the kind of setting in which such an inventory can do its work.

"It is a spiritual axiom that every time we are disturbed, <u>no matter what the cause,</u> there is something wrong with us. If somebody hurts us and we are sore, <u>we are in the wrong also</u>."[755]

"When I get upset, cross-grained and out of tune with my fellow man I know that I am out of tune with God. Searching where I have been at fault, it is not hard to discover and get right again."[756] Where we use our inventory process this becomes patently clear. After each "disturbance" we want to be able to look back and say: *"I knew something was terribly wrong, and the reason had to lie within myself."*[757] But it is likely that we will resist this fact. Old habits die hard. This is why we need to remind ourselves of it on a daily basis.

We found that: *"Acceptance was the Answer." "Acceptance is the answer to all my problems today. When I am <u>disturbed,</u> it is because I find some person, place, thing, or situation—some fact of my life—unacceptable to me, and I can find no serenity until I accept that person, place, thing, or situation as being exactly the way it is supposed to be at this moment. Nothing, absolutely nothing, happens in God's world by mistake...unless I accept life completely on life's terms, I cannot be happy. <u>I need to concentrate not so much on what needs to be changed in the world as on what needs to be changed in me and in my attitudes</u>."*[758]

"But are there no exceptions to this rule? What about "justifiable" anger? If somebody cheats us, aren't we entitled to be angry? Can't we be properly angry with self-righteous folk?"[759]

190

The answer to each of these questions is an emphatic and resounding **No!** Venting our anger is not OK, nor should it be repressed, stuffing it down and not dealing with it. ***"We have found that justified anger ought to be left to those better qualified to handle it... It mattered little whether our resentments were justified or not... As we saw it, our wrath was always justified. Anger, the occasional luxury of more balanced people, could keep us on an emotional orgy indefinitely."***[760] ***"It will become more and more evident as we go forward that it is pointless to become angry, or get hurt by people who, like us, are suffering from the pains of growing up."***[761]

"Many religions and philosophies urge us to get rid of anger in order to find a happier life. Yet a great number of people are certain that bottling up anger is very bad for emotional health, that we should get our hostility out in some way, or it will 'poison' our insides by turning inward toward ourselves, thus leading to deep depression."[762] We agree that anger needs to be dealt with but do not agree that it is healthy to "get it out." Punching pillows or using soft batons and hitting things may be effective for some, but we believe that it is at best a temporary measure, and if we do not deal with the root causes we will graduate from punching the pillow to more destructive behaviour.

"The minute... I... (feel) ***sorrow for myself, or... hurt by, or resentful towards anyone, I am in horrible danger."***[763] ***"Here is a look at some of the shapes and colours anger seems at times to arrive in:***

"Intolerance	*Snobbishness*	*Tension*	*Distrust*
"Contempt	*Rigidity*	*Sarcasm*	*Anxiety*
"Envy	*Cynicism*	*Self-pity*	*Suspicion*
"Jealousy	*Hatred*	*Discontent*	*Malice*
(Frustration)	(Self-righteousness)	(Injustice)	(Hurt)
(Betrayal)		(Fear)	

"Many of us believe anger is frequently an outgrowth of fear... Perhaps 'justifiable' resentment is the trickiest of all to handle... Even if we actually have been treated shabbily or unjustly, resentment is a luxury... we cannot afford. For us, __all__ anger is self-destructive...

"It's also remarkably effective, when we begin to get teed off at something, to pick up the phone and talk about it to our sponsor."[764]

We have found that: ***"Other kinds of disturbances—jealousy, envy, self-pity, or hurt pride—did the same thing."***[765] All lead to anger. So what do we do about these "feelings?" ***"A 'spot-check' inventory taken in the midst of such disturbances can be of very great help in quieting stormy emotions. Today's spot check finds its chief application to situations which arise in each day's march...***(we are reminded that it is a march not a drudge). ***The quick inventory is aimed at our daily ups and downs, especially those where people or new events throw us off balance and tempt us to make mistakes."***[766] There will be time later, at the end of the day, to more permanently repair and bolster our emotional and spiritual states.

"Simply repressing, glossing over, or damming up anger rarely (if ever) ***seems advisable. Instead, we try to learn not to act <u>on</u> it, but to do something <u>about</u> it."***[767] ***"Continue to take personal inventory and when we are wrong we promptly admit it."***[768] Does not the earlier statement say clearly that if our feelings are hurt we are <u>always</u> in the wrong also? This being so, we must be diligent. What we have found is that an outburst of anger is long after the events that loaded us to explode. Then it can be the most trivial thing that triggers the anger. As we were to look back over the days, weeks, even months and years before an eruption we find many examples of times we mistakenly thought we could hold it together and stuffed our feelings. The answer we find always to be the same, deal with the small "twinges" of discomfort, using the Steps and the big explosions don't happen.

We want to re-establish a point. When we speak of not having an angry flare-up we do not mean that we stuff our feelings, we mean to deal with them in a healthy and powerful way through the use of the process suggested in the Steps, early in the cycle of upset. Besides, ***"The positive value of righteous indignation is theoretical... It leaves every one of us open to the rationalisation that we may be as angry as we like provided we can claim to be righteous about it."***[769] Our experience demonstrates that even one well nursed "bad apple" of belief—this time, "I am right!" is enough to make the whole Spiritual barrel of ripe, delicious, desirable and wonderful "Apples"(the promises) of our lives to turn rotten.

FORMULA FOR SPOT-CHECK INVENTORY

There is a formula in the "Big Book" of *Alcoholics Anonymous* for a Spot Check Inventory and the maintenance of the promises gained from the previous Nine Steps. It suggests that we:

192

"Continue to watch for selfishness, dishonesty, resentment, and fear ("every time we are disturbed"[770]*). When these crop up...*

1) *"We ask God at once to remove them.*

2) *"We discuss them with someone immediately and*

3) *"Make amends quickly if we have harmed anyone.*

4) *"Then we resolutely* [4] *turn our thoughts to someone we can help.*[771]

"Love and tolerance of others is our code. And we have ceased fighting anything or anyone—even alcohol (or any of our addictions)*. For by this time sanity will have returned."*[772] Notice that fear—that *"evil and corroding thread"*[773] still crops up in our lives. What do we do about it? We treat it exactly the same as any other "disturbance," crediting it with no more power than it possesses, which is none at all. Most of us want to be courageous and in order to become so we must recognise that:

"Courage is resistance to fear, mastery of fear—not absence of fear."—Mark Twain

The way to conquer fear is by remembering that *"we are now on a different basis; the basis of trusting and relying upon God. We trust infinite God rather than finite selves."*[774] And we act accordingly. *"Now and then we fall under heavy criticism. When we are angered and hurt, it's difficult not to retaliate in kind. Yet we can restrain ourselves* (using this process) *and then probe ourselves, asking whether our critics were really right* (later that evening as seen ahead)*. If so, we can admit our defects to them. This usually clears the air for mutual understanding."*[775] Our bottom line experience is that, *"Nothing pays like restraint of tongue and pen."*[776] Or, given today's technology, it pays to refrain from clicking on the send button. *"The most heated bit of letter-writing can be a wonderful safety valve—providing the wastebasket is somewhere nearby."*[777]

EXPERIENCE SHOWS THIS IS A BAND-AID—A PLASTER—USED ONLY FOR EMERGENCY TREATMENT ON THE "BATTLEFIELD OF LIFE."

"We are sure God wants us to be happy, joyous, and free. We cannot subscribe to the belief that this life is a vale of tears, though it was once that for many of us."[778] Life tends to be a "battlefield" because we make it one. *"It is clear that we made our own misery. God didn't do it."*[779] So how do we heal these battle

---

[4] **Resolutely** = with determination, boldly, without vacillating, without shrinking, with firm purpose or purposefully, with resolve.

DEEP SOUL CLEANSING

scars <u>permanently</u>? The answer lies in the other two types of Tenth Steps.

SECOND IS THE "DAILY BALANCE SHEET"

"There's the one we take at day's end, when we review the happenings of the hours just passed. Here we cast a balance sheet, crediting ourselves with things well done, and chalking up debits where due."[780]

If, during the course of the day, we have acquired any resentment, we write a four-column inventory on them. That way the wound attended to with the *"Spot Check Inventory"* (often temporary band-aide) can be permanently healed with this process and amends made where necessary. However, just as often the band-aide was appropriate for the particular scrape. Remember that *"all inventories are alike in principle"*[781] therefore, the four column format is always appropriate for anything unresolved at the end of the day.

It is always the same with disturbance and resentment; we still think we're right. While *"admitting he may be somewhat at fault, he is sure that other people are more to blame."*[782] You would think that some day we would stop trying to be right, wouldn't you? In any situation where we believe things to be a certain way, we ask ourselves: "Is there another way this could be?" And we keep asking ourselves the question, until we have at least ten other possibilities. Then the odds are we are wrong, ten-to-one. We are not mind readers; thus it is a waste of time and mental acuity. Besides, is it really our business? *"So I don't just take the inventory at night—I take it continually throughout the day... For me,* (it) *has become a way of life."*[783]

We are working towards a life where we spend our time looking at *our* motives and plans and schemes. Those we can correct. Instead of attempting to "correct" others like we do; often, *"We 'constructively criticise' someone who needed it, when our real motive was to win a useless argument... We sometimes hurt those we love because they need to be 'taught' a lesson, when we really mean to punish."*[784] Even if it were true that we wanted to sincerely 'help' them, you would think that by now we would see that this never works. We really need to look at why we find it necessary to *"interfere with the growth of another human being."* [785] Besides, we need to decide whether we want a loving relationship or want to be their unsolicited "teacher." The *"Twelve Steps continually remind us of the stark need for ego deflation."*[786] *"Learning daily to spot, admit, and correct these flaws is the essence of character-building and good life."*[787]

We have created a simple and straightforward form for this purpose. It is suggested that **"When evening comes, perhaps just before going to sleep, many of us draw up a balance sheet for the day."**[788] **"Here we need only recognise that we did act or think badly, to visualise how we might have done better, and resolve with God's help to carry these lessons over into tomorrow, <u>making, of course, any amends still neglected</u>."**[789]

This work is completed with our Daily Prayer and Meditation as suggested in the *Big Book:* **"When we retire at night, we constructively review our day. Were we resentful, selfish, dishonest or afraid? Do we owe an apology? Have we kept something to ourselves, which should be discussed with another person at once? Were we kind and loving toward all? What could we have done better? Were we thinking of ourselves most of the time? Or; were we thinking of what we could do for others, of what we could pack into the stream of life? But we must be careful not to drift into worry, remorse or morbid reflection, for that would diminish our usefulness to others. After making our review we ask God's forgiveness and inquire what corrective measures should be taken?"**[790] The form which follows is taken directly from this paragraph.

This being a spiritual programme which needs constant attention, here is where we take our 'spiritual temperature,' if you will. A wise man told us that if we want to know how far we are away from God, we find out where we stand in our relationships. If the answer is that we are in conflict, we are far off. If we are at peace, we are close to God. A member from Sydney, Australia put it another way: **"The depth of our anxiety measures the distance we are from God."**[791]

Many members also practice keeping a journal, and this is said to be a very good technique for reviewing our day. This practice will also help us with our inventories when we go on our annual or semi-annual retreats. Basically, writing almost always helps.

ON GRATITUDE AND A GRATITUDE LIST *

Writing a gratitude list seems to some of us like a labour intensive task but can bring great rewards if practised. There are some that suggest we write one on a daily basis. It is extremely difficult to be both miserable and grateful at the same time.

"It took several years, but I learned to be grateful for my alcoholism and the programme of recovery it forced me into, for all the things that had happened to me and for me, for a life today that transcends and far exceeds anything I had previously known. I could not have that today if I had not experienced all the yesterdays."[792]

"When we retire at night we constructively review our day."[793] In this process we must always remember that: *"Love and tolerance of others is our code."*[794] *"And we have ceased fighting anything and anyone—even alcohol."*[795]

You'll find all the forms available and how to acquire it at the back of this publication. Included you'll find a website where you can download these forms for free.

Food	Money	
Breakfast	Item	Amount
Lunch		
Dinner		
Snack		
Exercise		
Litres Water Hours Sleep	Total Spent Today	

When we retire at night we constructively review our day. We remember we have ceased fighting anything and anyone—love and tolerance of others is our code.

We Draw Up a Balance Sheet

The "Negative Side" (-)	The "Positive Side" (+)
Were we resentful?	Have we stayed clean of our addiction today?
Were we selfish?	Were we kind?
Were we dishonest?	Were we loving toward all?
Were we afraid?	What did we pack into life?
Have we kept something to ourselves?	Did we pray and meditate?
Were we thinking of ourselves most of the time?	Did we call someone we could help today?
Were we "disturbed" today?	Did we think of how we could help others?
Do we owe an apology? And if so to whom?	Did we study literature today?
What could we have done better?	Did we go to a meeting today?
Did we blame our feelings on someone else?	Did we call our sponsor today?
Do we need to write 10th Step on something?	Did we do anything that is improved over our past?

Journal

After completing our "Daily Balance Sheet," we do any column work that is indicated. Otherwise there will be a constant build up of "twinges" that have not been handled, creating more and more "disturbance." As stated earlier, all inventories are basically the same, so we work a four column inventory on any type of disturbance. It comes as no surprise that this daily inventory is a Balance Sheet; this is exactly what we are looking for; balance, equanimity, our place as one among many, neither better than nor worse than anyone else: **_Every human being, no matter what his attitudes for good or evil, is a part of the Divine spiritual economy. Therefore, each of us has his place, and I cannot see that God intends to exalt one over another._**[796]

You'll find all the forms available and how to acquire it at the back of this publication. Included you'll find a website where you can download these forms for free.

DISTURBANCE CONTROL—STEWARDSHIP

Resentment (1) Or Fear:	The Cause (2)	Affects Our: (3)
Person, Place or Thing		❑ Self-Esteem ❑ Security ❑ Ambitions ❑ Personal Relations ❑ Sex Relations ❑ Pride/Shame ❑ Fear
Ask Ourselves: ** (AA 67.3) * (AA 62.2)	Putting out of our mind the wrong others had done, we resolutely looked for our own mistakes... We admitted our wrongs honestly...** **STEPS 4** and/or **10 - (**Column **4)**	
Where had we been selfish, self-centred or self-seeking? **		
Where had we been dishonest? **		
Where had we been frightened? **		
For what had we been responsible? **		
What decisions did I make based on self that later placed me in a position to be hurt?*		
When in the past did we make this decision? * (Earliest memory.)		
Where were we wrong**, **what was our part?**		

STEPS 6 & 7 List of Character Defects		

STEP 9 - Amend	STEP 8
	❑ Now ❑ Later ❑ Never

THIRD is the *"Annual or Semi-Annual House-Cleaning"*

Many of our programme friends go on a yearly retreat to tend to this important *"House-Cleaning"* (basically a renewal of the Steps). If we have survived for many years without relapsing, we may finally work all the Steps again. Like this member from Oklahoma *"I reviewed my entire life—the years before...and the twelve years in AA...For the first time in my life, it grew quite clear to me that I was an utter, complete, 100-percent, dyed-in-the-wool louse. I was so self-centred, so full of ego, that I had all but destroyed myself. During the years...I had learned little more than to 'keep the plug in the jug.' I had neglected to try to work all the Twelve Steps of the programme."*[797] *"Yes, I did go back and start all over on the Twelve Steps, and I felt the wonder of other discoveries—about myself and my Higher Power. I would have felt these years ago had I but followed the programme and had I been, as the Big Book states, 'willing to go to any length to get it.'"*[798]

"Then there are those occasions when alone, or in the company of our sponsor or spiritual advisor, we make a careful review of our progress since the last time. Many...go in for annual or semi-annual house-cleanings. Many of us also like the experience of an occasional retreat from the outside world where we quieten down for an undisturbed day or so of self-overhaul and meditation."[799]

Many of us have foolishly tried to work Step Tens in our heads, without putting them *in writing: "Admitting to God, to ourselves, AND another human being the exact nature of our wrongs."*[800] We then learned the hard way that: *"In actual practice, we usually find a solitary self-appraisal insufficient."*[801]

Though our decisions and choices were the cause of much of our problems in life we don't use that as an excuse not to be decisive in the present. *"We lose the fear of making decisions, great or small, as we realise that should our choice prove wrong we can, if we will, learn from the experience. Should our decision be the right one, we can* (and are careful to) *thank God for giving us the courage and the grace that caused us so to act."*[802] Remember, it is our intention today to be conscious of our choices and decisions.

"All of my family and loved ones, all of my friends, are nearer and dearer to me than ever before; and I have literally dozens of new friends."[803] We *want* to have, and *"develop the best possible relations with every human being we know."*[804] *"I know the purpose of life: The purpose of life is to create and the*

*by-product is happiness. **To** **create**: Everyone does it, some at the instinct level, and others in the arts. My personal definition...includes every waking activity of the human being; to have a creative attitude toward things is a more exact meaning, to live and deal with other human beings creatively, which to me means seeing the God in them, and respecting and worshiping this God."*[805] It is our responsibility, no matter what the other person is doing, to see the God in everyone.

We've come a long way. Let's not lose our momentum now. The so called "Pink Cloud" can be maintained with careful stewardship. ***"The secret of fulfilling my potential is acknowledging my limitations and believing that time is a gift, not a threat."***[806] To repeat what was said earlier: ***"The idea that we can be possessively loving of a few, can ignore the many, and can continue to fear or hate anybody has to be abandoned."***[807]

THE PRINCIPLE OF STEP TEN

Stewardship

The so-called "maintenance Steps" of the programme begin with Step Ten, teaching us perseverance and **stewardship**. Whereas perseverance is just plain "keeping on, keeping on;" **stewardship** is realising the need for a maintenance programme to keep the "Promises" we gained through working the previous Nine Steps. Dr. Bob said that ***"we are stewards of what we have."***[808] We look after what we have been given.

Chapter 14

Building Peace

Consciousness

STEP ELEVEN – PEACE BUILDER

"Sought Through Prayer And Meditation To <u>Improve</u> Our Conscious Contact With God, As We Understood (God)*, Praying Only For Knowledge Of* (God's) *Will For Us, and The Power To Carry That Out"*[809]

Read in preparation, in the "Big Book" of *Alcoholics Anonymous* –
Page 85-88

Twelve Steps and Twelve Traditions – Step Eleven –Pages 98-108

STEP ELEVEN – PEACE BUILDER

"Sought Through Prayer And Meditation To <u>Improve</u> Our Conscious Contact With God, As We Understood (God)*, Praying Only For Knowledge Of* (God's) *Will For Us, And The Power To Carry That Out"*[810]

𝕴n working Step Ten we carry out a daily self-examination. In Step Eleven, we find, *"There is a direct linkage among self-examination, meditation, and prayer... When they are logically related and interwoven, the result is an unshakable foundation for life."*[811] *"In Step Eleven we saw that if a higher Power had restored us to* (some semblance of) *sanity and had enabled us to live with some peace of mind in a sorely troubled world, then such a higher Power was worth knowing better, by as direct contact as possible. The persistent use of meditation and prayer, we found, did open the channel so that where there had been a trickle, there now was a river which led to sure power and safe guidance from God as we were increasingly better able to understand* (God)*."*[812]

IMPROVE CONSCIOUS CONTACT: PRAYER AND MEDITATION

"The other Steps can keep most of us sober and somehow functioning. But Step Eleven can keep us growing, if we try hard and work at it continually."[813] Even though *"we often tend to slight serious meditation and prayer as something not really necessary... Or perhaps we don't believe in these things at all."*[814] *"Prayer and meditation are our principal means of conscious contact with God."*[815] Most of our physical and mental problems can be traced back to a lack of spiritual health.

"Many people pray as though to overcome the will of a reluctant God, instead of taking hold of the willingness of a loving God."[816] *"When the spiritual malady is overcome, we straighten out mentally and physically."*[817] Therefore *"when we turn away from meditation and prayer, we...deprive our minds, emotions, and our intuitions of vitally needed support. As the body can fail its purpose for lack of nourishment, so can the soul."*[818]

"<u>The primary object of any human being is to grow</u>...<u>that being the nature of all growing things</u>... If the capability of loving is in the human being, then it must surely be in his Creator... Theology helps me in that many of its concepts cause me to believe that I live in a rational universe under a loving God, and that my own irrationality can be chipped away, little by little."[819]

We don't have to have perfect faith. But while there are any contrary subconscious beliefs, they will deny the affirmations of our lips. *"The important part is not to cancel our prayers by later worrying."*[820] *"The process of enlightenment is usually slow... The willingness to grow is the essence of all spiritual development."*[821] *"If we place instincts first, we have got to cart before the horse; we shall be pulled backwards into disillusionment. But when we are willing to place spiritual growth first—then and only then do we have a real chance."*[822] When the intellect is no longer contradicted by our past decisions and accompanying emotional reactions, unconscious doubts and fears, then the word of the mouth through affirmative prayer will immediately bear fruit.

Someone very close, simply says again and again, "God, God, God..."when in confusion. And this member says: *"Another sort of path toward God which I try to follow every day is the process of positive thinking. AA taught me that it is actually possible— though not always easy—to stop a negative or despairing train of thought and, by the use of a repeated slogan, recover a sense of gratitude, which permits me to begin a positive train of thought. The ultimate positive thought, of course, is 'God,' the word which affirms our faith that the universe is friendly to our being."*[823]

However: *"I, and maybe lots of other*(s)*...have still been missing something of top importance. Through lack of disciplined attention and sometimes through lack of the right kind of faith, many of us keep ourselves year after year in the rather easy spiritual kindergarten... But almost inevitably we become dissatisfied; we have to admit we have hit an uncomfortable and maybe a very painful sticking point.*

"Twelfth-Stepping, talking at meetings, recitals of drinking histories, confessions of our defects and what progress we have made with them no longer provide us with a released and the abundant life. Our lack of growth is often revealed by an unexpected calamity or a big emotional upset...

"As we usually don't get drunk on these occasions, our bright-eyed friends tell us how well we are doing. (Or, have we taken on other addictive behaviours?)

"But inside, we know better. We know we aren't doing well enough. We still can't handle life, as life is. There must be a serious flaw somewhere in our spiritual practice and development.

"What, then, is it?

208

"The chances are better than even that we shall locate our trouble in our misunderstanding or neglect of (the) *Step Eleven—prayer, meditation, and the guidance of God... If we expend even five percent of the time on Step Eleven that we habitually (and rightly) lavish on Step Twelve, the results can be wonderfully far-reaching. That is an almost uniform experience of those who constantly practice Step Eleven."*[824]

"Try Prayer. You can't lose, and maybe God will help you—just maybe."[825] And *"Pray with disbelief; but pray with sincerity; and the belief will come."*[826] *"Refusing to place God first, we had deprived ourselves of his help."*[827]

"I'd like to develop Step Eleven further—for the benefit of the complete doubter, the unlucky one who can't believe it (prayer and/or meditation) *has any real merit at all.*

"In lots of instances I think that people find their first great obstacle in the phrase 'God as we understand (God)*." The doubter is apt to say: 'On the face of it, nobody can understand God... I think people are kidding themselves when they say they can... As for those folks who claim God tells them where to drill for oil, or when to brush their teeth—well, they just make me tired.*

"So he looks upon meditation, prayer, and guidance as the means of a self-delusion. Now what can our hard-pressed friend do about this?

"Well, he can strenuously try meditation, prayer, and guidance, just as an experiment. He can address himself to whatever God he thinks there is. Or, if he thinks there is none, he can admit—just for experimental purposes—that he might be wrong. This is all-important. As soon as he is able to take this attitude, it means that he has stopped playing God himself; his mind has opened. Like any good scientist in his laboratory, our friend can assume a theory and pray to a 'higher power' that <u>may</u> exist and <u>may</u> be willing to help and guide him. He keeps on experimenting—in this case, praying—for a long time. Again he tries to behave like the scientist, an experimenter who is never supposed to give up so long as there is a vestige of any chance of success.

"As he goes along with his process of prayer, he begins to add up the results. If he persists, he will almost surely find more serenity, more tolerance, less fear, and less anger. He will acquire a quiet courage, the kind that doesn't strain him. He can look at so-called failure and success for what they really are.

Problems and calamity will begin to mean instruction, instead of destruction. He will feel freer and saner. The idea that he may have been hypnotizing himself by autosuggestion will become laughable. His sense of purpose and of direction will increase. His tensions and anxieties will commence to fade. His physical health is likely to improve. Wonderful and unaccountable things will start to happen. Twisted relations in his family and on the outside will unaccountably improve."[828]

By this point in our programme *"we had to face the fact that we must find a spiritual basis of life—or else."*[829] Or else what? Or else we would find ourselves just as miserable as ever, even though we are not using our substance of choice. Sooner or later *"we had to fearlessly face the proposition that either God is everything or else* (God) *is nothing. God either is or* (God) *isn't. What was our choice to be?"*[830] The most important purpose of this Step is to *"improve our conscious contact"* with a Power greater than we are. When we have completed the Steps we have merely skimmed the surface. Though we may even have had a *"Spiritual Experience"* of the flash of light variety, our spiritual life has just begun. We have a long journey of spiritual work ahead. The main thing we learn in the use of the Steps is that life continues, on life's terms. There are still times when we may go through hell sober. *"But what a difference there is between going through hell without a Power greater than one's self, and with It!"*[831]

For one member: *"All went well for a time, but he failed to enlarge his spiritual life. To his consternation he found himself* (relapsed)*."*[832] We trust that with due diligence on our part this won't happen to us. In our experience, we are either "enlarging" our spiritual life or it is lessoning.

A spiritual awakening is a continued process of becoming more spiritually awake; more conscious of our connection to a *"Power greater than ourselves."* The unconscious or subjective mind is like a CD that already has information recorded on it. Our conscious prayers and efforts at conscious control of our minds in meditation are like a CD Re-Writer with which we can re-record over those old beliefs. We accomplish this with conscious effort; it does not just happen to us. This is why it is suggested that we make a conscious effort to recognise our connection to God each morning and evening.

"Many...have long been striving for a better conscious contact with God and I trust that many more of us will presently join with that wise company."[833] The programme *"provided for me a means by which I could overcome the compulsion to drink and, more importantly, a means by which I could achieve a*

personality change or spiritual awakening—a surrender to life... I have faith in Something which remains a mystery to me and which I continue to seek."[834]

CONSCIOUS CONTACT = CONSCIOUS EFFORT

What we make conscious and continuous effort towards through prayer, will be established in our experience. Prayer or conscious thought establishes new beliefs, which brings new experience. Though we must be extremely cautious, and check out our "spiritual answers" with our Sponsor's or spiritual advisers. *"The moment I figure I have got a perfectly clear pipeline to God, I have become egotistical enough to get into real trouble. Nobody can cause more needless grief than* (one) *who thinks he has got it straight from God."*[835]

We should "walk our talk." *"I was astonished when I realised how little time I had been giving to my own elementary advice on meditation, prayer, and guidance—practices that I had so earnestly recommended to everyone else!*

"In this lack of attention I probably have plenty of company. But I do know that this is a neglect that can cause us to miss the finest experiences of life, a neglect that can seriously slacken the growth that God hopes we may achieve right here on earth; here in this great day at school, this very first of our Father's many mansions."[836]

As we have told newcomers: *"The very simple programme they advised me to follow was that I should ask to know God's will for me for that day, and then, to the best of my ability, to follow that, and at night to express my gratefulness to God for the things that had happened to me during the day."*[837] This is a very simplified version of the following suggestions for morning and night.

MORNING...

"On awakening let us think about the twenty-four hours ahead. We consider our plans for the day. Before we begin, we ask God to direct our thinking, especially asking that it be divorced from self-pity, dishonest or self-seeking motives. Under these conditions we can employ our mental faculties with assurance, for after all God gave us brains to use. Our thought-life will be placed on a much higher plane when our thinking is cleared of wrong motives.

"In thinking about our day we may face indecision. We may not be able to determine which course to take. Here we ask God for inspiration, an intuitive thought or a decision. We relax and take it easy. We don't struggle. We are often surprised how the right answers come after we have tried this for a while. What used to be the hunch or the occasional inspiration gradually becomes a working part of the mind. Being still inexperienced and having just made conscious contact with God, it is not probable that we are going to be inspired at all times. We might pay for this presumption in all sorts of absurd actions and ideas. Nevertheless, we find that our thinking will, as time passes, be more and more on the plane of inspiration. We come to rely upon it.

"We usually conclude the period of meditation with a prayer that we be shown all through the day what our next Step is to be, that we be given whatever we need to take care of such problems. We ask especially for freedom from self-will, and are careful to make no request for ourselves only. We may ask for ourselves, however, if others will be helped. We are careful never to pray for our own selfish ends. Many of us have wasted a lot of time doing that and it doesn't work. You can easily see why. [838] [5]

"If circumstances warrant, we ask our wives or friends to join us in morning meditation. If we belong to a religious denomination which requires a definite morning devotion, we attend to that also. If not members of religious bodies, we sometimes select and memorise a few set prayers which emphasise the principles we have been discussing. There are

---

[5] The underlined passage above can be very confusing to those of us wanting to do this work RIGHT. Does this mean that even if I need a job to feed my family I shouldn't ask? How about just to support myself? Can I even pray for another sober day according to the underlined? How do we know what the will of God is? *"Our immediate temptation will be to ask for specific solutions to specific problems, and for the ability to help other people as we have already thought they should be helped. In that case, we are asking God to do it our way. Therefore, we ought to consider each request carefully to see what its real merit is. Even so, when making specific requests, it will be well to add to each one of them this qualification: '...if it be Thy will... 'Thy will, not mine, be done.'"(Twelve Steps and Twelve Traditions – British Edition – Page 105.1)* If we are looking for the best answer possible, it probably won't come from our thinking alone. *"Among AA's there is still a vast amount of mix-up respecting what is material and what is spiritual. I prefer to believe that it is all a matter of motive. If we use our worldly possessions too selfishly, then we are materialists. But if we share these possessions in helpfulness to others, then the material aids the spiritual."*

212

many helpful books also. Suggestions about these may be obtained from one's priest, minister, or rabbi. Be quick to see where religious people are right. Make use of what they offer.

"As we go through the day we pause, when agitated or doubtful, and ask for the right thought or action. We constantly remind ourselves we are no longer running the show, humbly saying to ourselves many times each day 'Thy will be done.' We are then in much less danger of excitement, fear, anger, worry, self-pity, or foolish decisions. We become much more efficient. We do not tire so easily, for we are not burning up energy foolishly as we did when we were trying to arrange life to suit ourselves.

"It works-it really does."[839] – (Read Daily)

George F. also wrote:

"As human beings we have all developed many needs and wants. Those of us in the Western world all most always have our basic needs met. Our wants, are usually achieved through struggle. We want a luxury car, for instance we can't afford it but it's our dream. So we work a second job, we make sacrifices, and we scrimp and save. Finally, we achieve our goal. We show our family and friends. We watch ourselves as we drive by in the shop windows. We love to get out at the petrol station or at shopping centre so others can see what we've achieved. Then, after a short period of time we notice we're spending more for petrol, services are three times as expensive and insurance costs have doubled. We have to keep our second job and have little time for play. Now the luxury car has become a burden. We are disillusioned. The same scenario may take place with clothes, houses, jewellery, or a boat and other recreational vehicles. It is always the same cycle of want, struggle, accomplishment and disillusion. Nothing external ever fixes it for us; it's all provides the same, fleeting satisfaction!!

"When we see this truth, a change can occur. In the stillness and light of this truth we can see that our endless wants keep us struggling to find satisfaction in our daily lives. There is no satisfaction, peace, harmony, safety, love or happiness to be found in our struggle to achieve our wants. Struggling is ego!

"A conscious contact with the Power of the Universe is all we *need*. When we have *that* we have it all. Money is no longer a problem; it is just paper; a kind of spiritual energy. If we think we need a huge bank account to feel secure, our security is not based in Spirit, it is based in want. This Divine Presence is our satisfaction, peace, harmony, safety, love, and happiness. It is far more rewarding than cars, jewellery, clothes, shoes, people or money. When we have this connection to our Real Self and this Higher Power lives through us, in us, as us, all the rest is added unto us. When the gifts of life come this way there is no disillusionment, no accomplishment, yet much is accomplished. There is no struggle, yet lots of activity but no want. It is God's good pleasure to give us Its kingdom."

Chuck C. said: *"Three words... 'Life, Good, God,' insofar as I'm concerned, are synonymous. They all mean the same thing."*[840] If we assume God to be the Principle of Life, then the Will of Life has to *BE* Life. Consequently, we can interpret the Will of God to be everything that expresses life without hurt or harm to ourselves or others. Anything that will enable us to express greater life, greater happiness, greater freedom, and greater power must be the will of God.

Naturally if we have any sense at all, we will seek to free ourselves from misery and unhappiness. But to try to find that happiness at the expense of others, defeats the very purpose of freedom, for at the basis of All is the principle of Unity. So **"such a request should have a qualification: that it be granted only if it was** (God's) **will and if others would be helped."**[841]

Therefore, the decisive factor for dealing with whether a thing is God's Will is: Does the thing we wish to do, express more life, more happiness, and more peace to us and at the same time harm no one? If it does—it is right. It is NOT SELFISH and would fall into the category of God's will for us. Or do we find that, **"With the best of intentions, he tends to force his own will into all sorts of situations and problems with the comfortable assurance that he is acting under God's specific direction."**[842] **"While most of us believe profoundly in the principle of 'guidance,' it was soon apparent that to receive it accurately, considerable spiritual preparation was necessary."**[843] We believe it is important to check out our spiritual 'guidance' with a spiritual advisor. Discussion with our sponsors is always suggested as a buffer in these situations.

"I learned that it would be well to begin the day with morning devotion, which is the custom in our house now."[844] Who would think that such a simple thing would bring so much to our families? This is where that earlier suggestion about Step 10 comes in.

NIGHT

That portion of Step 10 – **"When we retire at night, we constructively review our day. Were we resentful, selfish, dishonest or afraid? Do we owe an apology? Have we kept** *something to ourselves, which should be discussed with another person at once? Were we kind and loving toward all? What could we have done better? Were we thinking of ourselves most of the time? Or; were we thinking of what we could do for others, of what we could pack into the stream of life? But we must be careful not to drift into worry, remorse or morbid reflection, for that would diminish our usefulness to others. After making our review we ask God's forgiveness and inquire what corrective measures should be taken?"*[845]

ON DREAMS

There is nothing wrong with dreams. In fact there are those of us that believe, *"the dreamers are the saviours of the world."*[846] *"Before any dream can come true, there must first be a dream."*[847] However, there is a big difference between a dream and a fantasy. A fantasy is living inside a lie and a dream is for something new, it is not living in appearances but living in the possibility. Anything we can dream of is *not* too big for us to embark on, if it hurts no-one—brings happiness into our lives—and we are willing to share its benefit—it is Life's will for us.

ABOUT PRAYER AND MEDITATION...

We would like to remind ourselves to keep an open mind. *"Do not let any prejudice you may have against spiritual terms deter you from honestly asking yourself what they mean to you."*[848] It is important to remember that if any of the words, spiritual or otherwise, "disturb" us, there is something for us to deal with and we have the tools to do so. Of course we can always keep our prejudices, but then we will probably remain uncomfortable when others use those words, within our hearing, giving them power to "disturb" us.

A member in New York said: *"I must bear in mind that it is the spirit within me, which comes from God, that is going to be the healing force."*[849] *"We found the Great Reality* (God) *deep down within us. In the last analysis it is only there that* (God) *may be found."*[850] Another spiritual big book says the kingdom of God, the kingdom of heaven, is within us. In other words, God constitutes my individual being and yours. Our presence is an expression of Its presence.

Said still another way, your connection to God is within you. It is unique to you. We are not suggesting your connection is the same as ours. But all paths lead to the top of the same mountain. To know this intellectually is of little benefit. We must seek first the realisation of God and then practice the presence. This comes about by practicing the principles of our programme in all our affairs. When we clean our inner house through inventory and amends, the grace of this Universal Intelligence is unveiled in us and expels our problems, our obsessions.

Keeping the awareness (consciousness) of this Reality gives us the realisation that **"of myself I am nothing."** But through our oneness with God all that is, is ours. **"The point is that we are willing to grow along spiritual lines.** "[851] The demonstration of this willingness is open-minded study and practice, practice, practice. **"Through prayer and meditation, I open channels; then I establish and improve my conscious contact with God."**[852]

"NOW, WHAT OF PRAYER?...

"Prayer is the raising of the heart and mind to God—and in this sense it includes meditation."[853] Prayer is a vital part of the programme "it Works if you Work it." Here again we need use our will, since **"it is especially required of the atheist and agnostic that he become open-minded on the subject of God. This seems to require a considerable exertion indeed. If then we** (dare to) **suggest that he address himself to whatever God there may be, in meditation and prayer, he usually finds this takes a lot of discipline to do, even as an experiment."**[854] **"We have found that the actual good results of prayer are beyond question. They are matters of knowledge and experience. All those who have persisted have found strength not ordinarily their own. They have found wisdom beyond their usual capability. And they have increasingly found a peace of mind which can stand firm in the face of difficult circumstances."**[855]

"It has been well said 'almost the only scoffers at prayer are those who never tried it enough.'"[856] There are stories of people attempting to prove that prayer doesn't work. There was **"a man engaged in proving to a friend that there was no power in prayer. He told of having been thrown from a runaway dog sled in a lonely area of the Arctic. Lying in the snow with a broken leg, he knew he would perish if a miracle did not happen. So he prayed for one, but went on lying there. No miracle answered his prayer.**

"His listener said, 'But you were saved, or you wouldn't be here to tell about it.'

"'Not through prayer, pal. If it hadn't been for an Eskimo who just happened to come over the ridge and see me, I'd have

216

died.'"[857] He never seemed to ask himself how the Eskimo "happened" to find him in a blinding blizzard.

There's another example that really points it out for me; although some might have a more difficult time seeing it. There was a "docudrama" that came out in 2003 called "Touching the Void." It was the true story of two young mountain climbers, Joe Simpson and Simon Yates. Joe, during their descent of a new route on the West Face of the Siula Grande in the Peruvian Andes slipped breaking his leg. Joe, while being lowered down the mountain, in an ice storm where there was 0 feet visibility, broke through an ice shelf and was hanging there over the mountains edge. Not knowing what was happening, Simon waited for Joe to lift his weight off the rope.

As time went on Simon's position on the face of the mountain became more and more precarious. Finally fearing for his own life he cut the rope. Simon Yates is probably best known, much to his chagrin, as 'the guy who cut the rope' on that fateful day. But that's not the story here.

Joe fell some 150 feet into a much deeper ice chasm. Surprised to be alive, he struggled to climb back out of the crevasse he found it impossible with 80 feet of over hanging ice. As it would, the question came to him: "what should I do?" The answer came in a thought for him to go down into the abyss; this turned out to be the perfect choice that eventually led him to safety. As he lowered himself deeper into what seemed to be an icy tomb, he reaches a point where a bright shaft of light was seen. There he saw a gradual slope up to that sunlight, which he was able to make his way to the surface and gradually back down to the base camp where Simon had arrived.

Joe bragged in the film that he never stooped to asking "God" for help. Our only question is: where does he think the unreasonable idea to go down, into the ice, instead of up, out of the chasm came from? From my perspective the *question is the prayer* and the answer came, as with most *answers to prayer, are in an unusual or new idea or thought solution.* All answers come from within. For us these stories represent a difference in perspective.

As we have been building our conscious contact with a Power Greater than ourselves we have added several prayers and readings to both our morning Meditation and our evening prayers and inventory. By the time we reach this Step in "A Vision of Recovery" is the statement: ***"that the spiritual malady should be my main concern and that the more faith I have, the fewer problems I will have...as my faith grows, my fears lessen."***[858] The more we studied spiritual matters, prayed and meditated the more we began to see that *"underneath the material world and life as we see it, there is an All Powerful, Guiding, Creative Intelligence."*[859]

"We shouldn't be shy on this matter of prayer... It works, if we have the proper attitude and work at it."[860]

SERENITY PRAYER:

When we first enter the programme one of the first prayers we learn is the Serenity Prayer. ***"God grant me the Serenity to accept the things I cannot change; the Courage to change the things I can; and the Wisdom to know the difference."***[861]

"It was discovered in the 'In Memoriam' column of an early June 1941 edition of the New York Herald-Tribune. The exact wording was 'Mother— God grant me the Serenity to accept the things I cannot change, Courage to change the things I can, and Wisdom to know the difference. Goodbye.'[862]

How are we to interpret this simple but dynamic prayer?   Our experience shows that pain and disturbances in life comes from NOT MINDING **OUR** *OWN BUSINESS*. There are three kinds of business in the Universe: **Our** *Business,* **Their** *Business,* and **God's** *Business.* **God's** *Business* is easy enough to figure out; it is anything outside of **Our** control, and **Their** control.

So what is **Their** *Business?* **Their** *Business* can be identified when we are thinking, or even worse saying out loud, things like: "**They** need to get a Job, we want **Them** to be X, **They** should be Y, or **They** need to Z." If **Our** thoughts are in **Their** *Business,* we become disturbed when **They** fail to do what we think is right. *Our* Serenity fades. **If _They_ are Mentally Living _Their_ Life and _We_ are Living _Their_ Life, Who is Living _Our_ Life?**

We have discovered that we are too often mentally minding **Their** *Business,* and **They** are minding **Our** *Business.* And we all wonder why our lives don't work!

To think that we know what's best for anyone else, even in the name of love, is pure arrogance. The result is pain, tension, anxiety, and fear. We have enough problems with **Our** *Own Business* without taking on **Theirs**—let alone be so blatantly arrogant as to take on **God's.**

"I am happy; I thought I could never be happy. A happy man is not likely to do harm to another human being."[863]

"It appears to me that most of the wrenching turmoil in people's lives—whether or not they are alcoholic—derives from too stubborn persistence in trying to resolve <u>insoluble</u> *problems.*

218

That is why the philosophy contained in the Serenity Prayer is one of the most important guidelines I've found...

"Accept the things you cannot change. So simple. If the problem cannot be solved—<u>today</u>—why, simply drop it. I grant that this is not always easy; it takes self-discipline...

"On the other hand, problems which can be solved provide the real excitement in life. The daily challenge to grapple with and master the conflicts encountered from dawn to dark is stimulating.

"But the last line of the Serenity Prayer contains the clinker—the <u>wisdom</u> to know the difference between soluble and insoluble situations. As one who is most suspicious of... (my own) *wisdom (since sobering up anyway), I find that substituting the word 'honesty' for 'wisdom' often furnishes the clue to the answer I'm seeking...*

"Serenity to me, therefore, is the absence of insoluble conflict. And it is up to me to first determine whether, after an honest look at myself, I can cope with the problem, then to decide whether it is to be tackled, passed over to another day, or dismissed forever."[864]   This professor said: *"I tried to change everything and everybody, <u>except myself</u>—the only thing I <u>could</u> change."*[865]

"We treasure our Serenity Prayer so much. It brings a new light to us that can dissipate our old-time and nearly fatal habit of fooling ourselves. In the radiance of this prayer we see that defeat, rightly accepted, need be no disaster. We now know that we do not have to run away, nor ought we again try to overcome adversity by still another bulldozing power drive that can only push up obstacles before us faster than they can be taken down."[866]

STEP THREE PRAYER:

"God I offer myself to Thee to build with me and to do with me as Thou wilt. Relieve me of the bondage of self that I may better do Thy will. Take away my difficulties, that victory over them may bear witness to those I would help of Thy Power, Thy Love, and Thy Way of life. May I do Thy will always!"[867]

IN STEP SEVEN WE *HUMBLY ASKED*:

"My creator, I am now willing that you should have all of me good and bad. I pray that you now remove from me every single defect of character, which stands in the way of my usefulness to you and my fellows. Grant me strength as I go out from here to do your bidding. Amen"[6] [868]

STEP ELEVEN PRAYERS – *"knowledge of Gods will for us..."*

The Prayer of St. Francis of Assisi

"Lord, make me a channel of thy peace—that where there is hatred, I may bring love—that where there is wrong, I may bring the spirit of forgiveness—that where there is discord, I may bring harmony—that where there is error, I may bring truth—that where there is doubt, I may bring faith—that where there is despair, I may bring hope—that where there are shadows, I may bring light—that where there is sadness, I may bring joy. Lord, grant that I may seek rather to comfort than to be comforted—to understand, than to be understood, to love, than to be loved. For it is by self-forgetting that one finds. It is by forgiving that one is forgiven. It is by dying that one awakens to Eternal Life."[869]

The following prayer, paraphrased from *Share* magazine (the UK's AA magazine), it was recommended to a Sponsee for use when things weren't going as planned.

"Dear God, please have me set aside everything I think I know about _____(Blank)_____ so that I may be open to a new experience."

"Step Eleven... surely means that we ought to look toward God's perfection as our guide rather than as a goal to be reached in any foreseeable time."[870]

There are many spiritual paths. The important thing is to *"be quick to see where religious people are right."*[871] *"We are only operating a spiritual kindergarten in which people are enabled to get over drinking* (and other addictions) *and find the grace to go on living to better effect. Each man's theology has to be his own quest, his own affair."*[872]

---

[6] The meaning of Amen is, and so be it. If uncomfortable saying amen say and so it is or and so be it. But either way get that prayer is a proclamation not a petition.

But like this member, *"I centre my thoughts on a Higher Power. I... surrender all to this power within me... May the Steps I take today strengthen my words and deeds."*[873]

"Thy Will Be Done."[874]

We often pray: *"How can I best serve Thee—Thy will (not mine) be done."*[875] True prayer must be *"Thy will, not mine, be done."*[876] But the implication relative to the Will of God in this prayer is not a submission to the inevitability of evil, bad, or limitation; we pray in the knowledge that the will of God is always Good.

We pray *"thy will be done,"* but within this 'will' we find (as earlier) that there is plenty of scope for self-expression—room to move around and express life to its fullest. There is nothing we can learn that will be of more value to us than the art of positive prayer. We pray to change ourselves, that we may be receptive to the Divine right action of God. Prayer is the act and the art of changing the thought patterns of the one praying—transforming our receptivity. In other words, it is what helps to change OUR ATTITUDE, reminding us that another view of the acronym 'AA' is, "Altered Attitudes." Prayer is where we find that our attitude is changed through the Grace of God.

How many of us are afraid to be branded 'Pollyanna's' after the character in the story? Pollyanna is often accused of sappy optimism and outdated, old-fashioned emotionalism. But what does the story really reveal?

By an accident of a faulty delivery system, one Christmas Pollyanna finds herself the recipient of a pair of child's crutches instead of the China doll she coveted. At the urging of her missionary minister father, she found one reason to be glad for the crutches—that she didn't have reason to need them.

What a great inspiration she is for anyone attempting the spiritual practice of gratitude! Pollyanna's story embodies the paradoxical nature of life; we have the freedom to choose where we place our attention, and thus our creative power. There are always at least two ways of seeing a person, place, thing or situation in our lives. What we choose to see, decide, and pay attention to is what tends to happen. Pollyanna could easily, and justifiably, have opted to choose disappointment, victimisation, anger, or resentment about her situation. Not unlike what most of us have done in similar disappointing circumstances. Any of those options would have resulted in, what they always create—more disappointment, victimisation, anger and resentment. As they have in many of our lives.

Another way of describing this scenario is as a separation from love, joy, gratitude and good; in other words, an apparent separation from

God.   Others may find our practice to be unrealistic, cockeyed optimism, and will perhaps accuse us of being a 'Pollyanna' in a derogatory sense.   But be glad, for our choice keeps us in gratitude, and being grateful keeps us in Unity with God.

Many say to us: "Prayer doesn't work for me." Yet when we talk with them at length we find that their prayers <u>were</u> answered, only they were expecting a revelation like: "writing on the wall" or a "burning bush."   Yes, circumstances of life often change in answer to our prayers. But more often then not they are answered through a thought or intuitive answer. The work we do in prayer is done in our own minds and the answer comes from **"the Great Reality deep within us. In the last analysis it is only there that** (God) **may be found."**[877]

"We are often surprised how the right answers come after we have tried this for a while. What used to be the <u>hunch or the occasional inspiration gradually becomes a working part of the mind.</u>"[878]   Doesn't this clearly indicate where the answers to our prayers are to be found? However, many of us reject those answers that come to us with: "Nope, that's surely not the right answer." Don't we?

"Certainly, (God) **does not...save us from all troubles and adversity. Nor, in the end...save us from so-called death—since this is but an opening of a door into a new life, where we shall dwell among** (God's) **many mansions."**[879]   Regarding prayer and faith **"I simply ask this question: 'In your own life, have you ever really tried to think and act as though there might be a God? Have you experimented?'**[880] And not just for a few days, but really, NO—I mean REALLY—experimented? Some of us would rather keep fighting, both old-timers and **"new people who say they are atheistic or agnostic. Their will to disbelieve is so powerful that apparently they prefer a date with the undertaker to an open-minded and experimental quest for God. Happily for me, and for most of my kind who have since come along...the constructive forces brought to bear in our Fellowship have nearly always overcome this colossal obstinacy.   Beaten into complete defeat... confronted by the living proof of release, and surrounded by those who can speak to us from the heart, we have finally surrendered. And then, paradoxically, we have found ourselves in a new dimension, the real world of spirit and of faith. Enough willingness, enough open-mindedness—and there it is!"**[881]

THE LORD'S PRAYER

In many meetings in the USA where the programme began we find that, **"They opened with a little prayer, and I thought it was very fine that we stood, all of us together, and closed with the Lord's Prayer."**[882]   **"Meetings in Cleveland...opened with an audible prayer... The speaker...spoke for 45 minutes, and we closed with the Lord's Prayer."**[883]   Many who come to the rooms have to deal with underlying resentments about God and religion right from the start. Since many have objection against its mention. It is suggested that we **"...lay aside prejudice, even against organised religion."**[884]   And take a new look at more traditional prayers and see what they may mean to you, as we did with this prayer. We have attached our interpretation in the Appendix, as the prayer is not written in any of AA's approved writings, though it is mentioned.

"All of us, without exception, pass through times when we can pray only with the greatest exertion of will. Occasionally we go even further than this. We are seized with a rebellion so sickening that we simply won't pray. When these things happen we should not think too ill of ourselves. We should simply resume prayer as soon as we can."[885]   And, of course, work through any obvious disturbances we experience. We truly recognise that: **"The moment we catch even a glimpse of God's will, the moment we begin to see truth, justice, and love as the real and eternal things in life, we are no longer deeply disturbed by all the seeming evidence to the contrary that surrounds us in purely human affairs."**[886]

MEDITATION

The Big Book of *Alcoholics Anonymous* states: **"Be quick to see where religious people are right. Make use of what they offer."**[887]   Where many of us first came into the Programme we were told time and time again to "take what we could use and leave the rest." We can do the same with what is offered by religions.

Meditation is one of the mystical processes of Spiritual development that is suggested in Step Eleven. And it is one of the most beneficial: **"Through deep meditation, I take the effortless path toward God. I meditate for half an hour every morning and evening. The purpose of transcendental deep meditation is to allow the attention to be led deep within the mind to the source of all thought, which is experienced as blissful being, and to bring the blissful nature of that state out into normal waking consciousness for enjoyment throughout the day.**

"The Upanishad, part of the Hindu scriptures, concludes: 'From Joy all things are born; by Joy all things are sustained; to Joy all things return.' The more thoroughly I can surrender to this proposition, the more thoroughly I enjoy my life. Ultimately, my God as I understand (God) *is Joy and the expansion of Joy."*[888]

Simply put, *"meditation means awareness, attention, listening."*[889] We could skip briefly over it here and have you search out your own method of meditation. Ultimately, we each will have to find a satisfactory form of meditation of our own. But let us look a little closer at this much-maligned spiritual practice. *"Bill found...that Wally and Annabelle G. helped sober up a lot of people... 'I think that there may have been times when we attributed it to their morning hour of meditation,' Bill said. 'I sort of always felt that something was lost...when we stopped emphasizing the morning meditation.' (Bill and Lois themselves, however, continued this practice together until his death, 1971.)"*[890]

There are literally hundreds of forms of spiritual meditation; let's look at two practices.

CENTRING:

The objective of centring is to consciously move one's awareness to the core of oneself—the centre where a *"Power greater than yourself"* is felt. Remember: *"We found the Great Reality deep down within us. In the last analysis it is only there that* (God) *may be found."*[891]

Here we attempt to feel the presence of God. This may be done by any means that moves thought from our own preoccupations to a focused centre within. It is as though one enters an inner room, a place of quiet and serenity within one's own consciousness. Once there the Presence can be wholly realised, and one can feel integrated and unified with the Truth of our Being. Here *"The consciousness of your belief is sure to come to you."*[892] We found that *"our God consciousness was a steady growth after we became associated with"*[893] the programme. It's the programme—the Steps that expands our consciousness. The fruits of that programme are a deeper and deeper understanding as we centre ourselves on the *"Great Reality deep down within."*

CONTEMPLATION:

This is a much more acceptable method in a western society where left-brain activity is held in such high regard. The object of contemplation is a deeper comprehension of, or breakthrough in, our understanding of a given object or subject. It may be reflection on a paragraph, a section or a sentence of the Big Book, **As Bill Sees It** or a daily meditation book like **Daily Reflections.** Likewise, praying or communing with nature is a form of contemplation. It is a practice that serves to transform perception and the understanding of the nature of Reality.

Each morning you choose something to read and reflect on it throughout the day, see life through the lens of this thought. We read and study all the material. For instance there is great wisdom in all of the Big Book, including the personal stories. *"Each individual, in the personal stories, describes in his own language and from his own point of view the way he established his relationship with God."*[894] To reflect on these stories could be helpful in our own shift in consciousness. This is contemplation, a path to understanding oneness with All That Is.

Given that meditation is essentially learning to train the mind to focus where we choose, perhaps we are wise to select our focus carefully. *"When I focus on what's good today, I have a good day, and when I focus on what's bad, I have a bad day. If I focus on a problem, the problem increases; if I focus on the answer, the answer increases."*[895]

Now let's look at a more traditional form of meditation, and how to practice it. Meditation exercises offer a new and deeper way to seek the *"Great Reality deep down within."*[896] When you first begin to meditate, it will seem you are getting nowhere, simply because meditative silence is so foreign to our normal state of consciousness. However, there is no more rewarding activity (or inactivity) for us to participate in. So many of us say, "I don't have the time to meditate." By now we should be aware of how much time and energy it takes to run on self-will and that it leads only to despair; whereas meditation leads to peace and enlightenment.

My Sponsor George F. wrote:

> "One of the most popular forms of meditation is focusing on the breath. In this practice we clear the mind of all thought. Once we have purged our memory of all the disinformation, all conceptual thought and discriminatory thought activity we will have arrived at a place of stillness beyond all human activity. The experience can be one of walking hand in hand with our creator and the realisation of there being only One Power, Presence and Intelligence in the universe, and we are one with It. This gives us an entirely new perspective. Do we really need

to earn our living by the sweat of our brow? Must we now live in fear? Do we really need to live in fear: fear of the unknown, fear whether we are good enough, smart enough, or strong enough? Once we have reached this state of consciousness, are we actually still condemned to struggle and strive and live an insecure existence? Is our lot in life in fact really to feel isolated, alone and separate?

"Experience shows that when we think "the good life" is up to *us* we continue feeling separate, alone, insecure and not good enough. We then continue being fearful and struggle to "make it" in life. As long as we continue to hold on to the old belief that we were right, that life ***is*** a struggle, it will ***be*** a struggle. When life becomes intolerable and we can't go on, we either give up or embark on a quest for a solution. We find that solution in the Twelve Steps."

Some of us say: 'I've been reading a daily meditation book every morning for some time and it doesn't seem to be bringing much reward.' We find that, ***"Meditation is something which can always be further developed... Aided by such instruction and example as we can find, it is essentially an individual adventure, something which each one of us works out in his own way... Meditation is in reality intensely practical. One of its first fruits is emotional balance."***[897] Something we could all use a little more of.

Meditation is the process whereby we begin to gain ***"knowledge of*** (God's) ***will for us and the Power to carry that out."*** Many suggest that in prayer we make our request and in meditation we listen for the answers, ***"the knowledge of*** (God's) ***will for us and the power to carry that out."*** When one reaches this stage ***"He can now accept himself and the world around him. He can do this because he now accepts a God who is All—and who loves all."***[898]

We would like to share some of the writings about Dr. Bob's ***"spiritual quest."***

"Dr. Bob was a man in search of God, and it was in this area that he, like Bill Wilson, was probably among the least conservative of men. This is not remarkable when we consider that New England...fostered many of the 'new thought' philosophies...mentioned by William James in 'The Varieties of Religious Experience.'"[899] ***"He felt that in far distant centuries, the science of mind would be so developed as to make possible contact between the living and the dead."***[900]

"The revelation in Dr. Bob's life came when he made (a) ***discovery: that spirituality couldn't be absorbed by someone***

226

emulating a sponge, but that one might find it in healing and helping to free those afflicted and in bondage.

"This, of course, was what Dr. Bob meant when he said that Bill had brought him the idea of service. 'I think the kind of service that really counts,' Dr. Bob said, 'is giving of yourself, and that almost always requires effort and time...And I think that is what Bill learned in New York and I didn't learn in Akron until we met.'

"Dr. Bob's experience differed from Bill's: He never had the flash of light... Rather, it was spiritual growth that Dr. Bob talked about...he said, his spiritual values changed as time went by.

"As Dr. Bob himself said, 'I don't think we can do anything very well in this world unless we practice it. And I don't believe we do AA too well unless we practice it.... We should practice...acquiring the spirit of service. We should attempt to acquire some faith, which isn't easily done.... But I think faith can be acquired; it can be acquired slowly; it has to be cultivated.

"We're all after the same thing, and that's happiness. We want peace of mind. The trouble with us...was this: We demanded the world give us happiness and peace of mind in just the particular way we wanted to get it.... But when we take time to find out some of the spiritual laws, and familiarise ourselves with them, and put them into practice, then we do get happiness and peace of mind... There seem to be some rules to follow, but happiness and peace of mind are always here, open and free to anyone.'"[901]

"'Dad told me that what he was after was a spiritual revelation, which could come suddenly to some people,' said Smitty. 'He hoped it would be revealed to him that way. He worked hard to attain it... He studied for at least an hour every day on some religious subject. It was a long slow process. The net result was he had a wide and deep understanding of religious and spiritual matters. He had actually achieved the goal, although it was never revealed to him in a sudden manner.'"[902]

"Dr. Bob sought to discover and familiarise himself with the spiritual laws in great part through his reading, which was extensive...

"'He read about every religion.' Said Smitty, 'not only Christian religion. He could tell you about the Koran, Confucius, even Voodooism, and many other things.'"[903] Many of us follow a similar

path to this Canadian member: *"I became interested in Christian mysticism, which led me into the study of techniques of deep meditation and of comparative religions. I began to realise that the so-called mystics of whatever tradition—Christian, Jewish, Buddhist, Hindu, Taoist, or Muhammadan—all ultimately talked the same language. In one way or another, they all described the same blissful One behind the Many, who could be directly known in deep prayer and meditation."*[904]

"According to Paul S., 'Dr. Bob's morning devotion consisted of a short prayer, 20 minute study of a familiar verse...and a quiet period of waiting for directions as to where he, that day, should find use for his talent. Having heard, he would religiously go about his Father's business, as he put it.'"[905]

"Whenever he got stuck about something, he always prayed about it."[906] *"He always said, 'Give God a chance.'"*[907] *"I should not be surprised to find myself coming to the astounding conclusion that God, whoever or whatever He* (She or It) *may be, is eminently more capable of running this universe than I am. At last I believe I am on my way."*[908]

"For me, AA is a synthesis of all the philosophy I've ever read, all of the positive, good philosophy, all of it based on love. I have seen that there is only one law, the law of love, and there are only two sins; the first is to interfere with the growth of another human being, and the second is to interfere with one's own growth."[909]

THE PRINCIPLE OF STEP ELEVEN

Consciousness

Prayer and meditation are a wonderful source of *enlightenment*. Enlightenment can only come to a **conscious** mind. Great benefit comes from the *patient* use of these tools as we give up our desire for instant gratification. We must **"Let Go and Let God"** as we become more **conscious** of our beliefs, actions, and attitudes. As a result we become more and more **conscious** of God, more **"spiritually awakened."**

Chapter 15

Get It...Give It...
Live It...

Service

STEP TWELVE

"Having Had A Spiritual Awakening As The Result Of These Steps, We Tried To Carry This Message To Other Alcoholics, And To Practice These Principles In All Our Affairs."[910]

Read in preparation, in the "Big Book" of *Alcoholics Anonymous* –
Pages   89-103

Read in preparation, in the *Twelve Steps and Twelve Traditions* –
Step Twelve   Pages 109-130

STEP TWELVE

"Having Had A Spiritual Awakening As The Result Of These Steps, We Tried To Carry This Message To Other Alcoholics, And To Practice These Principles In All Our Affairs."[911]

his is the programme's third and final "Maintenance Step." *"Joy of living is the theme of the Twelfth Step. Action its key. Giving that asks no reward. Love that has no price tag."*[912] *"The joy of living is the theme of* (the) *Twelfth Step, and action is the key word... Here we begin to practice all Twelve Steps of the programme in our daily lives so that we and those about us may find emotional sobriety."*[913] As we stressed earlier, concerted effort is required to maintain the gifts we received as a result of working the first nine Steps or we lose it all. Let us clearly tackle the full meaning of this Step in three parts:

"Having had a Spiritual Awakening as the Result of These Steps"[914]

"Our Twelfth Step...says that as a result of practicing all the Steps, we have each found something called a spiritual awakening."[915] *"The greatest gift that can come to anybody is a spiritual awakening."*[916] When we give freely of ourselves *"A new state of consciousness and being is received as a free gift."*[917] We see clearly that a desired quality of *"permanent sobriety can be attained only by a most revolutionary change in the life and outlook of the individual—by a spiritual awakening."*[918] Our psychiatrist friend *"Dr. Harry Tiebout... says, 'A religious, or spiritual experience, is the act of giving up reliance on one's own omnipotence.'"*[919]

"When a man or woman has a spiritual awakening, that most important meaning of it is that he has now become able to do, feel, and believe that which he could not do before on his unaided strength and resources alone... He finds himself in possession of a degree of honesty, tolerance, unselfishness, peace of mind, and love of which he had thought himself quite incapable."[920] We find that having thoroughly done the work *"nearly everyone has experienced this touch of God—the fleeting feeling of insight, love, joy, and 'The world is right.' Once...thought...unusual...I now think, they are forecasts of what one can have if one is willing to take the time and make the effort."*[921]

WHAT IS A SPIRITUAL AWAKENING?

What We Were...		**What We Become...**
Old Attitudes...		New Attitudes...
Old Ideas...	We Work the	New Ideas...
Old Emotions...	12 Steps	Feelings of Love...
Old Beliefs...		New Beliefs...

We "Experience"
ourselves
differently...
**A Spiritual
Experience**

We no longer look at ourselves and others in a negative light...

We are not saints; we claim spiritual progress, not Spiritual perfection...

What if I doubt the existence of God? One member says: **"Doubting God's existence was no barrier at all to a spiritual experience. Also, I can say that having such an experience didn't lead me to any certainty about God.**"[922]

We first must attempt to define a "spiritual awakening"– **"In my view, some of the evidences of a spiritual awakening are: maturity; an end to habitual hatred; the ability to love and to be loved in return; the ability to believe, even without understanding, that Something lets the sun rise in the morning and set at night, makes the leaves come out in the spring and drop in the fall, and gives the birds song. Why not let this Something be God?**"[923]

We have already discussed in earlier Steps that our search is for conscious contact with a **"Power greater than ourselves."** A contact with a Power we can count on in our lives. Many define this as the purpose of the programme. There are a number of philosophical ideas that have worked for many. They would constitute as **"spiritual,"** what still others have defined as, **"awakening,"** or as with Bill W. as a **"spiritual experience."** However, let us take the word more at face value.

Awakening simply means—to awaken... So, to *awaken* to a Power greater than ourselves working in our lives is a **"Spiritual**

Awakening." If by some quirk of fate we have not been awakened, at least to this degree, by the time we reach this final Step then we work with our sponsors to find which of the previous Steps has not been put solidly in place. The real way to tell whether or not we have completed the Steps thus far is to read the promises and ask ourselves if they have come true for us. As stated there they **"always materialise if we work for them... sometimes quickly, sometimes slowly."**[924] The speed depends on how quickly we work through the Steps. The sooner we complete them thoroughly the sooner the "Promises" are fulfilled.

Bill's spiritual awakening was sudden. **"In his helplessness and desperation, Bill cried out, 'I'll do anything, anything at all!' He had reached a point of total, utter deflation—a state of complete, absolute surrender. With neither faith nor hope, he cried, 'If there be a God, let Him** (Her of It) **show Himself!'"**[925]

Whereupon he recounted in more detail later: **"'Then, seen in the minds eye, there was a mountain. I stood upon the summit, where a great wind blew. A wind, not of air, but of spirit... it blew right through me. Then came the blazing thought 'You are a free man'... I became acutely conscious of a Presence which seemed like a veritable sea of living spirit... 'This,' I thought, 'must be the Great Reality.'**

"I seemed to be possessed by the absolute, and the curious conviction deepened that no matter how wrong things seemed to be, there could be no question of the ultimate rightness of God's universe."[926]

"Ebby...not quite prepared for Bill's description of what happened...brought Bill a book that offered further clarification. It was William James' 'Varieties of Religious Experiences.'

"As Bill read...he saw that all the cases described by James had certain common denominators, despite the diverse ways in which they manifest themselves... Of the <u>three common denominators</u> in the case histories, the <u>first</u> was calamity; each person James described had met utter defeat in some area of his life. All human resources had failed to solve his problems. Each person had been utterly desperate.

"The <u>next</u> common point was admission of defeat. Each of the individuals acknowledged his own defeat as utter and absolute.

"The <u>third</u> common denominator was an appeal to a Higher Power. This cry for help could take many forms, and it might or might not be in religious terms.

"Whatever the type of experience, however, it brought the sufferer into a state of consciousness, and so opened the way to release from the old problems."[927]

Many people express a desire for this kind of spiritual experience, but we suggest that this just might be for the same reason we hope for a million pounds. Because, we believe that then our troubles will be over. However, our experience is that a sudden spiritual experience or the rather more gradual realisation we will look at below, are not an end to pain and suffering. Either type takes continued effort to maintain its completeness. *"I believe completeness is waiting for anyone who will take the time to make the effort, through quiet thinking, honest prayer, chosen reading, and exercise. These are the ingredients. It is an adventure so worthwhile that all else fades in comparison, yet it makes all else worthwhile."*[928]

We are simply talking about *"God-centeredness versus self-centeredness."*[929] As this member from Toronto said: *"For the first time in my adult life, I was unmistakably aware of the living presence of God within myself and the universe."*[930] *"Spiritual Experience and Spiritual Awakening...* (constitute) *the personality change sufficient to...recovery from alcoholism* (or any dilemma).*"*[931]

We find that: *"Most of our experiences are what the psychologist William James (1902) calls the 'educational variety' because they develop slowly over a period of time."*[932] *"Awareness of a Power greater than ourselves is the essence of spiritual experience. Our more religious members call it 'God consciousness.'"*[933]

In our different programmes *"such breakthroughs are everyday events. They are all the more remarkable when we reflect that a working faith had once seemed an impossibility of the first magnitude to perhaps half of our present membership...as soon as they could cast their main dependence upon a 'higher power'—even upon their own...groups—they had turned that blind corner which had always kept the open highway from their view. From this time on—assuming they tried hard to practice the rest of the...programme with a relaxed and open mind—an ever deepening and broadening faith, a veritable gift, had invariably put in its sometimes unexpected and often mysterious appearance."*[934]

But we realise that *"if an alcoholic failed to perfect and enlarge his spiritual life through work and self-sacrifice for others, he could not survive the <u>certain trials and low spots ahead</u>."*[935] A

236

relief from self-obsession, a willingness to help others, and a dependence on a Power Greater than ourselves is as big a Spiritual Awakening as one could ever ask. We are certainly not claiming that our way is the only way to obtain such an awakening. *"It doesn't matter too much how the transforming spiritual experience is brought about so long as one gets one that works."*[936] But giving that we have tried many other ways that haven't worked, why not use this one which has proved effective?

"Somehow the alcoholic (or any addictive personality) *must get enough objectivity about himself to abate his fears and collapse his false pride."*[937]   As the Twelve Steps produce more and more results with a growing list of addictive behaviours, big and small, the *"world is becoming more appreciative of our methods... In this respect they are commencing to teach us humility."*[938]

The *"manner of making ready to receive this gift lies in the practice of the Twelve Steps in our programme."*[939] These Steps become a chosen way of life, a selected set of principles to guide us. Once we complete the Steps for the first time and choose to consistently work __all__ the Steps, *"then we were ready to devote ourselves in service to others, using the understanding and language of the heart, and seeking no gain or reward."*[940]

Who are they, these people who answer our desperate calls for help in the middle of the night and come to visit us? Who are they that share with me and "love me until I can love myself?" What is it that they have? *"They had something! ...suddenly, it seemed to me, I had the answer. These men were but instruments. Of themselves they were nothing.*

"Here at last was a demonstration of spiritual law at work."[941] What goes around comes around; do unto others as you would have them do unto you; karma. Each one of these phrases, express the same spiritual law, only the words are different. *"These men* (and women) *were like lamps supplied with current from a huge spiritual dynamo and controlled by the rheostat of their souls. They burned dim, bright, or brilliant, depending upon the degree and progress of their contact. And this contact could only be maintained just so long as they obeyed that spiritual law.*

"These men (and women) *were thinking straight—therefore their actions corresponded to their thoughts. They had given themselves, __their minds,__ over to a higher power for __direction__. Here, it seemed to me, in the one word 'Thought'—was the crux of the whole spiritual quest. That 'As a man thinketh in his*

heart, so is he' and his health, his environment, his failure, or his success in life.

"How foolish I had been in my quest for spiritual help. How selfish and egotistical I had been to think that I could approach God <u>*intellectually*</u>*. In the very struggle to obtain faith I had lost it. I had given to the word faith a religious significance only. I had failed to see that faith was 'our common everyday manner of thinking.' That good and evil were but the results of certain uniform and reliable spiritual laws... Like everyone's thinking, it was a mixture of good and bad, but mainly it was uncontrolled.*

"I had been sticking my chin out and getting socked by spiritual law until I was punch drunk. If one could become humble, if he could become 'as a little child' before this powerful spiritual thought force, the pathway could be discovered.

"Where my life had been full of mental turmoil there is now an ever-increasing depth of calmness. Where there was a hit or miss attitude toward living there is now new direction and force.

"The approaches of man to God are many and varied. My conception of God as Universal Mind is after all but one man's approach to and concept of the Supreme Being. To me it makes sense, opens up a fascinating field of endeavour and is a challenge, the acceptance of which can make of life the 'Adventure Magnificent.'"[942]

What greater awakening could there be than this? *"Today I think of life in terms of happiness, contentment, freedom from fear and despair, sane thinking, ability to face problems as they occur, the opportunity to help other*(s)*... and to be decent...*

"These...years...have been the happiest of my life. I have been helped morally, spiritually, mentally and materially through"[943] the programme. This is a spiritual awakening indeed.

"WE TRIED TO CARRY THIS MESSAGE..."

"Now, what about the rest of the Twelfth Step? The wonderful energy it releases and the eager action by which it carries our message to the next suffer(er)*...and which finally translates the Twelve Steps into action upon all our affairs is the pay-off, the magnificent reality."*[944] *"We know this because we see monotony, pain, and even calamity turned to good use by those who keep on trying to practice* (the) *Twelve Steps."*[945]

238

As Bill W. demonstrated in the very beginning of the programme it is not necessary that one <u>succeeds</u> in carrying the message to others. The benefit to the one "trying" to do so is the same. If you recall he himself tried and failed for the first six months of his sobriety before he finally met Dr. Bob and had his first success. We must always remember that ***"recovery begins when one alcoholic talks with another alcoholic, sharing experience, strength, and hope."***[946] From this experience with Dr. Bob, Bill learned from a lesson that established the successful way he and Dr. Bob worked with people and created the style for the layout of the Big Book. It literally follows exactly the way newcomers were worked with at that time.

Where did the idea of one drunk or addict talking to another come from? After Bill's spiritual experience he made one of the biggest understatements of all time. He said: ***"While I lay in the hospital the thought came that there were thousands of hopeless alcoholics who might be glad to have what had been so freely given to me. Perhaps I could help some of them. They in turn might work with others."***[947]

"With this illumination came the vision of a possible chain reaction, one alcoholic working with the next. I was convinced that I could give to fellow sufferers that which Ebby had given to me, (Bill always called Ebby his sponsor) ***and for months afterward I tried to carry the message. But nobody sobered up, and a wonderful lesson came out of the experience: I was painfully learning <u>how not to communicate</u>. No matter how truthful the words of my message, there could be no deep communication if what I said and did was coloured by pride, arrogance, intolerance, resentment, imprudence, or desire for personal acclaim—even though I was largely unconscious of these attitudes."***[948]

We repeat: ***"The joy of good living is the theme of*** (the) ***Twelfth Step."***[949] In fact, ***"Showing others who suffer how we were given help is the very thing which makes life seem so worth while to us now."***[950] The very past that had been such a burden is now a <u>tool</u>. We can ***"Cling to the thought that, in God's hands, the dark past is the greatest possession you have—the key to life and happiness for others. With it you can avert death and misery for them."***[951]

"I have had the joy of seeing many a human being, down and out; learn to stand straight again, and to proceed under his own power to happiness in life."[952]

"Life will take on new meaning. To watch people recover, to see them help others, to watch loneliness vanish, to see a fellowship grow up about you, to have a host of friends—this is an experience you must not miss. We know you will not want to miss it. Frequent contact with newcomers and with each other is the bright spot of our lives."[953]

Those of us that work this Step find this to be true *"beyond our wildest dreams." "Commitment and service were part of recovery. I was told that to keep it we have to give it away."*[954] The question is always asked: "When should we begin working with others?" Or, should we work with others before we have taken *all* the Steps? The moment we decide that we want what the programme has to offer and are *"willing to go to any lengths to get it,"*[955] we are ready to work with others. Not that we try to carry a message that we haven't yet got, but that we can carry them to the message. *"But, obviously you cannot transmit something you haven't got."*[956] Which just means don't lie—just share your experience. This is *not an excuse to delay working with others*, the salvation of our entire programme—even sobriety itself.

Think about this for a moment, it was obvious to Bill that if he had not immediately worked with others he never would have stayed clean and sober. Dr. Bob was clear that he was going to the same place and doing the same things Bill was, *with the exception of service*, and he could not stay sober until he started working with others at once. If you are having a problem staying off your particular "drug of choice" maybe, just maybe, working with others is the solution. We cannot wait until we feel good enough about our programme to help others. This very attitude may be, in itself, the reason you keep relapsing.

So long as we share our experience with each Step along the way and stays ahead of the newcomer in working the Steps it is good for us to work with others. With the First Step, for example, in our admission of complete defeat *"it was discovered that very new people could drive the opening wedge into a fresh case almost as well as anybody."*[957] *"Even the newest of newcomers finds undreamed rewards as he tries to help...the one who is even blinder than he."*[958] *"In telling newcomers how to change their lives and attitudes, all of a sudden I found I was doing a little changing myself."*[959]

Dr. Bob described to a newcomer the great benefit of "passing it on." *"A person never knew a lesson until he tried to pass it on to someone else. And that he had found out every time he tried to pass this on it became more vivid to him."*[960] Our experience shows that the very thing we need to "learn" comes out of our mouth when helping another.

The noted psychologist Carl Rogers believed that when working with another there are *"potent and orderly forces which are evident in this whole experience, forces which seem deeply rooted in the universe as a whole."*[961] *"Happy, joyous and free"*[962] seems to come with a price tag—unselfish service to others.

"Bill D. said... 'I think I have the answer. Bill Wilson,' he said, 'was very, very grateful that he had been released from this terrible thing, and he had given God the credit for having done it, and he's so grateful about it he wants to tell other people about it.'"[963] *"With Bill D., there were now three recoveries, and all three felt that they had to carry the message or perish themselves."*[964]

The commitment of those early members is a powerful example to follow. Listen to this member's experience: *"I remember well one fellow ...walking nearly three miles through slush, wet and snow to come to the hospital to see a man that he had never seen before in his life, and that impressed me very much. He walked to the hospital to save bus fare and did it gladly in order to be helpful to an individual he had never even seen."*[965] Another in the hospital said: *"I believe every member of the Akron Group did come to see me, which impressed me terrifically...because they would take the time to come and talk to me without even knowing who I was."*[966]

What are some of the kinds of *"Twelfth Step Work"* that we can do to maintain our emotional sobriety and demonstrate our gratitude?

SERVICE

Dr. Bob recalled that both he and Bill W. belonged to the *"Oxford Group, 'Bill in New York, for five months, and I in Akron, for two and a half years.' But there was a significant difference: 'Bill had acquired their idea of service. I had not."*[967] From the beginning of the programme, service is a major element in staying sober. Central to service is taking on a commitment at a meeting or two. We would like to say something about this thing called commitment; if I take on a commitment that means to me that I am committed to that job, whatever it is, to be taken care of. If I can't be there then I find someone to take my place. I don't just announce my absence. I make it my responsibility to have that position filled.

Anything you can do to ensure that there is a meeting and that it is running smoothly for the newcomer is worthwhile. You are never too sober to stack chairs, set-up, be a greeter, act as literature secretary, treasurer, make coffee, and be secretary, GSR etc. And please don't fall into the trap of thinking there is some kind of hierarchy based on length of sobriety. This is where the idea of a Home Group comes in; a Home Group is a family of sufferers dedicated to being there and carrying the message to others who still suffer. We in a Home Group are working together to build a community to help bring newcomers home.

The most important service of all is making newcomers feel welcome, as Dr. Bob's wife Anne points out to Dorothy: *"I was so thrilled at my friends that after every meeting, I'd rush up to them and get into these mad conversations. One night, Anne called me over, 'Dorothy, people have been awfully good to you, haven't they? You've been pretty lucky, and you made so many friends.' Of course, I agreed 100 percent. 'Don't you think that you could pass that on, a little bit? There's a woman sitting over there in the corner, and nobody's talking to her.'*

"From Anne, I learned it was the new people that counted. To really try and make them feel welcome and wanted—that's one way I can try to pay back."[968] So remember to go up to someone you don't know at our meetings. Just say: "I haven't met you before, how are you doing?" It could make all the difference in the world to them. It could even determine whether they return or not. Besides, you just might make a new friend.

WORKING ONE-TO-ONE WITH OTHERS

Working one-to-one with another is great medicine. One member describes how Dr. Bob *"came and sat beside my bed. He...insisted that I could do it if I really wanted to stop drinking. Without telling me what it was, he said he had an answer to my problem and condition that really worked. Then he told me very simply the story of his own life...how he had found and applied the remedy with complete success. He felt sure I could do the same. Day after day he called on me in the hospital and spent hours talking to me."*[969] This simple method of sharing our stories one-to-one is the key to working with others. But what is the correct attitude to have regarding our "failures" or "successes" with new people? Listen to this story: *"'I worked with about 17 newcomers,' Oscar said. 'I helped them with the rent, brought them food and coal, and helped them get jobs. They all got drunk.*

"'I went down to Akron and complained to Dr. Bob, who told me that I was doing this for myself and they were doing me a favour.

"'But I'm helping them.'

"'No!' He said. 'Those men showed you what will happen if you pick up a drink. They did you a favour. And when they don't pick up a drink, they show you how the programme works. Either way, they do you a favour.'

"Another quote...attributed to Dr. Bob...was 'There are two kinds of people to watch...those who make it, and those who don't.'[970]

"Gratitude should go forward, rather than backward. In other words, if you carry the message to still others, you will be making the best possible repayment for the help given to you."[971] Just before Bill W. went to Akron, Ohio, on business and 12 Stepped Dr. Bob he was in deep despair. He asked Lois what he should do and she suggested he see Dr. Silkworth and ask for his advice.

This is what Bill learned, in his words: *"Just before leaving for Akron, Dr. Silkworth had given me a great piece of advice. Without it, AA might never have been born. 'Look, Bill,' he had said, 'you're having nothing but failure because you are preaching at these alcoholics. You are talking to them about the Oxford Group precepts of being absolutely honest, absolutely pure, absolutely unselfish, and absolutely loving. This is a very big order. Then you top it off by harping on this mysterious spiritual experience of yours. No wonder they point their finger to their heads and go out and get drunk. Why don't you turn your strategy the other way around? Aren't you the very fellow who once showed me that book by James which says that deflation at great depth is the foundation of most spiritual experiences? ... Bill, you've got to deflate these people first. So give them the medical business, and give it to them hard. Pour it right into them about the obsession that condemns them to drink and the physical sensitivity or allergy of the body that condemns them to go mad or die if they keep drinking. Coming from another alcoholic, one alcoholic talking to another, maybe that will crack those tough egos deep down. Only then can you begin to try the other medicine, the ethical principles you have picked up."*[972]

"After failure on my part to dry up any drunks, Dr. Silkworth reminded me of Professor William James' observation that truly transforming spiritual experiences are nearly always founded on

calamity and collapse."[973] If we stop to look, the layout of the Big Book reveals this: The first forty three pages, more than a quarter (26%) of the book (Plus the Preface and Forwards) are very light on the spiritual angle; the focus is on the hopelessness of the condition. The next forty six pages, again more than a quarter (28%) are spent discussing the spiritual solution. The final seventy five pages, nearly half the overall content (46%) focus on the different aspects of working with others. Although one might say that the stories are dedicated to the Twelfth Step, sharing *"What we used to be like, what happened, and what we are like now."*[974] This would make the major part of the book, well over 80% focused on Step Twelve, carrying the message.

Twelve Step work, where we go to see someone who has called in for help, is immensely rewarding. It is usually suggested today that two members go on these first-time calls, relaying their own stories: *"What we used to be like, what happened, and what we are like now."*[975] Then we take the newcomer to a meeting, introduce them around and generally help them get started. This is one of the ways that "Sponsorship" first started. The person that came on the first 12 Step Call and introduced us around to meetings also guided us through the Steps. Most important of all, and the reason that we have the Programme today is that: *"Nothing in their lives took precedence over their response to a call for help from some alcoholic in need. They would drive miles and stay up all night with someone they had never laid eyes on before and think nothing of it."*[976] Bill W. was a firm believer that "when all else fails—work with another."

If we want the great happiness and joy these pioneers had then we need to put the programme first as they did. When we are committed to helping others stay sober, we gain even more than those we help. *"A sober member...sat me down in her office and told me her story—how she drank, what happened and how she got sober."*[977] *"Two men came to my apartment and stayed with me, drinking coffee until after the bars closed. They kept coming, taking me to meetings for a month."*[978]

The Cleveland groups thought this work was better started sooner than later. *"We find that putting the new fellows to work right away is the answer—putting them on their own and creating enthusiasm."*[979] *"Bill concluded, 'The Cleveland pioneers had proved three essential things: (1) the value of personal sponsorship, (2) the worth of the AA book in indoctrinating newcomers, and finally, (3) the tremendous fact that AA, when the word really got around, could now soundly grow to great*

244

size.'"[980] *"I think I would have had much more difficulty in getting straightened out if I hadn't been <u>almost immediately put to work</u>... While I was still shakily trying to rebuild...* (Dr. Bob) *sent me to see another alcoholic who was in the hospital. All the doctor asked me to do was tell my story. I told it, not any too well perhaps, but as simply and as earnestly as I knew how.'"*[981]

Remember, when we are working with others there is a formula laid out in the Big Book that works. It tells us *"Our stories disclose in a general way what we used to be like, what happened, and what we are like now."*[982] These stories provide a blueprint for working with others.

The path is as follows:

A. The first member to contact the prospect, known as a "Pigeon" in NY, a "Cash Customer" in Akron and a "Baby" in California— would bring home the hopelessness of the dis-ease by telling her own story, encouraging the newcomer to see their complete defeat.

B. Out of this hopelessness she would carry the message of the solution: The 12 Steps (6 before the writing of the "Big Book").

C. Then she would bring many other recovered members to the alcoholic's bedside, who would tell their stories and stress how much happier their lives had become.

Their sponsor's (in the early days simply the first to call) would first immerse them in the first Step, which in the beginning was deflation, the foundation of recovery. If the alcoholic still believes that she is in control, the whole structure of her recovery will eventually collapse. We must catch them when they're down. *"The <u>first</u> Step had to do with calamity and disaster; the <u>second</u> was an admission of defeat—that one could not go on living on the strength of one's resources; and the <u>third</u> was an appeal to a Higher Power for help."*[983]

Let's look at part of the story of the man who started the programme in Chicago. *"I can still remember very distinctly getting into Akron at eleven p.m. and rousting...Howard out of bed to do something about me. He spent two hours with me that night telling me his story. He said he had finally learned that drinking was a fatal illness made up of an allergy plus an obsession, and once the drinking had passed from habit to obsession, we were completely hopeless and could look forward only to spending the balance of our lives in mental institutions—or to death."*[984]

"The next afternoon and evening, two other men visited me, and each told me his story and the things that they were doing to try to recover from this tragic illness."[985]

"In the next two or three days the balance of this handful of men contacted me, encouraged me, and told me how they were trying to live this programme of recovery <u>and the fun they were having doing it.</u>"[986] So, who went on a Twelve Step call at that time? <u>Everyone in the group</u> went to visit newcomers to tell their stories. They didn't wait "until they were ready," what ever that means. Whether they sobered up on that occasion or not *"when one alcoholic had planted in the mind of another the true nature of his malady, that person could never be the same again."*[987]

If you remember Bill's story, in the beginning he and Lois worked with a number of people and not one got sober. Bill said later: *"Lois and I used to blame ourselves, thinking that somehow we failed. Only the other night, she and I looked over a list of the people we worked with in those days... The number of them who have since dried up was truly astonishing. This made us realise that in God's economy, nothing is wasted."*[988] Dr. Bob would *"get up at two or three in the morning to help another alcoholic...* (He) *used to visit the alcoholic ward every day. This was in addition to his regular practice—it was entirely voluntary...work. He couldn't do enough for them."*[989]

However, we learned *"that 'the press of newcomers and inquiries was so great that we have to swing more to the take-it-or-leave-it attitude, which, curiously enough, produces better results than trying to be all things at all times at all places to all men.'"*[990]

ABOUT "WET-NURSING"

It has been a hard learned lesson that working with people that are still drinking is difficult if not impossible. It is called "Wet-Nursing," and over the years there have been many *"examples of the ineffectiveness of wet-nursing, 'which was given up in later years.'"*[991] At least, this is true in most cases. Many of us are still pulled in by the plight of some suffering soul whom we think we are going to save!

"Doc used to say, 'If they're ready, work with them; if they're not, you might as well walk away, because they're not going to stop drinking.'"[992] This does NOT mean that we don't talk to anyone that has been using. It means, we don't try to convince someone who

is NOT ready and *"**willing to go to any lengths**"*[993] that they should be.

SPONSORSHIP

"In the earliest days...the term 'sponsor' was not in the AA jargon. Then a few hospitals...began to accept alcoholics (under that diagnosis) as patients—if a sober...member would agree to 'sponsor' the sick man or woman... All through the early months of recovery, the sponsor stood by, ready to answer questions or to listen whenever needed.

"Sponsorship turned out to be such a good way to help people get established...that it has become a custom followed throughout the...world, even when hospitalisation is not necessary."[994] And remember, many of them only had a few weeks of sobriety. Don't hesitate to work with others; it just might save *your* life.

Just as our sponsors took us through the Steps, so we can do the same for others. That is what this material can be used for, a kind of guide, to assist in this aim. If we have received the benefit of Sponsorship, then we may want to give back in this way. It is part of our Programme. Those that we work with come to us with all sorts of "problems." We share our experience but we make it clear that *"Of course we cannot wholly rely on friends (advisers or sponsors) to solve all our difficulties. A good adviser will never do all our thinking for us. He will therefore help to eliminate fear, expediency, and self-deception, so enabling us to make choices which are loving, wise, and honest."*[995]

Many of us believe that we cannot get sober without resolving certain problems. We must *"Burn the idea into the consciousness of every man that he can get well regardless of anyone"*[996] or anything. But we each learned *"As the newcomer and I examine each Step, both she and I receive new insight and find an additional facet of this jewel of sobriety."*[997] The problems take care of themselves.

A suggestion we often hear in the rooms is that men should be sponsored by men and women by other women. Where did this come from? *"The idea that men should help men and women help women evolved as a means of...self-preservation...experience proved it wise for the newcomers' sake."*[998] We've heard people use the excuse that in the beginning there were only men, to work with the women. Well, that is not exactly true. Dr. Bob *"Smith says that men can rarely work satisfactorily with women... The sex problem makes it difficult. He, as a physician, can and has helped, but his wife and other wives must handle most of this."*[999] Very early in our development *"Members saw that the difficulty in working with women was primarily because of sexual problems. It was considered safer for the non-alcoholic wives to work with them."*[1000]

Even the appearance of impropriety can be fatal. Let's look at what happened when a man went on a Twelfth Step call. *"To give some idea of the dangers involved...He called on her after her husband had left for work...The neighbours saw this and told the husband. One night, the husband lay in the weeds outside the house, waiting for the guy, and when the AA came along to take the woman to a meeting, the husband blew him in half with a shotgun."*[1001] His intentions were good but the result was not. What is the old expression? "The road to hell is paved with good intentions."

A sponsor is not a "misery buddy" she is there to guide the Sponsee through the Steps. *"Years ago I used to commiserate with all people who suffered. Now I commiserate only with those who suffer in ignorance, who do not understand the purpose and ultimate utility of pain."*[1002] To continually listen to someone commiserate about their life and not guide them to do anything about it is not helpful. We always guide them to the Steps, that's our purpose.

"We found that the principles of tolerance and love had to be emphasized in actual practice. We can never say (or insinuate) to anyone that he must agree to our formula or be excommunicated."[1003] Sponsorship to me is a commitment and commitments mean commitment. I do not find it necessary to "fire" any Sponsor or Sponsee, I simply add another person, if need be, to assist in my or their growth. I certainly don't know everything nor do I expect anyone else to be so wise. This is how I have chosen to handle the situation. We each have to follow our own path.

We see no hierarchy in Sponsorship *"all true communication must be founded on mutual need. Never could we talk down to anyone, certainly not to a fellow alcoholic. We saw that each sponsor would have to humbly admit his own needs as clearly as those of his prospect."*[1004]

We discover that judging or checking up on others' behaviour to be a very ineffective method of assistance. *"When setting out to 'check' others, I found myself often motivated by fear of what they were doing, self-righteousness, and even downright intolerance. Consequently, I seldom succeeded in correcting anything."*[1005]

"If we would favourably affect others, we ourselves need to practise what we preach—and forget the 'preaching,' too."[1006] The question remains: When are we ready to sponsor? The answer is that there is no definitive answer.   The newcomer can often help someone even newer than they more effectively than an old-timer can. Someone who has just completed Step One can often be very helpful to the person just looking at it for the first time. So it is good to begin helping another as soon as we can; the worst that can happen is we'll get out of our own self-centredness, which can never be a bad thing!

There would be no groups anywhere if the fellowship was based on a formal hierarchy. Bill knew nothing when he started and it all worked out just fine. The reality is we each find our own way by doing—not by getting ready. In Los Angeles for example: *"There was no phone, so the local AA's had an ad running in the paper. 'Then they would bring the letters up and open them...you made a call every night.' Al said that he himself went on a Twelve Step call the second week he was in the programme."*[1007] It was very much all hands on deck.

Remember that back then it was the person who made the Twelve Step call that usually became the newcomers sponsor. So lighten-up and get busy! If you have been introduced to this material at our retreat, you already have more knowledge of the programme than most did back then.

ANONYMITY?

What about letting others know that you are in the programme? The man who started the programme in Detroit hesitated to tell people he was in the programme. *"If I go around shouting from the rooftops about my alcoholism, it might very possibly prevent me from getting a good job.   But supposing that just one man died because I had, for selfish reasons, kept my mouth shut? No. I was supposed to be doing God's will, not mine.* (God's) *road lay clear ahead of me, and I'd better quit rationalising myself into any detours."*[1008]

When All Else Fails...

When Dr. Bob first sobered up, their first group formed quickly. *"'We had to', Bill said. 'We were under awful compulsion. And we found that we had to do something for somebody or actually perish ourselves."*[1009] *"Practical experience shows that nothing will so much insure immunity from drinking as intensive work with other alcoholics."*[1010] We find, as Bill did, that when *"plagued by waves of self-pity and resentment... I soon found that when all other measures failed, work with another...would save the day."*[1011]   Earlier we saw that when Dr. Bob discovered the idea of service, he *"was so eager to help others because he found it the best way to stay sober. Dr. Bob held on to this discovery and developed it into the deep conviction shown in his last talk, saying that the Twelve Steps 'when simmered down...resolve themselves into the words 'love' and 'service.''"*[1012]   When we begin to see love in others eyes, we are told that: *"The reason you see love in these people's eyes is because you are beginning to love them. The love that we see in their eyes is the reflection of our own love. We have got to love to be loved."*[1013]

Service is the answer. *"The best thing about...service jobs is that, for a period of time, I got out of myself."*[1014]   Getting out of ourselves and out of our own way is when self-obsession begins to release its grip on us. Life is good. *"The central characteristic of the spiritual experience is that it gives the recipient a new and better motivation out of all proportion to any process of discipline, belief, or faith.*

"These experiences cannot make us whole at once; they are a rebirth to a fresh and certain opportunity."[1015]   We are *"ruled, not by people, but by principles, by truths and, as most of us would say, by God."*[1016]   Also, *"It was found that...members didn't always have to learn through their own experience. They could learn and grow through the experience of others."*[1017] This is something that before we worked the programme we never quite seemed to master.

This may all seem too much like hard work. But *"In Step Twelve— carrying the...message to others—I've found little else than great joy."*[1018]   *"Of course...even the best, fall short of such achievements as a consistent thing... We often get quite off the beam. Our troubles sometimes begin with indifference... We temporarily cease to grow because we feel satisfied that there is no need for all of* (the) *Twelve Steps for us... The best-intentioned of us can fall for the...illusion."*[1019]

Dr. Bob gave his last talk at the First International Convention, in Cleveland. He ended by saying: *"None of us would be here today if somebody hadn't taken time to explain things to us, to give us a little pat on the back, to take us to a meeting or two, to do numerous little kind and thoughtful acts in our behalf. So let us never get such a degree of smug complacency that we're not willing to extend, or attempt to extend, to our less fortunate brothers* (and sisters) *that help which has been so beneficial to us. Thank you very much."*[1020]

250

Twelfth Step work is almost certainly one of the clearest demonstrations of gratitude we can express. **"To express my gratitude, I wanted to spend the rest of my life trying to help someone else, and I knew that one of the best places to work was in the Fellowship...without my old, shallow ideas of 'success.'"**[1021] If you are anything like me, this realisation in itself is an amazing spiritual awakening. **"Never in my life, before...had I really done anything _for_ anyone."**[1022] Our attitude was always: "What's in it for me?"

INSTITUTIONS—CHURCHES, HOSPITALS, PRISONS AND OTHERS

Working with Doctors, Hospitals, Prisons, Courts and Treatment Centres today is not much different than in the past. But the way people are introduced to the programme is changing. However let us not forget that we work **with** these professionals. **"Though we work out our solution on the spiritual as well as an altruistic plane, we favour hospitalisation for the alcoholic who is very jittery or befogged. More often than not, it is imperative that a man's brain be cleared before he is approached, as he has then a better chance of understanding and accepting what we have to offer."**[1023] The point is that we don't get into conflict with these institutions and the people who work in them. We cooperate fully, accepting their contribution to our fellowships growth. **"We cooperate widely with the men of medicine as well as with the men of religion."**[1024] We must always remember that we have **"no opinion on outside issues; hence the AA name ought never be drawn into public controversy."**[1025]

"Practically every...member declares that no satisfaction has been deeper and no joy greater than in a Twelfth Step job well done. To watch the eyes of men and women open with wonder as they move from darkness into light, to see their lives quickly fill with new purpose and meaning, to see whole families reassembled, to see the...outcast received back into his community in full citizenship, and above all to watch these people awaken to the presence of a loving God in their lives— these things are the substance of what we receive as we carry (the) **message."**[1026]

There was an amazing process that they used to follow at the hospitals. There was a steady stream of visitors, telling their stories. **"The visits developed into a continuous discussion...with the patients from noon until ten o'clock at night. One member who had been** *active at St. Thomas in the 1940's said there was an average of at least 15 visitors a day. So at the end of a five-day period, the prospect...had met from 60 to as many as 100 visitors few of whom at least would click."*[1027] What an amazing commitment. *"In five days at St. Thomas, you would hear as many talks as you would hear in six months outside."*[1028] Is our commitment as great?

Those early experiences were very intense. *"Before leaving the hospital, two of these men, convinced of my sincerity of purpose, imparted to me the necessary knowledge and mental tools which have resulted in my complete sobriety."*[1029]

It is good to do service in prisons, *"Some things about...prison are different: mandatory attendance or you're thrown off the list; anonymity being no more than just another long word when your name is on a facility-wide 'call-out' sheet each week. But the general feel of a street...meeting can definitely be preserved in a prison setting. The people make the meeting. AA people give people in prison hope."*[1030]

"One thing I am certain of: Inmates in prison who attend...have their chances of remaining free greatly enhanced—this is a proven fact...It is estimated that two-thirds of the men in prison were under the influence of alcohol and/or drugs when they committed their offences."[1031] A so-called *"Five-Time Loser"* describes past prison recidivism: *"We...nearly always, had good intentions when we were released from prison. But with the first drink, our good intentions dissolved; our personalities changed. We reverted to the old way of life we knew—a life full of anger, vindictiveness, resentment, fear, dependence, denial, self-will, irresponsibility. And we found ourselves back in prison."*[1032] We can help our fellows get off this merry-go-round.

GO TO MEETINGS

"We sit in...meetings and listen, not only to receive something ourselves, but to give reassurance and support which our presence can bring."[1033] Yes, the simple act of going to meetings is a small form of service, even if we don't share. We will hear some people that have been around for a while saying things such as "I don't get as much out of the meetings as I use to so I don't go to as many." Well, the truth is that once we have reaped the benefits of the programme it is time for us to give back. We begin going to meetings to help those that still suffer. Looking to get something out of the meetings for ourselves is evidence of backsliding into old ideas. *"Selfish, self*

centred that we think is the root of our problem."[1034] Remember, *"Some of us have tried to hold on to our old ideas and the result was nil until we let go absolutely."*[1035] Maybe we have a **"root"** that still remains and needs to be dug out?

It is made very clear in "The Long Form" of the Twelve Traditions what the real reason is for meetings: *"Each...group ought to be a spiritual entity having but one primary purpose—that of carrying its message to the alcoholic who still suffers."*[1036] Once we have worked our way through the Steps we attend meetings in order to help the newcomer or those **"still suffering."** The more we shift our attention away from ourselves, the better we feel. This *is* the reason for meetings. *"We meet frequently so (that) newcomers may find the fellowship."*[1037]

In the early days *"The meeting consisted of eight or nine alcoholics and seven or eight wives."*[1038] The early Chicago group reported: *"'At the present time, we have ten rummies—three women and seven men—and five non-alkies in the group,' he said, 'all working hard on the eight new prospects that we have at the present writing."*[1039] Where would all the Twelve Step programs be today had they not had the blessing and assistance of the husbands and wives? The groups grew with the help of the entire family.

There are fewer of these kinds of meetings now. Closed meetings started that kept out non-alcoholics. Then, years later, even open meetings became less and less welcoming to family members. We think this is a shame. It is very important that the family be involved in our spiritual way of life. *"In Youngstown (Ohio), it was usual for two couples to visit the prospective member before he attended his first meeting. The husband would tell the man about AA, and the woman would talk with the wife. 'That way, they would know what it was all about when they finally got to AA."*[1040]

When we began both partners developed spiritually, making life at home progressively better and better. After the meetings, or in the absence of them, members and their spouses would socialise. *"Every evening we would meet at the home of one of the members and have coffee and doughnuts and spend a social evening."*[1041] Most of the conversation centred on the topic of how to bring other alcoholics and their families into the groups. These meetings after the meetings also brought families closer together.

Meetings were family affairs right from the very beginning. *"The (non-alcoholic) wives' role was extremely important in the earliest days... It is no exaggeration to say that there would have been no AA without those wives... Often the wives...helped with the meetings, opened their homes to recovering drunks, did Twelve Step work, and considered themselves as much a part...as their husbands...their influence was strong.*

"'The meetings were definitely open. They insisted on it,' said Ernie G. the second, 'Doc didn't believe in closed meetings. He told me, 'You bring Ruth. If you don't I'm going to come and get her.' He was emphatic about it. That was good...when she came to a few meetings, she found out there was hope.'

"'I told him I felt the presence of God at the meeting, more than any other place I've ever been,' said Ruth. 'This is for us...let's grow up here together.' We decided, and we both made it our life's work—to build our lives around the spiritual aspects of Alcoholics Anonymous.'"[1042] The Pan-Fellowship meetings are trying to bring this flavour back to the rooms.

Why keep going to meetings then? Late in life Dr. Bob was asked: *"'Do you have to go to all these meetings? Why don't you stay home and conserve your strength?'*

"'Dr. Bob considered the question for a time, then said, 'The <u>first</u> reason is that this way is working so well. Why should I take a chance on any other way? The <u>second</u> reason is that I don't want to deprive myself the privilege of meeting, greeting, and visiting with fellow alcoholics. It is a pleasure to me. And the <u>third</u> reason is the most important. I belong at the meeting for the sake of the new man or woman who might walk through that door. I am living proof that (it) *will work as I work* (it)*, and I owe it to the new person to be there.   I am the living example.'"*[1043]

"I like the face-to-face sharing before and after the meetings. That way, I get to meet the new members and give them a warm welcome, a handshake, and a smile."[1044]

SPEAKING AT MEETINGS

"Our stories disclose in a general way what we used to be like, what happened and what we are like now."[1045] "Doing the chair," as it is called in England, or otherwise know as "Speaking at Meetings" and sharing can have a profound effect on people. *"If our turn comes to speak at a meeting, we again try to carry* (the) *message."*[1046]   Sometimes, someone speaking from the most unspectacular background can be telling the newcomers story. Some of us have been given a simple suggestion by our sponsors. "You don't

turn down a programme request." And very importantly to, lighten up! **"So many sceptical, suspicious newcomers have found confidence and comfort in the laughter and talk. This is Twelfth Step work in the very best sense of the word."**[1047]

Some of us have had problems with meetings from time to time. Those problems have generally arisen when *listening to the people in the programme instead of listening to the programme in people.* It is vital that we **"identify, not compare...Identifying, they said, was trying to see how I was like the people I was with. Comparing, they told me, was looking for differences, usually seeing how I was better than others."**[1048] Recognising that we are no worse, and no better, than our fellows is our goal.

The meetings originally focused on what was currently happening in every day life more than the problem for which we originally came to the programme. We hear many people complain today that they don't hear enough about alcohol in the meetings. Most of them **"'would be surprised how little talk there was of drinking experience even among ourselves.' Wally said. 'That was usually kept for...new prospects in the hospital. We were more interested in our everyday life than we were in reminiscing about drinking.'"**[1049]

In our book another member says: **"with a...meeting. The more I focus my mind on the defects—late start, long drunk-a-logs,** (with no talk of the problem of our addiction or no talk of the "Programme") **cigarette smoke—the worse the meeting becomes. But when I try to see what I can add to the meeting, rather than what I can get out of it, and when I focus on what's good about it, rather than what's wrong with it, the meetings keep getting better."**[1050]

TELEPHONE SERVICE

Most areas have a telephone service at the Intergroup or Central Office level. In the majority of cases, you only need a year's sobriety, and in many of our programmes less time is required, to perform this service. There is usually training available. This is part of the front line services we can do. It can be quite rewarding and again may just save *your* life.

In the beginning of the programme, everyone was involved in phone work, husbands and wives. **"Dorothy O. (Judd's wife) recalled how 'another girl and I did all the calling to see that members would visit patients in the hospitals. It wasn't left to chance. Then we went to meetings and assisted there.'"**[1051]

"TO PRACTICE THESE PRINCIPLES IN ALL OUR AFFAIRS"

"Our basic troubles are the same as everyone else's, but when an honest effort is made 'to practice these principles in all our affairs,' (the) *well grounded...seem to have the ability, by God's grace, to take these troubles in stride and turn them into demonstrations of faith. ...But...we often discover a greater challenge in the lesser and more continuous problems of life. Our answer is in still more spiritual development. Only by this means can we improve our chances for really happy and useful living."*[1052]

The programme *"had all the answers for me, that, if I would be willing and try, I could stay sober—one day at a time. However, I found that this involved the effort to practice the programme."*[1053]

What are these principles? Many of us have ignored and misunderstood the Principles that have been alluded to in each of these Steps and which this study mentions at the end of each Step. These are the principles that we now try to live our lives by. The six, Bill was introduced to when he got sober, and since there are now Twelve Steps there are now twelve principles.

For some sobriety equals not using and that is all that matters. **"The chief purpose of AA is sobriety.** (Keep in mind our definition of *"sobriety: a peaceful, calm, contented, serene and well-balanced life."*) *all realise that without sobriety we have nothing.*

"However, it is possible to expand this simple aim into a great deal of nonsense, so far as the individual member is concerned...

"This is why (the) *Twelfth Step urges that we 'practice these principles in __ALL__ our affairs.' We are not living just to be sober; we are living to learn, to serve, and to love."*[1054]

"It became clear that if we ever were to feel emotionally secure among grown-up people, we would have to put our lives on a 'give-and-take basis'; we would have to develop the sense of being in partnership or brotherhood with all those around us. We saw that we would need to give constantly of ourselves without demands for repayment. When we persistently did this we gradually found that people were attracted to us as never before. And even if they failed us, we could be understanding and not...seriously affected."[1055]

The programme *"is a wonderful thing to know and apply... in your life. You've got to live it out in the street. You see somebody having a little problem, help them, no matter who they are. That's AA."*[1056] We must learn to apply the programme at home as well, **if** we truly want to maintain the promises. One who "grew up" around the programme found that she and her partner learned to do just that. *"We agreed to never be higher than third on each other's list, with God always first and Alcoholics Anonymous second. He is my partner and my best friend. We both sponsor several people, and our house is filled with love and laughter. Our telephone never stops ringing. We share the joy of a common solution."*[1057]

"My friend had emphasised the absolute necessity of demonstrating these principles in all my affairs. Particularly was it imperative to work with others as he had worked with me...if an alcoholic failed to perfect and enlarge his spiritual life through work with others, he could not survive the certain trials and low spots ahead."[1058]

Another "big book" of spiritual concepts says: *"If a brother or sister is ill-clad and in lack of daily food, and one of you says to them, go in peace, be warmed and filled, without giving them the things needed for the body, what does it profit? So, faith by itself, if it has no works, is dead."*[1059] As a result of the Fellowship and Twelve Step recovery *"There is a sense of belonging, of being wanted, needed and loved. In return for a bottle and a hangover, we have been given the Keys of the Kingdom."*[1060]

Except *"we feel that elimination of our drinking* (or whatever our addiction) *is but a beginning. A much more important demonstration of our principles lies before us in our respective homes, occupations and affairs."*[1061] If we are not *"happy, joyous and free"*[1062] and demonstrating these qualities we have not truly grown. One way to insure peace is to recognise *"The spiritual life is not a theory. We have to live it. Unless one's family expresses a desire to live upon spiritual principles we think we ought not to urge them. We should not talk incessantly to them about spiritual matters. They will change in time. Our behaviour will convince them more than words."*[1063] Leave them be, and keep yourself spiritually fit.

The writer of this study had many conversations with his Sponsor about why it is that our statistical average of recovery has dropped so drastically since they were first reported in the Forward to the Second edition of *Alcoholics Anonymous*. Then as we were looking to insert the information and give our brilliant argument as to why they seem no longer to be true. We finally read the statistics as they were written and not as we read them.

This may point to many misinterpretations of both the Steps and Traditions. Let us show you exactly what it says. **"Of alcoholics who came to AA _and really tried_, 50% got sober at once and remained that way; 25% sobered up after some relapses, and among the remainder, those who stayed on with AA showed improvement. Other thousands came to a few AA meetings and at first decided they didn't want the programme. But great numbers of these—about two out of three—began to return as time passed."**[1064] We completely discounted the "other thousands" who came to a few meetings and decided they didn't want the programme, just as it seems they did.

Many "old-timers" complain about the courts, hospitals and treatment centres making money from the programme. But **"more than half of new members were reaching AA with the help of professionals."**[1065] We tend to agree with an early Cleveland member. In 1977, after some forty years of sobriety, he said: **"'I think the programme is just the same...The principles are there; the Steps are there; the practices are there; and the opportunities are there. If you do as the Big Book says, then it is the same programme that existed...in 1939.'**

"'The people who wanted to stay sober then were the ones who did what the programme suggested. Today, the people who want to stay sober are the ones who do what the programme tells them to do.'"[1066] The programme never changes but the work may be becoming more intense for those of us wanting to attain our expanded definition of sobriety. **"We think that AA has changed, but the root of it hasn't."**[1067]

It is easier to be critical than to recognise that this programme is obviously Divinely Inspired and it will continue—for good. **"In the end we can only be worth as much as our spiritual example has justified... I have become a pupil of the AA movement rather than the teacher I once thought I was."**[1068] We cannot teach anyone, anything. We cannot make others understand. We cannot convince anyone. When we try to force our "awareness" on another, or "make them see what they are doing" our experience shows that: **"Who is convinced against his will is of the same opinion still."**[1069] We only learn through open-mindedness, not through others insistence.

"The Twelfth Step...seems to carry this implicit warning: 'If you are not having at least the beginnings of a spiritual awakening, it would be well to look back over the Steps and find out where you are failing.'... There is a kind of built-in guarantee that, if you are living the Steps to the best of your ability, no matter

how difficult it may be at times, you will eventually have this awakening of the spirit."[1070] With the implementation of the Twelve Steps in our lives we find we have our *"Instincts restored to true purpose. Understanding is the key to right attitudes, right action key to good living."*[1071] In service we find ourselves *"going out of our way to understand and help"*[1072] others.

"We have been considering so many problems that it may appear that AA consists mainly of racking dilemmas and trouble shooting. To a certain extent, that is true. We have been talking about problems because we are problem people who have found a way up and out, and who wish to share our knowledge of that with all who can use it."[1073] The following member puts it another way. *"After being in the hospital for several days, a plan of living was outlined to me. A very simple plan, that I still find much joy and happiness in following. It is impossible to put on paper all the benefits I have derived...physical, mental, domestic, spiritual, and monetary. This is no idle talk. It is the truth."*[1074] It is the truth for many of us.

"Whatever this spiritual awakening may mean to anyone else...to me it means that the God of my understanding has given me, by (God's) *special presence in AA and through...people and the Twelve Steps, a gift that surpasses understanding—an awakening of my human spirit!—A priest"*[1075] wrote this. I personally love the fact this is said by a priest. It is wonderful to me when anyone that has spent their adult life looking for a spiritual awakening does so in our programme. These Steps are the most powerful tools ever organised into a simple, if not easy, plan for life.

THE PRINCIPLE OF STEP TWELVE

Service

In Step Twelve we learn the true meaning of the word charity. As we carry the message through being of **service** we become a beacon to others, by sharing the changes that have begun to take place in our own lives. We must *"give it away to keep it."* **"Our real purpose is to fit ourselves to be of maximum service to God and the people about us."**[1076]

"The tremendous fact for every one of us is that we have discovered a common solution. We have a way out on which we can absolutely agree, and upon which we can join in...harmonious action. This is the great news... (the Big Book) **carries to those who suffer from alcoholism"**[1077] and numerous other dilemmas. A great many of us have learned that: **"What opinions I may hold, what techniques I may use one year or five years from now, I have no way of knowing. But I have noticed, during the past seven years, that I have always been happiest when my commitment to AA and its Twelve Steps has been greater than my involvement in any other activity or group."**[1078]

Chapter 16

The Principles

THE PRINCIPLES OF THE PROGRAMME

𝕿he following are *"the Principles by which...members recover."*[1079] as we see them. The *"Twelve Steps are a group of principles, spiritual in nature, which, if practised as a way of life, can expel the obsession to drink* (or, we believe, any obsession) *and enable the sufferer to become happily and usefully whole."*[1080] *"The basic principles...as they are known today, were borrowed mainly from the fields of religion and medicine."*[1081]

When we began there were six principles. Today, now that we have Twelve Steps, we believe there are twelve principles. *"We begin to see that the...principles are good ones. Though we are still beset with much rebellion, we increase the practice of these principles out of a sense of responsibility to ourselves, our families, and our groups."*[1082] These principles are the *"common denominators of all religions...potent enough to change the lives of men and women.* [1083] It is nearly impossible to put these powerful principles created by the Steps into single words, but here is an attempt to do so.

The initial six comprised: *Defeat* (now our Step One); *Honest* self-survey (now our Step Four); *Confession* (now our Step Five); *Restitution* (now our Step Nine); *Conscious contact* with a Higher Power (now our Step Eleven) and *Service* (now our Step Twelve). These principles went with the original Six Steps. We consider the additional principles to be: *Open-mindedness* (Step Two); *Surrender,* (Step Three); *Willingness* (Step Six); *Humility* (Step Seven); *Forgiveness* (Step Eight); *Stewardship* (Step Ten).

The Principles of the Programme are:

1) **Defeat** (Step 1)

   Here the acceptance of our powerlessness and the knowledge of our *defeat* are paramount. I cannot make it on my own. "We" begin a life-long process. **Ego deflation** is the removal of a belief in separation. We are not alone or separate. We must be clear that *"any life run on self-will can hardly be a success"*[1084] and therefore not worth living.

2) **Open Mindedness** (Step 2)

   Step Two is the smallest beginning of a pattern of faith *and **open-mindedness*** that builds. First is *faith* in the programme, where we see *a power greater than ourselves* at work. To be **O**pen Minded is the **KEY**.

3) **Surrender** (Step 3)

When we walk through the doors of our first meeting, or even with our first call for help, something begins to happen. That "something" becomes clearer by the time of our decision in Step Three. We decided to **surrender** to, and *trust* in, the process of the Steps, *a power greater than ourselves*. The bottom line for **surrender** is the recognition that "I could be wrong."

4) **Honesty** (Step 4)

It can be argued that each of these "Principles" is buried in all the Steps; "**H**onesty" is the **KEY**. However, Step Four begins a lifetime of **honest self-survey**, one day at a time.

5) **Confession** (Step 5)

Our journey begins with the *courage* to ask for help. For some of us this journey begins with our first meeting. For others of us when we ask for help from a sponsor, but certainly for all of us that *courage* is there by the time we begin the **confession** of our "short comings" in Step Five.

6) **Willingness** (Step 6)

All our answers are found deep inside, **Willingness** is the **KEY**. We must be willing to go against the demands of our self-will to use the weapons we have created to, we think, survive; our defects of character.

7) **Humility** (Step 7)

Step 7 reminds us to give up our attempts at fixing ourselves and turn it over to God, an act of **humility** and open-mindedness that most of us never understood.

8) **Forgiveness** (Step 8)

Forgiveness begins here when we release our resentments and hurts, "real or imagined," and become ready to make our amends.

9) **Restitution** (Step 9)

Amend, means "to mend" our past behaviour. Our new found life long experience of "mending" and making **restitution** for our past (and not so past) actions begins on Step Nine. This is where the "promises" are received, giving us an understanding of **freedom** never before experienced.

10) Stewardship (Steps 10)

The so-called "maintenance Steps" of the programme begin with Step 10, teaching us perseverance and **stewardship**. *Perseverance* is just plain "keeping on, keeping on," where as **stewardship** is the learning of the necessity for us to **_continue_** daily maintenance of the "Promises." Dr. Bob said that **_"We are stewards of what we have._**"[1085]

11) Conscious Contact (Step 11)

Now that we have a belief in a Higher Power we **_"improve our conscious contact"_** with that Power greater than ourselves through Prayer and meditation. This is where we find a wonderful source of **Conscious** *enlightenment*. Enlightenment can only come to a **conscious** mind. A greater **conscious contact** is the benefit of the *patient* use of daily prayer and meditation, as we give up our desire for instant gratification. We must "Let Go and Let God." We become more **conscious** of our beliefs, of our actions, and attitudes. And most importantly we become more and more God **conscious**, "a spiritual awakening."

12) Service (Step 12)

Our entire life, through the **_"practice of these principles in all our affairs"_**[1086] becomes one of service, including our jobs, and our home life, everywhere. We learn the true meaning of the word *charity*, as we carry the message through **service** and become a beacon to others in the programme. In Step Twelve it is made clear that we must "give it away to keep it**." "Our real purpose is to fit ourselves to be of maximum service to God and the people about us.**"[1087]

Appendices

APPENDICES

APPENDIX I—

The Lords Prayer* a Look at it From a Member's Perspective

(Written for those of us that have a "problem" with this prayer being said in meetings and wish to resolve it)

Our Father	This points us to the Unity of all. In fact if God is our Parent then as with of all nature we are descendant from the parent and therefore, the same species. **"We are unique because of the Universal Law that like begets like...If God is a Spiritual Being, then we are Spiritual Beings."**[1088]
Which Art In Heaven	The person who wrote this prayer made it clear that the kingdom of "Heaven" was within us. So that is where we will find our "Conscious Contact" with God, in our own consciousness.
Hallowed Be Thy Name	This is to honour **"Infinite God rather than our finite selves"**[1089] for the life we live. This reminds us of the principle of **"Humility."**
Thy Kingdom Come	The Kingdom of God for most alcoholics can be found in our programme. We give up an unprincipled life for one with principles to live by; spiritual principles.
Thy Will Be Done	We must remind ourselves to be willing to "Let Go and Let God." **"We constantly remind ourselves that we are no longer running the show, humbly saying to ourselves many times each day 'Thy Will Be Done.'"**[1090]
On Earth As It Is In Heaven	Earth is where we live. Heaven is found within our own consciousness. Therefore, life will be as we believe within our own minds. When our attitude changes, our life changes.
Give Us This Day Our Daily Bread	Give "Us" reminds us of the **"we";** of the fellowship. Together we can survive and be happy. We Live Life **"One Day at a Time"** as our slogan says.
Forgive Us Our Trespasses As We Forgive Those Who Trespass Against Us	This is a reminder of our Steps 8 & 9. Step 8 is where we forgive, and reminds us that we cannot be forgiven before we forgive. Step 9 is where we ask for forgiveness ourselves. This portion of the "Lords Prayer" actually reminds us of the order of forgiveness.
Lead Us Not Into Temptation	A reminder of Steps 1, 2, 3, 6, 7 and 11 where we constantly work on maintaining our conscious contact with God. Therefore we are not tempted to pick up our old weapons of survival—our character defects.
Deliver Us From Evil	"Evil" is twisted thinking which comes from the Ego. Therefore, when saying this prayer ask to be delivered from Ego or a belief in our separation from God.
For Thine Is The Kingdom And The Power And The Glory Forever	A final reminder to leave life in God's hands. Therefore, a request for and demonstration of Humility and with humility an elimination of the humiliation that goes with a lack of Humility.
Amen	Means, so be it. Therefore all that we've asked believing is done. Done! And, so it is.

When the Big 'I' Becomes Nobody

By Harry M. Tiebout

(A culled version)

"*THE...PROGRAMME OF HELP is touched with elements of true inspiration...My thesis is that anonymity, thoughtfully preserved, supplies two essential ingredients to that maintenance. The two ingredients, actually two sides of the same coin, are: first, the preservation of a reduced ego; second, the continued presence of humility or humbleness...*

"*This ego is not an intellectual concept, but a state of feeling—a feeling of importance—of being 'special.'*"[1091]

The ego is not only a set of beliefs by which we live our lives but also a belief in our "specialness." And ours is a programme of ego <u>de</u>flation, not <u>in</u>flation. "*Today, AA in practice is well aware of the dangers of singling anyone out for honours and praise. The dangers of re-inflation are recognised.*

"*Now let's take a closer look at this ego which causes trouble. The feelings associated with this state of mind are of basic importance in understanding the value of anonymity for the individual—the value of placing him in the rank and file of humanity.*

"*Certain qualities typify this ego which views itself as special and therefore different. It is high on itself and prone to keep its goals and visions at the same high level. It distains what it sees as grubs who plod along without the fire and inspiration of those sparked by ideals lifting people out of the commonplace and offering promise of better things to come.*

"*Often the same ego operates in reverse. It despairs of man, with his faults and failings, and develops a cynicism which sours the spirit and makes of its possessor a cranky realist who finds nothing good in this vale of tears. Life never quite meets his demands upon it, and he lives an embittered existence, grabbing what he can out of the moment, but never really part of what goes on around him. He seeks love and understanding and prates endlessly about his sense of alienation from those around him. Basically, he is a disappointed idealist—forever aiming high and landing low. Both of these egos confuse humbleness with humiliation.*"[1092]

"Clearly, the sense of being special, of being 'something,' has its dangers, its drawbacks... Yet the opposite, namely, that one is to be nothing has little counter appeal.

"The self as nothing is not easily developed. It runs counter to all our desires for identity, for an apparently meaningful existence, one filled with hope and promise. To be nothing seems a form of psychological suicide. We cling to our Somethingness with all the strength at our command. The thought of being a nothing is simply not acceptable. But the fact is that the person that does not learn to be as nothing cannot feel that he is but a plain, ordinary, everyday kind of person who merges with the human race—and as such is humble, lost in the crowd, and essentially anonymous. When that can happen, the individual has a lot going for him.

"People with 'nothing' on their minds can relax and go about their business quietly and with a minimum of fuss and bother. They can even enjoy life as it comes along. In AA, this is called the 24-hour programme, which really signifies that the individual does not have tomorrow on his mind. He can live in the present and find his pleasure in the here and now. He is hustling nowhere. With nothing on his mind, the individual is receptive and open-minded.

"The great religions are conscious of the need of nothingness if one is to attain grace...

"Zen teaches the release of nothingness. A famous series of pictures designed to show growth in man's nature ends with a circle enclosed in a square. The circle depicts man in a state of nothingness; the square represents the framework of limitations man must learn to live within. In this blank state, 'Nothing is easy, nothing is hard,' and so Zen, too, has linked nothingness, humbleness, and grace.

"Anonymity is a state of mind of great value to the individual in maintaining sobriety. While I recognise its protective function, I feel that any discussion of it would be one-sided if it failed to emphasize the fact that the maintenance of a feeling of anonymity—of a feeling 'I am nothing special'—is a basic insurance of humility and so a basic safeguard against further trouble... This kind of anonymity is truly a precious possession."[1093]

The ego will believe in anything rather than be wrong. *"The gnome theory has its appeal. It is less damaging to the ego to believe privately in elves than to entertain the possibility that I could be wrong."*[1094]

FURTHER ON ANONYMITY

"Anonymity is humility at work."[1095]   AA is NOT a secret organisation, though the work is done without fanfare. It is NOT about NOT telling anyone you are a member. In Dr. Bob's day, *"As far as anonymity was concerned, <u>we</u> knew who we were. It wasn't only AA, but our social life. All of our lives seemed to be spent together. We took people home with us to dry out. 'The...group had the names, addresses, and phone numbers of all the members,' said Warren. 'In fact, I remember Dr. Bob saying, 'If I got up and gave my name as Dr. Bob S.,* (at a meeting) *people who needed help would have a hard time getting in touch with me.'*

"'(Dr. Bob) said there were two ways to break the anonymity Tradition: (1) by giving your name at the public level of press or radio; (2) by being so anonymous that you can't be reached by other drunks.'

"Dr. Bob (further) *commented on the Eleventh Tradition as follows:*

"Since our Tradition on anonymity designates the exact level where the line should be held, it must be obvious to everyone who can read the English language that to maintain anonymity at any other level is definitely a violation of this Tradition.

"The AA who hides his identity from his fellow AA by using only a given name violates the Tradition just as much as the AA who permits his name to appear in the press in connection with matters pertaining to AA.

"The former is maintaining his anonymity <u>above</u> the level of press, radio, and films, and the latter is maintaining his anonymity <u>below</u> the level of press, radio, and films—whereas the Tradition states that we should maintain our anonymity <u>at</u> the level of press, radio, and films."[1096]

More clarity can be on this subject may be found in "The Long Form" of The Twelve Traditions: *"Our relations with the general public should be characterised by personal anonymity. We think AA ought to avoid sensational advertising. Our names and pictures as AA members ought not to be broadcast, filmed, or publicly printed. Our public relations should be guided by the principle of attraction rather than promotion. There is never a need to praise ourselves. We feel it better to let our friends recommend us."*[1097] Which obviously points out that our friends should know. Some of us are greatly surprised when someone will be talking about a friend or sometimes even their family and says that they haven't told them that they are in the Programme. That means that there is someone out there that may die of alcoholism because they weren't aware we were an alcoholic.

"In some sections of AA, anonymity is carried to the point of real absurdity. Members are on such a poor basis of communication that they don't even know each other's last names or where each lives. It's like the cell of an underground."[1098] We are becoming more open with each other—not less. *"Some groups, especially newer ones, conduct themselves like secret societies. They do not wish their activities know even to friends."*[1099] Dr. *"...Bob...said...he didn't think we would get anyplace if people didn't know we belonged to AA. He had the firm conviction that you should let yourself be known as an AA member in the community, and he was always sure to tell you about it every time you met him."*[1100]

"And finally, we of Alcoholics Anonymous believe that the principle of anonymity has an immense spiritual significance. It reminds us that we are to place principles before personalities; that we are actually to practice a genuine humility. This to the end that our great blessings may never spoil us; that we shall forever live a thankful contemplation of Him (Her or It that) *presides over us all."*[1101] Anonymity is about humility NOT about hiding the fact that we are an alcoholic or a member of the Fellowship. *"But supposing that just one man died because I had, for selfish reasons, kept my mouth shut? No. I was supposed to be doing God's will not mine."*[1102]

"For Dr. Bob, a professional man, one of the greatest stumbling blocks had been his prideful need to conceal his drinking—from people who probably knew about it anyhow. ... (Very quickly) *he openly admitted his problem to the very people he had wanted to hide it from.*

"It was a difficult thing to do: 'He trembled as he went about, for this might mean ruin, particularly to a person in his line of business.'

"When he came home that night, his entire outlook had changed."[1103] At a Pan-Fellowship meeting there is a phone list that is passed out and some people feel uncomfortable with that. Where would we be if the founding groups had felt the same? *"'Another*

thing that they did moved me so,' said Dorothy. 'They handed out little address books with everybody's name in it. Very few people, of course, had phones then. We were all too poor. But the ones who had phone numbers, there they were. And when they said, 'Drop in on us—anytime,' they meant it. I knew they did.'"[1104]

"The word 'anonymous' has for us an immense spiritual significance."[1105] Doing something for someone else and not taking credit for it is the real principle of anonymity. We find that, *"...the keeping of one's anonymity* (in this respect) *often means a sacrifice of one's desire for power, prestige, and money."*[1106]

"I believe most of us would agree that the general idea of anonymity is sound, because it encourages alcoholics and the families of alcoholics to approach us for help. Still fearful of being stigmatised, they regard our anonymity as an assurance their problems will be kept confidential, that the...skeleton in the family closet will not wander the streets."[1107]

"When we consult an AA (or other programme) *friend, we should not be reluctant to remind him of our need for full privacy. Intimate communication is normally so free and easy among us that an... adviser may sometimes forget when we expect him to remain silent."*[1108]

Gossip is not always lying about someone. It often doesn't matter what we are saying. When we really look at it, we, *"...find that big people discuss ideals, average people discuss things, and little people— they talk about other people."*[1109] So, which is it that we choose to be?

Integrity is the principle we need to follow, *"...the truth can be used to injure as well as heal... In AA,* (or other 12 Step Fellowships) *for instance, we talk a great deal about each other. Provided our motives are thoroughly good, this is not in the least wrong. But damaging gossip is quite something else. Of course, this kind of scuttlebutt can be grounded in fact. But no such abuse of the facts could ever be twisted into anything resembling integrity."*[1110] We suggest extreme caution and self-analysis when speaking of others. Always remember that *"Gossip barbed with anger,* (is) *a polite form of murder by character assassination..."*[1111]

APPENDIX III—**GROUP CONSCIENCE VS MEETING CONSCIENCE**

Group Conscience is a decision making process by the members are committed to the group as their Home Group. This includes those that do meeting service and regular participating members devoted to the group's well-being. Groups lose their cohesiveness when the things that made the meeting so successful are forgotten. When this group conscious is made some think they can defeat the group conscious. As in this example where, **"An old-timer, in disagreement, took the matter before the people attending that night's meeting whether they were members of that group or not. The people attending voted to reverse the decision of the group conscience... That meeting conscience weakened the effectiveness of that group conscience, and...people left the group."**[1112]

This seems to us to be the demise of perfectly good groups doing perfectly good work. Too often many of us are confused as to what the difference is between a **group** conscience and a **meeting** conscience and there is no talk of a **meeting** conscience in the Traditions. **"If we as a Fellowship don't carefully pass on to newer members the responsibilities that come with being a group, many more groups will go..."**[1113] **"'You get out of this programme what you put into it,' ...I'm lucky to be in a meeting where a lot of guys are putting in a lot."**[1114]

APPENDIX IV—ON DISCRIMINATION

"𝕸ost AA's simply wanted to get people into the programme, rather than keep them out. This might mean overcoming inbred prejudices and crossing social, religious, racial, and national boundaries in order to carry the message of recovery to anyone, anywhere, who needed help. It also meant doing the very same things in order to accept help. And if AA as a fellowship never had any greater achievement, it could say that most members have done more than pay lip service to this idea."[1115]

"I also learned that alcoholism is an equal opportunity illness, does not discriminate—is not restricted to race, creed, or geography. At last I was released from the bondage of my uniqueness."[1116]

"There are no colour bars in AA. If you give us a try, you will see that we are really human beings, and we will welcome you with open arms and hearts."[1117] Besides, if we do still have prejudices this will give us a chance to work them out with our sponsors. Most of us found that fellowship people "had no desire to know anything, except whether I was definite about my desire to quit..."[1118]

"We are people who normally would not mix. But there exists among us a fellowship, a friendliness, and an understanding which is indescribably wonderful."[1119] There are not even any concerns about ex-cons, or ex-criminals. Bill wrote, in a "Letter to a prison group: ...when you members come into the world of AA on the outside, you can be sure that no one will care a fig that you have done time. What you are trying to be—not what you were—is all that counts with us."[1120]

"Noting that 'we were biased then' Oscar recalled the April 1945 Cleveland Bulletin (an AA newsletter)...said, 'We whites, if we preach brotherly love, must practice it. And should a Negro (the unfortunate language of the time) appeal to us for help and guidance, it is our...duty to give the best that is in us, recognising that a human soul is given into our hands to help or destroy."[1121]

"We have a way out on which we can absolutely agree, and upon which we can join in brotherly and harmonious action."[1122]

How about women? "Women alcoholics had to overcome a double standard that was even more rigid in the 1930's than it is *today—the notion that nice women didn't drink to excess. This made it difficult for a woman to admit to the problem in the first place, to say nothing of being accepted in AA.*[1123]

"...it was four whole years before AA brought permanent sobriety to even one alcoholic woman. Like the high-bottoms the women said they were different; AA couldn't be for them. But as the communication was perfected, mostly by the women themselves, the picture changed."[1124]

"NO GENDER GAPS, NO GENERATION GAPS, NO SOCIAL CHASMS..."

This ninety year old member reports: *"I LOOK AROUND THE room at my home group. About forty of us. A dozen or so have been regulars since the group's first meeting ten years ago. Most of us have been sober for more than five years. A few count their sobriety in days, weeks, or months.*

"I tick them off in my mind: an eighteen-year-old girl still in high school; a single woman of twenty-two, employed, living alone; a young housewife with two children under the age of six; a man who has lived for eighty-four years, over twenty of which have passed in Alcoholics Anonymous; a pretty matron in her forties whose teenage children cause constant turmoil in her household; a man in his fifties recently laid off from a job he had thought was his for life; another in his sixties whose wife recently and unexpectedly died; one in his early thirties who hates the conditions on his job but is afraid to protest them; a woman in her seventies so busy with club work and golf and travel that she barely has time for a weekly meeting.

"Financial standings among those individuals range from zero to affluence. Educational backgrounds cover everything from high school dropout to Ph.D. From all of them, we catch references to problems, sorrows, big and little triumphs. Often we sense heartbreak or uncertainty over "relationships"- marital, paternal, social, business, and erotic."[1125] No matter what, we have all been accepted.

"Looking around my AA group brought these thoughts to mind; and I see, astonishingly, that there are no gender gaps, no generation gaps, no social chasms here."[1126] The one thing that seems to be waning is growth in some areas, areas where nearly all meetings have closed to the family of members. The wife of AA number three, Bill D., believed that the rapid growth of AA was because it was open to the spouses. *"Henrietta said... 'I always felt that it*

never would gone over so big if Dr. Bob hadn't said that they didn't want separate meetings, that husbands and wives had been separated long enough. Many years later, they had some closed meetings...but they didn't have any then."[1127]

References

REFERENCES

The page number is before the decimal and paragraph number after.

[1] Language of the Heart – Page 236.3
[2] Pass It On—Bill Wilson and the AA Message – Page 299.4,5
[3] Pass It On—Bill Wilson and the AA Message – Page 299.2
[4] As Bill Sees It – Page 308.2
[5] Alcoholics Anonymous – Page 59.1
[6] Language of the Heart – Page 135.4
[7] Alcoholics Anonymous – Page 133.1
[8] Language of the Heart – Page 224.3
[9] Language of the Heart – Page 224.3
[10] Language of the Heart – Page 224.4-6
[11] Language of the Heart – Page 225.2
[12] Language of the Heart – Page 225.6
[13] Language of the Heart – Page 225.9
[14] Language of the Heart – Page 225.9
[15] Language of the Heart – Page 231.2
[16] DR. BOB and the Good Oldtimers – Page 253.3
[17] As Bill Sees It – Page 105.2
[18] Language of the Heart – Page 98.2
[19] Experience, Strength, & Hope – Page(s) ix.2
[20] Experience, Strength, & Hope – Page(s) 220.2
[21] Experience, Strength, & Hope – Page(s) x.3
[22] Best of the Grapevine – Page(s) – 171.7
[23] Twelve Steps and Twelve Traditions – Page 17.2 – British Edition
[24] The Language of the Heart – Page 333.3
[25] Experience, Strength, & Hope – Page(s) 309.5
[26] Pass It On—Bill Wilson and the AA Message – Page 356.2
[27] Alcoholics Anonymous – Page 348.2 – 4th Edition
[28] Alcoholics Anonymous – Preface – Page xii.2
[29] Alcoholics Anonymous – Page 58.2
[30] Alcoholics Anonymous – Page 425.5 – 4th Edition
[31] Alcoholics Anonymous – Page 525.3 – 4th Edition
[32] Alcoholics Anonymous – Page 557.1 – 4th Edition
[33] Experience, Strength, & Hope – Page(s) 342.3
[34] Came to Believe... – Page(s) – 120.3
[35] Experience, Strength, & Hope – Page(s) 165.2
[36] Alcoholics Anonymous – Page 510.1 – 4th Edition
[37] Alcoholics Anonymous – Page 45.1-2
[38] Alcoholics Anonymous – Page 546.2 – 4th Edition
[39] As Bill Sees It – Page 72.1
[40] Twelve Steps and Twelve Traditions – Page 45.2 – British Edition
[41] Twelve Steps and Twelve Traditions – Page 44.4 – British Edition
[42] Twelve Steps and Twelve Traditions – Page 54.3 – British Edition
[43] Alcoholics Anonymous – Page 419.5 – 4th Edition
[44] Best of the Grapevine – Page(s) – 26.6 – 27.1
[45] Best of the Grapevine – Page(s) – 129.1
[46] Best of the Grapevine – Page(s) – 133.2,9, 134.1, 135.2,6,7
[47] Alcoholics Anonymous – Page 69.3
[48] Twelve Steps and Twelve Traditions – Page 55.1 – British Edition
[49] Twelve Steps and Twelve Traditions – Page 72.2-3 – British Edition
[50] Twelve Steps and Twelve Traditions – Page 77.4 – British Edition
[51] Alcoholics Anonymous – Page 127.2

[52] Experience, Strength, & Hope – Page(s) 34.3
[53] AA Comes of Age – Page 311.2
[54] Alcoholics Anonymous – Page 547.1 – 4th Edition
[55] Alcoholics Anonymous – Page 30.3
[56] Alcoholics Anonymous – Page 62.2
[57] Alcoholics Anonymous – Page 62.3
[58] Alcoholics Anonymous – Page 27.5
[59] Twelve Steps and Twelve Traditions – Page 33.1 – British Edition
[60] Alcoholics Anonymous – Page 396.3 – 4th Edition
[61] Alcoholics Anonymous – Page 521.3 – 4th Edition
[62] Alcoholics Anonymous – Page 45.2-3
[63] Best of the Grapevine – Page(s) – 49.6
[64] Alcoholics Anonymous – Page 308.2-5 – 4th Edition
[65] Twelve Steps and Twelve Traditions – Page 5 – British Edition
[66] Alcoholics Anonymous – Page 541.2 – 4th Edition
[67] Alcoholics Anonymous – Page 541.2 – 4th Edition
[68] Alcoholics Anonymous – Page 457.4 – 4th Edition
[69] Alcoholics Anonymous – Page 510.1 – 4th Edition
[70] The Language of the Heart – Page 8.4
[71] Experience, Strength, & Hope – Page(s) 138.7
[72] Twelve Steps and Twelve Traditions – Page 116.4 – 117.1 – British Edition
[73] As Bill Sees It – Page 191.1
[74] Experience, Strength, & Hope – Page(s) 12.3
[75] Alcoholics Anonymous – Page 17.2
[76] Alcoholics Anonymous – Page 133.1
[77] Alcoholics Anonymous – Page 429.2 – 4th Edition
[78] Alcoholics Anonymous – Page 493.4 – 4th Edition
[79] Alcoholics Anonymous – Page 58.1
[80] As Bill Sees It – Page 35.1
[81] The Language of the Heart – Page 301.4
[82] Came to Believe… – Page(s) – 5.2
[83] Alcoholics Anonymous – Page 275.1 – 4th Edition
[84] Language of the Heart – Page 196.2
[85] Language of the Heart – Page 197.3
[86] Alcoholics Anonymous – Page 263.1 – 4th Edition
[87] Language of the Heart – Page 201.2-3
[88] Twelve Steps and Twelve Traditions – Page 6 – British Edition
[89] Language of the Heart – Page 197.5 – 198.1
[90] Alcoholics Anonymous – Page 498.2 – 4th Edition
[91] Twelve Steps and Twelve Traditions – Page 37.3 – British Edition
[92] Came to Believe… – Page(s) – 85.6
[93] Alcoholics Anonymous – Page 83 – 84
[94] As Bill Sees It – Page 291.1
[95] Alcoholics Anonymous – Page xiv
[96] As Bill Sees It – Page 238
[97] Alcoholics Anonymous – Page 58.3
[98] Twelve Steps and Twelve Traditions – Page 15.6 – 16.1 – British Edition
[99] Alcoholics Anonymous – Page 164.3
[100] Pass It On—Bill Wilson and the AA Message – Page 352.4,5
[101] Pass It On—Bill Wilson and the AA Message – Page 352.5
[102] DR. BOB and the Good Oldtimers – Page 192.7,8
[103] DR. BOB and the Good Oldtimers – Page 227.2,3
[104] Came to Believe… – Page(s) – 118.5
[105] Best of the Grapevine – Page(s) – 125.1

106 Best of the Grapevine – Page(s) – 125.2
107 Best of the Grapevine – Page(s) – 126.4
108 Best of the Grapevine – Page(s) – 127.2,3
109 Experience, Strength, & Hope – Page(s) 378.2
110 Experience, Strength, & Hope – Page(s) 378.3
111 Best of the Grapevine – Page(s) – 128.2
112 Experience, Strength, & Hope – Page(s) 390.3,4
113 Came to Believe... – Page(s) – 26.2
114 Alcoholics Anonymous – Page 164.4
115 Alcoholics Anonymous – Page 164.4
116 Alcoholics Anonymous – Page 164.4
117 Alcoholics Anonymous – Page 59 – 60
118 Came to Believe... – Page(s) – 64.7
119 Alcoholics Anonymous – Page 59.4.1
120 Alcoholics Anonymous – Page 59.4
121 The Language of the Heart – Page 297.4
122 Twelve Steps and Twelve Traditions – Page 5 – British Edition
123 Came to Believe... – Page(s) – 87.1
124 Came to Believe... – Page(s) – 3.1
125 Alcoholics Anonymous – Page 59.4
126 Alcoholics Anonymous – Page 30.2
127 Alcoholics Anonymous – Page 416.4 – 4th Edition
128 Alcoholics Anonymous – Page 417.1-2 – 4th Edition
129 Alcoholics Anonymous – Page 443.2 – 4th Edition
130 Experience, Strength, & Hope – Page(s) 98.3
131 Alcoholics Anonymous – Page 402.1 – 4th Edition
132 Alcoholics Anonymous – Page 397.1 – 4th Edition
133 Alcoholics Anonymous – Page 443.2 – 4th Edition
134 Alcoholics Anonymous – Page 514.4 – 4th Edition
135 Best of the Grapevine – Page(s) – 182.4
136 Alcoholics Anonymous Comes of Age – Page 311.2
137 Alcoholics Anonymous – Page 553.4 – 4th Edition
138 DR. BOB and the Good Oldtimers – Page 146.3
139 Alcoholics Anonymous – Page xxvi
140 Alcoholics Anonymous – Page xxviii
141 DR. BOB and the Good Oldtimers – Page 92.5
142 Alcoholics Anonymous – Page 33.2
143 DR. BOB and the Good Oldtimers – Page 113.6 – 114.1
144 Alcoholics Anonymous – Page 271.1 – 4th Edition
145 Alcoholics Anonymous – Page 269.2, 270.2 – 4th Edition
146 Alcoholics Anonymous – Page 269-272.1 – 4th Edition
147 Alcoholics Anonymous – Page 443.2 – 4th Edition
148 Alcoholics Anonymous – Page xxvi
149 Alcoholics Anonymous – Page xxx.3 – xxx.6
150 Alcoholics Anonymous – Page 30.1
151 Alcoholics Anonymous – Page 24
152 Alcoholics Anonymous – Page 45
153 The Language of the Heart – Page 285.2
154 DR. BOB and the Good Oldtimers – Page 39.2
155 Twelve Steps and Twelve Traditions – Page 23 – British Edition
156 Alcoholics Anonymous – Page 18.4
157 Alcoholics Anonymous – Page 42.2
158 Alcoholics Anonymous – Page 42.2
159 The Language of the Heart – Page 280.5

[160] The Language of the Heart – Page 281.3
[161] Alcoholics Anonymous – Page 27.5
[162] As Bill Sees It – Page 32.3
[163] Twelve Steps and Twelve Traditions – Page 22.2 – British Edition
[164] Alcoholics Anonymous – Page 451.2 – 4th Edition
[165] Alcoholics Anonymous – Page 561.2 – 4th Edition
[166] Alcoholics Anonymous – Page 562.1 – 4th Edition
[167] Alcoholics Anonymous – Page 302.2
[168] Alcoholics Anonymous – Page 39
[169] Alcoholics Anonymous – Page 30.2
[170] Alcoholics Anonymous – Page 467.3 – 4th Edition
[171] Came to Believe... – Page(s) – 3.1
[172] As Bill Sees It – Page 98.2-3
[173] As Bill Sees It – Page 184
[174] Pass It On—Bill Wilson and the AA Message – Page 252.6
[175] As Bill Sees It – Page 99.1
[176] Twelve Steps and Twelve Traditions – Page 69.3 – British Edition
[177] Experience, Strength, & Hope – Page(s) 54.5, 55.1
[178] Experience, Strength, & Hope – Page(s) 341.4 – 342.2
[179] Alcoholics Anonymous – Page 59.4.1
[180] Alcoholics Anonymous – Page 59.4.1
[181] Twelve Steps and Twelve Traditions – Page 23.2 – British Edition
[182] Experience, Strength, & Hope – Page(s) 390.2
[183] Alcoholics Anonymous – Page 556.2 – 4th Edition
[184] As Bill Sees It – Page 114.2
[185] Alcoholics Anonymous – Page 550.2 – 4th Edition
[186] Twelve Steps and Twelve Traditions – Page 77 – British Edition
[187] Experience, Strength, & Hope – Page(s) 423.5
[188] Alcoholics Anonymous – Page 64.1
[189] Language of the Heart – Page 234.2
[190] Alcoholics Anonymous – Page 549.3 – 4th Edition
[191] Twelve Steps and Twelve Traditions – Page 21.2 – British Edition
[192] Twelve Steps and Twelve Traditions – Page 21.3 – British Edition
[193] As Bill Sees It – Page 251.3
[194] Alcoholics Anonymous – Page 60.3
[195] Alcoholics Anonymous – Page 60.5
[196] AA Comes of Age – Page 46
[197] Alcoholics Anonymous – Page 25.2
[198] As Bill Sees It – Page 283.4
[199] Came to Believe... – Page(s) – 86.4
[200] The Language of the Heart – Page 273.1,2
[201] Came to Believe... – Page(s) – 3.3
[202] Twelve Steps and Twelve Traditions – Page 22.2 – British Edition
[203] Alcoholics Anonymous – Page 60.4
[204] Twelve Steps and Twelve Traditions – Page 21.2 – British Edition
[205] Twelve Steps and Twelve Traditions – Page 21.4 – British Edition
[206] Twelve Steps and Twelve Traditions – Page 23.1 – British Edition
[207] Alcoholics Anonymous – Page 42.3
[208] Twelve Steps and Twelve Traditions – Page 24.3 – British Edition
[209] Twelve Steps and Twelve Traditions – British Edition – Page 110.3
[210] Best of the Grapevine – Page(s) – 182.5 – 183.1
[211] Came to Believe... – Page(s) – 27.1
[212] Twelve Steps and Twelve Traditions – Page 22.1 – British Edition
[213] Alcoholics Anonymous – Page 60.5

[214] Alcoholics Anonymous – Page 59.4.2
[215] Alcoholics Anonymous – Page 59.4.2
[216] Alcoholics Anonymous – Page 25.2
[217] Twelve Steps and Twelve Traditions – Page 25.1 – British Edition
[218] Alcoholics Anonymous – Page 44.1
[219] Alcoholics Anonymous – Page 366.2 – 4th Edition
[220] Alcoholics Anonymous – Page 25
[221] Alcoholics Anonymous – Page 43.3
[222] Alcoholics Anonymous – Page 42.1
[223] Came to Believe… – Page(s) – 119.5
[224] Alcoholics Anonymous – Page 10.4
[225] Twelve Steps and Twelve Traditions – Page 5 – British Edition
[226] Twelve Steps and Twelve Traditions – Page 22.2 – British Edition
[227] Twelve Steps and Twelve Traditions – Page 5 – British Edition
[228] Twelve Steps and Twelve Traditions – Page 27.1 – British Edition
[229] As Bill Sees It – Page 137.2
[230] Alcoholics Anonymous – Page 406.3 – 4th Edition
[231] DR. BOB and the Good Oldtimers – Page 194.1,2
[232] DR. BOB and the Good Oldtimers – Page 204.7 – 205.1
[233] Twelve Steps and Twelve Traditions – Page 26 – British Edition
[234] Alcoholics Anonymous – Page 397.3 – 4th Edition
[235] Alcoholics Anonymous – Page xxix.4 – 4th Edition
[236] Twelve Steps and Twelve Traditions – British Edition – Page 110.3
[237] Alcoholics Anonymous – Page 12.3,5
[238] Alcoholics Anonymous – Page 47.2
[239] Alcoholics Anonymous – Page 46.2
[240] Alcoholics Anonymous – Page 306.3 – 307.1 – 4th Edition
[241] Experience, Strength, & Hope – Page(s) 11.1 – 3
[242] Twelve Steps and Twelve Traditions – Page 27.2 – British Edition
[243] Alcoholics Anonymous – Page 47.3
[244] Alcoholics Anonymous – Page 568.3 – 4th Edition
[245] Twelve Steps and Twelve Traditions – Page 28.3 – 29.1 – British Edition
[246] As Bill Sees It – Page 4.3
[247] Came to Believe… – Page(s) – 98.2
[248] Experience, Strength, & Hope – Page(s) 13.2
[249] Experience, Strength, & Hope – Page(s) 14.2
[250] The Language of the Heart – Page 273.6
[251] Experience, Strength, & Hope – Page(s) 103.2, 104.1
[252] Experience, Strength, & Hope – Page(s) 104.4
[253] Experience, Strength, & Hope – Page(s) 105.2
[254] Experience, Strength, & Hope – Page(s) 106.2,3, 107.1
[255] Experience, Strength, & Hope – Page(s) 107.2
[256] Experience, Strength, & Hope – Page(s) 106.1
[257] Alcoholics Anonymous – Page 568.5 – 4th Edition
[258] Experience, Strength, & Hope – Page(s) 130.2
[259] Experience, Strength, & Hope – Page(s) 265.2
[260] Alcoholics Anonymous – Page 30.1
[261] Twelve Steps and Twelve Traditions – Page 31.1 – British Edition
[262] Twelve Steps and Twelve Traditions – Page 25.1 – British Edition
[263] Experience, Strength, & Hope – Page(s) 74.3
[264] Alcoholics Anonymous – Page 550.2 – 4th Edition
[265] Twelve Steps and Twelve Traditions – Page 33.2 – British Edition
[266] Twelve Steps and Twelve Traditions – Page 31.2 – British Edition
[267] Twelve Steps and Twelve Traditions – Page 32.2 – British Edition

[268] Alcoholics Anonymous – Page 366.3 – 4th Edition
[269] Best of the Grapevine – Page(s) – 50.2
[270] Alcoholics Anonymous – Page 46.3
[271] Alcoholics Anonymous – Page 47.1
[272] Alcoholics Anonymous – Page 59.4.3
[273] Alcoholics Anonymous – Page 59.4.3
[274] Twelve Steps and Twelve Traditions – Page 35 – British Edition
[275] Alcoholics Anonymous – Page 367.2 – 4th Edition
[276] Experience, Strength, & Hope – Page(s) 42.2
[277] Experience, Strength, & Hope – Page(s) 42.2
[278] Twelve Steps and Twelve Traditions – Page 73.3 – British Edition
[279] Alcoholics Anonymous – Page 551.1 – 4th Edition
[280] Experience, Strength, & Hope – Page(s) 81.3, 82.2
[281] Alcoholics Anonymous – Page 53
[282] Came to Believe... – Page(s) – 3.3
[283] Alcoholics Anonymous – Page 55
[284] Came to Believe... – Page(s) – 36.4
[285] Best of the Grapevine – Page(s) – 181.2
[286] Came to Believe... – Page(s) – 83.1
[287] Alcoholics Anonymous – Page 60.6
[288] Alcoholics Anonymous – Page 61.1
[289] Twelve Steps and Twelve Traditions – Page 6.1 – British Edition
[290] Twelve Steps and Twelve Traditions – Page 41.1 – British Edition
[291] Twelve Steps and Twelve Traditions – Page 41.2 – British Edition
[292] Twelve Steps and Twelve Traditions – Page 41.2 – British Edition
[293] Twelve Steps and Twelve Traditions – Page 41.3 – British Edition
[294] Twelve Steps and Twelve Traditions – Page 37.2, 3 – British Edition
[295] Twelve Steps and Twelve Traditions – Page 41.3 – British Edition
[296] Alcoholics Anonymous – Page 467.4 – 4th Edition
[297] Twelve Steps and Twelve Traditions – Page 41.3-42.2 – British Edition
[298] Alcoholics Anonymous – Page 60.8-62.3
[299] The Language of the Heart – Page 8.2
[300] Twelve Steps and Twelve Traditions – Page 39.2 – British Edition
[301] Experience, Strength, & Hope – Page(s) 40.2
[302] Alcoholics Anonymous – Page 63.4
[303] Alcoholics Anonymous – Page 417.3 – 4th Edition
[304] Experience, Strength, & Hope – Page(s) 201.2
[305] Experience, Strength, & Hope – Page(s) 201.2
[306] Alcoholics Anonymous – Page 63.4-64.2
[307] Twelve Steps and Twelve Traditions – Page 36.1 – British Edition
[308] Alcoholics Anonymous – Page 63.2-3
[309] Came to Believe... – Page(s) – 86.4
[310] Came to Believe... – Page(s) – 115.6 -116.1,4
[311] Experience, Strength, & Hope – Page(s) 22.2
[312] Experience, Strength, & Hope – Page(s) 47.1,2
[313] Alcoholics Anonymous – Page 64.1
[314] Twelve Steps and Twelve Traditions – Page 6 – British Edition
[315] Pass It On—Bill Wilson and the AA Message – Page 297.2
[316] The Language of the Heart – Page 279.3
[317] Revised from the Science of Mind magazine November 1999 Vol. 72 No. 11
[318] Alcoholics Anonymous – Page 46.3
[319] Alcoholics Anonymous – Page 68.3
[320] Twelve Steps and Twelve Traditions – Page 37.4 – British Edition
[321] Twelve Steps and Twelve Traditions – Page 37.3 – British Edition

[322] As Bill Sees It – Page 63
[323] Alcoholics Anonymous – Page 47.1
[324] Alcoholics Anonymous – Page 47.1
[325] DR. BOB and the Good Oldtimers – Page 85.7
[326] DR. BOB and the Good Oldtimers – Page 92.11 – 93.1
[327] Came to Believe... – Page(s) – 24.6
[328] Experience, Strength, & Hope – Page(s) 254.5
[329] Experience, Strength, & Hope – Page(s) 112.7, 113.1
[330] Came to Believe... – Page(s) – 100.3
[331] Came to Believe... – Page(s) – 102.6
[332] Came to Believe... – Page(s) – 60.2,6,7, 61.2
[333] Came to Believe... – Page(s) – 15.7
[334] Alcoholics Anonymous – Page 59.2
[335] Twelve Steps and Twelve Traditions – Page 35.2 – British Edition
[336] Best of the Grapevine – Page(s) – 17.4 – 18.1
[337] DR. BOB and the Good Oldtimers – Page 101.3,4, 102.1
[338] Came to Believe... – Page(s) – 29.2
[339] Twelve Steps and Twelve Traditions – Page 51.2 – British Edition
[340] Twelve Steps and Twelve Traditions – Page 44.2 – British Edition
[341] Alcoholics Anonymous – Page 63.4 – 64.2
[342] DR. BOB and the Good Oldtimers – Page 88.11 – 89.1
[343] Alcoholics Anonymous – Page 516.4 – 4th Edition
[344] Alcoholics Anonymous – Page 63.2
[345] Alcoholics Anonymous – Page 59.4.4
[346] Alcoholics Anonymous – Page 59.4.4
[347] DR. BOB and the Good Oldtimers – Page 102.1
[348] Alcoholics Anonymous – Page 88.4
[349] Alcoholics Anonymous – Page 534.2 – 4th Edition
[350] Alcoholics Anonymous – Page 373.5
[351] Alcoholics Anonymous – Page 64.1
[352] Alcoholics Anonymous – Page xxvi
[353] Twelve Steps and Twelve Traditions – Page 55.3 – British Edition
[354] As Bill Sees It – Page 140.3
[355] Twelve Steps and Twelve Traditions – British Edition – Page 111.1
[356] The Carl Rogers Reader, from Client-Centred Therapy—1951
[357] The Language of the Heart – Page 135.1
[358] Twelve Steps and Twelve Traditions – Page 48.3 – British Edition
[359] Twelve Steps and Twelve Traditions – Page 48.3 – British Edition
[360] Twelve Steps and Twelve Traditions – Page 48.4 – British Edition
[361] Twelve Steps and Twelve Traditions – Page 32.3 – British Edition
[362] Twelve Steps and Twelve Traditions – Page 32.4 – British Edition
[363] Twelve Steps and Twelve Traditions – Page 33.1 – British Edition
[364] Alcoholics Anonymous – Page 547.2 – 4th Edition
[365] As Bill Sees It – Page 68.2
[366] The Language of the Heart – Page 255.3
[367] Experience, Strength, & Hope – Page(s) 212.3
[368] Language of the Heart – Page 238.2
[369] Best of the Grapevine – Page(s) – 27.5
[370] Alcoholics Anonymous – Page 63-65
[371] Twelve Steps and Twelve Traditions – Page 6 – British Edition
[372] Experience, Strength, & Hope – Page(s) 218.2
[373] Experience, Strength, & Hope – Page(s) 309.1
[374] Experience, Strength, & Hope – Page(s) 327.3
[375] Twelve Steps and Twelve Traditions – Page 6 – British Edition

[376] Twelve Steps and Twelve Traditions – Page 45.2 – British Edition
[377] Twelve Steps and Twelve Traditions – Page 65.2 – British Edition
[378] Came to Believe... – Page(s) – 86.3
[379] Twelve Steps and Twelve Traditions – Page 43.1 – British Edition
[380] Twelve Steps and Twelve Traditions – Page 43.1 – 44.2– British Edition
[381] Alcoholics Anonymous – Page 65.8 – 66.4
[382] Alcoholics Anonymous – Page 64.3
[383] Twelve Steps and Twelve Traditions – Page 46.1 – British Edition
[384] Twelve Steps and Twelve Traditions – Page 55.3 – British Edition
[385] Alcoholics Anonymous – Page 263.2 – 4th Edition
[386] Alcoholics Anonymous – Page 468.2 – 4th Edition
[387] Alcoholics Anonymous – Page 66.5 – 67.3
[388] Alcoholics Anonymous – Page 467.3 – 4th Edition
[389] The Language of the Heart – Page 259.5 – 260.1
[390] The Language of the Heart – Page 260.3
[391] Alcoholics Anonymous – Page 62.1
[392] Alcoholics Anonymous – Page 62.3
[393] Alcoholics Anonymous – Page 62.2
[394] Twelve Steps and Twelve Traditions – Page 39.1 – British Edition
[395] Twelve Steps and Twelve Traditions – Page 39.1 – British Edition
[396] Experience, Strength, & Hope – Page(s) 212.2
[397] Experience, Strength, & Hope – Page(s) 424.2
[398] Came to Believe... – Page(s) – 98.1
[399] Best of the Grapevine – Page(s) – 25.5,7
[400] Alcoholics Anonymous – Page 544.3 – 4th Edition
[401] Twelve Steps and Twelve Traditions – Page 6 – British Edition
[402] Experience, Strength, & Hope – Page(s) 130.3
[403] Experience, Strength, & Hope – Page(s) 131.1
[404] Alcoholics Anonymous – Page 62.2
[405] The Language of the Heart – Page 261.2
[406] Twelve Steps and Twelve Traditions – Page 77.4 – British Edition
[407] The Language of the Heart – Page 265.1,3,4
[408] Alcoholics Anonymous – Page 67.4 – 68.3
[409] The Language of the Heart – Page 271.1
[410] Twelve Steps and Twelve Traditions – Page 128.1 – British Edition
[411] Alcoholics Anonymous – Page 68.4
[412] The Language of the Heart – Page 267.2
[413] The Language of the Heart – Page 268.3
[414] The Language of the Heart – Page 268.1,2
[415] Came to Believe... – Page(s) – 103.11 – 104.1
[416] Alcoholics Anonymous – Page 68.2
[417] Alcoholics Anonymous – Page 68.2
[418] Alcoholics Anonymous – Page 62.2
[419] Alcoholics Anonymous – Page 62.3
[420] Best of the Grapevine – Page(s) – 128.2
[421] Experience, Strength, & Hope – Page(s) 40.3, 41.1
[422] Experience, Strength, & Hope – Page(s) 335.3
[423] Experience, Strength, & Hope – Page(s) 332.1
[424] Experience, Strength, & Hope – Page(s) 213.1
[425] Twelve Steps and Twelve Traditions – Page 53.4 – British Edition
[426] Experience, Strength, & Hope – Page(s) 330.3
[427] Experience, Strength, & Hope – Page(s) 214.2
[428] Think and Grow Rich – Napoleon Hill
[429] Alcoholics Anonymous – Page 62.2

430 Twelve Steps and Twelve Traditions – Page 127.2 – British Edition
431 DR. BOB and the Good Oldtimers – Page 158.2
432 Alcoholics Anonymous – Page 65
433 Alcoholics Anonymous – Page 68
434 Alcoholics Anonymous – Page 80.5 – 81.1
435 Alcoholics Anonymous – Page 68-70
436 Twelve Steps and Twelve Traditions – Page 83.1 – British Edition
437 Alcoholics Anonymous – Page 69.4
438 Alcoholics Anonymous – Page 69.3
439 Alcoholics Anonymous – Page 67.2 and 68.5 – 69.3
440 Twelve Steps and Twelve Traditions – Page 52.2 and 53.4 – 54.1 – British Edition
441 Twelve Steps and Twelve Traditions – Page 82.3 – 83.1 – British Edition
442 Alcoholics Anonymous – Page 62, 69
443 Twelve Steps and Twelve Traditions – Pages 52.3 – 53.2 – British Edition
444 As Bill Sees It – Page 84.2
445 Best of the Grapevine – Page(s) – 77.1
446 Twelve Steps and Twelve Traditions – Page 125.2 – 126.2 – British Edition
447 The Home Group: Heartbeat of AA – Page 54.2
448 The Home Group: Heartbeat of AA – Page 56.3,4
449 Twelve Steps and Twelve Traditions – Page 128.3 – 129.1 – British Edition
450 DR. BOB and the Good Oldtimers – Page 128.7
451 Best of the Grapevine – Page(s) – 77.3
452 Experience, Strength, & Hope – Page(s) 117.1
453 Twelve Steps and Twelve Traditions – Pages 52.3 – British Edition
454 Experience, Strength, & Hope – Page(s) 31.6
455 Twelve Steps and Twelve Traditions – Pages 52.3 – 53.2 – British Edition
456 Alcoholics Anonymous – Page 70-71
457 The Language of the Heart – Page 264.7
458 Twelve Steps and Twelve Traditions – Page 6 – British Edition
459 Twelve Steps and Twelve Traditions – Page 51.2 – British Edition
460 As Bill Sees It – Page 172.1
461 Alcoholics Anonymous – Page 59.4.5
462 Alcoholics Anonymous – Page 59.4.5
463 Twelve Steps and Twelve Traditions – Page 111.1 – British Edition
464 Alcoholics Anonymous – Page 72.1
465 Twelve Steps and Twelve Traditions – Page 56.1 – 57.2 – British Edition
466 Alcoholics Anonymous – Page 72.2
467 Twelve Steps and Twelve Traditions – Page 62.3 – British Edition
468 Alcoholics Anonymous – Page 72.1
469 Alcoholics Anonymous – Pages 72.2 – 73.4
470 Twelve Steps and Twelve Traditions – Page 57.3 – British Edition
471 Twelve Steps and Twelve Traditions – Page 60.2 – British Edition
472 Twelve Steps and Twelve Traditions – Page 61.3 – British Edition
473 Alcoholics Anonymous – Pages 73.4 – 74.1
474 Twelve Steps and Twelve Traditions – Page 60.3 – British Edition
475 Twelve Steps and Twelve Traditions – Page 61.2 – British Edition
476 Alcoholics Anonymous – Page 74.1
477 Alcoholics Anonymous – Page 74.2
478 Alcoholics Anonymous – Page 74.3
479 Twelve Steps and Twelve Traditions – Page 62.2 – British Edition
480 Twelve Steps and Twelve Traditions – Page 47.3 – British Edition
481 Twelve Steps and Twelve Traditions – Page 47.3 – British Edition
482 Twelve Steps and Twelve Traditions – Page 6 – British Edition
483 Alcoholics Anonymous – Page 74.3 – 75.1

[484] Alcoholics Anonymous – Page 75.2,3
[485] As Bill Sees It – Page 44.1
[486] As Bill Sees It – Page 111.3
[487] Twelve Steps and Twelve Traditions – Page 63.1 – British Edition
[488] Twelve Steps and Twelve Traditions – Page 57.4 – British Edition
[489] Twelve Steps and Twelve Traditions – Page 58.1 – British Edition
[490] Experience, Strength, & Hope – Page(s) 21.3
[491] Twelve Steps and Twelve Traditions – Page 58.2 – British Edition
[492] Twelve Steps and Twelve Traditions – Page 59.1 – British Edition
[493] Twelve Steps and Twelve Traditions – Page 6 – British Edition
[494] Experience, Strength, & Hope – Page(s) 282.2
[495] Alcoholics Anonymous – Page 75.4
[496] Alcoholics Anonymous – Page 73.5 – 74.1
[497] Came to Believe… – Page(s) – 27.1
[498] Alcoholics Anonymous – Page 75.4
[499] Alcoholics Anonymous – Page 468.2 – 4th Edition
[500] Alcoholics Anonymous – Page 71.1
[501] Alcoholics Anonymous – Page 71.1
[502] Daily Reflections Page 243.2,3
[503] Came to Believe… – Page(s) – 97.6 – 98.1
[504] DR. BOB and the Good Oldtimers – Page 102.3
[505] Twelve Steps and Twelve Traditions – Page 6 – British Edition
[506] Alcoholics Anonymous – Page 59.4.6
[507] Alcoholics Anonymous – Page 59.4.6
[508] Alcoholics Anonymous – Page 164.3
[509] Twelve Steps and Twelve Traditions – Page 64
[510] Twelve Steps and Twelve Traditions – Page 66
[511] Twelve Steps and Twelve Traditions – Page 45.3 – British Edition
[512] As Bill Sees It – Page 10.3
[513] Twelve Steps and Twelve Traditions – Page 111.1 – British Edition
[514] Experience, Strength, & Hope – Page(s) 274.1
[515] Twelve Steps and Twelve Traditions – Page 7 – British Edition
[516] Twelve Steps and Twelve Traditions – Page 45.3 – British Edition
[517] Alcoholics Anonymous – Page 72.1
[518] Twelve Steps and Twelve Traditions – Page 64.1 – British Edition
[519] Twelve Steps and Twelve Traditions – Page 7 – British Edition
[520] Twelve Steps and Twelve Traditions – Page 56.2 – British Edition
[521] Twelve Steps and Twelve Traditions – Page 49.4 – British Edition
[522] Twelve Steps and Twelve Traditions – Page 50.2 – British Edition
[523] Twelve Steps and Twelve Traditions – Page 50.3 – 51.1 – British Edition
[524] Twelve Steps and Twelve Traditions – Page 64.1 – British Edition
[525] The Language of the Heart – Page 259.1
[526] Twelve Steps and Twelve Traditions – Page 59.3 – British Edition
[527] Twelve Steps and Twelve Traditions – Page 59.3 – British Edition
[528] Alcoholics Anonymous – Page 76
[529] Alcoholics Anonymous – Page 59.4.7
[530] Alcoholics Anonymous – Page 59.4.7
[531] Daily Reflections Page 202.2
[532] Twelve Steps and Twelve Traditions – Page 71.1-3 – British Edition
[533] Twelve Steps and Twelve Traditions – Page 72.3,4 – British Edition
[534] Twelve Steps and Twelve Traditions – Page 73.2 – British Edition
[535] Twelve Steps and Twelve Traditions – Page 73.3 – British Edition
[536] Twelve Steps and Twelve Traditions – Page 7 – British Edition
[537] Twelve Steps and Twelve Traditions – Page 74.2 – British Edition

[538] Twelve Steps and Twelve Traditions – Pages 75.3 – 76.1 – British Edition
[539] Language of the Heart – Page 254.6 – 255.1
[540] Twelve Steps and Twelve Traditions – Page 76.2 – British Edition
[541] Twelve Steps and Twelve Traditions – Page 115.2 – British Edition
[542] Came to Believe... – Page(s) – 12.1
[543] Twelve Steps and Twelve Traditions – Page 76.3-4 – British Edition
[544] Twelve Steps and Twelve Traditions – Page 77.2 – British Edition
[545] Twelve Steps and Twelve Traditions – Page 77.4 – British Edition
[546] Twelve Steps and Twelve Traditions – Page 78.2 – British Edition
[547] Alcoholics Anonymous – Page 72.1
[548] Alcoholics Anonymous – Page 72.2
[549] DR. BOB and the Good Oldtimers – Page 222.5
[550] Alcoholics Anonymous – Page 66.1
[551] As Bill Sees It – Page 211.2
[552] Twelve Steps and Twelve Traditions – Page 78.2 – British Edition
[553] Alcoholics Anonymous – Page 76.2
[554] The Language of the Heart – Page 300.3
[555] DR. BOB and the Good Old Timers – Page 179.5,6
[556] The Carl Rogers Reader, from Client-Centred Therapy—1951
[557] Alcoholics Anonymous – Page 76.2
[558] Alcoholics Anonymous – Page 59.4.8
[559] Twelve Steps and Twelve Traditions – Page 79.1 – British Edition
[560] Twelve Steps and Twelve Traditions – Page 111.1 – British Edition
[561] Alcoholics Anonymous – Page 76.3
[562] Twelve Steps and Twelve Traditions – Page 7 – British Edition
[563] Twelve Steps and Twelve Traditions – Page 79.1 – 80.2 – British Edition
[564] Twelve Steps and Twelve Traditions – Page 95.2 – British Edition
[565] Daily Reflections Page 230.2
[566] Came to Believe... – Page(s) – 27.1
[567] Came to Believe... – Page(s) – 86.3,5
[568] Alcoholics Anonymous – Page 13.4
[569] Alcoholics Anonymous – Page 76.4
[570] Alcoholics Anonymous – Page 66.5 – 67.2
[571] Twelve Steps and Twelve Traditions – Page 80.4 – 81.1 – British Edition
[572] Twelve Steps and Twelve Traditions – Page 7 – British Edition
[573] Twelve Steps and Twelve Traditions – Page 48.2 – British Edition
[574] Twelve Steps and Twelve Traditions – Page 81.2,3 – British Edition
[575] Twelve Steps and Twelve Traditions – Page 48.2 – British Edition
[576] Twelve Steps and Twelve Traditions – Page 61.3 – 62.1 – British Edition
[577] Alcoholics Anonymous – Page 69.4
[578] Twelve Steps and Twelve Traditions – Page 84.1 – British Edition
[579] Twelve Steps and Twelve Traditions – Page 80.3 – British Edition
[580] Alcoholics Anonymous – Page 76.3-4
[581] Twelve Steps and Twelve Traditions – Page 80.2 – British Edition
[582] Alcoholics Anonymous – Page 67.3
[583] Alcoholics Anonymous – Page 69.4
[584] Alcoholics Anonymous – Page 552.2–3 – 4th Edition
[585] Twelve Steps and Twelve Traditions – Page 84.1 – British Edition
[586] Alcoholics Anonymous – Page 13.4
[587] Alcoholics Anonymous – Page 70.4
[588] Twelve Steps and Twelve Traditions – Page 82.1,2 – British Edition
[589] Twelve Steps and Twelve Traditions – Page 82.1,2 – British Edition
[590] Alcoholics Anonymous – Page 59.4.9
[591] Alcoholics Anonymous – Page 59.4.9

[592] Twelve Steps and Twelve Traditions – Page 79.1-2 – British Edition
[593] Twelve Steps and Twelve Traditions – Page 8 – British Edition
[594] Experience, Strength, & Hope – Page(s) 60.3
[595] Experience, Strength, & Hope – Page(s) 217.2
[596] Experience, Strength, & Hope – Page(s) 285.2
[597] Alcoholics Anonymous – Page 445.4 – 4th Edition
[598] Twelve Steps and Twelve Traditions – Page 86.1 – British Edition
[599] Alcoholics Anonymous – Page 74.2
[600] Twelve Steps and Twelve Traditions – Page 88.1 – British Edition
[601] Twelve Steps and Twelve Traditions – Page 86.2 – British Edition
[602] Alcoholics Anonymous – Page 67.3
[603] Alcoholics Anonymous – Page 13.4
[604] Alcoholics Anonymous – Page 79.2
[605] Alcoholics Anonymous – Page 74.2-3
[606] Alcoholics Anonymous – Page 80.1 2
[607] Alcoholics Anonymous – Page 526.2 – 4th Edition
[608] Twelve Steps and Twelve Traditions – Page 8.2 – British Edition
[609] Alcoholics Anonymous – Page 13.6 – 14.1
[610] Alcoholics Anonymous – Page 13.5
[611] Alcoholics Anonymous – Page 76.3
[612] Alcoholics Anonymous – Page 83.3
[613] Alcoholics Anonymous – Pages 77.3-78.1
[614] Alcoholics Anonymous – Page 83.1
[615] Twelve Steps and Twelve Traditions – Page 88.2 – British Edition
[616] Alcoholics Anonymous – Page 83.3
[617] Alcoholics Anonymous – Page 77.1-2
[618] Twelve Steps and Twelve Traditions – Page 88.2 – British Edition
[619] Daily Reflections Page 237.2
[620] Alcoholics Anonymous – Page 347.2 – 4th Edition
[621] Came to Believe… – Page(s) – 95.3
[622] Daily Reflections Page 244.2
[623] Alcoholics Anonymous – Page 83.1
[624] Alcoholics Anonymous – Page 80.5 – 81.1
[625] Came to Believe… – Page(s) – 24.4
[626] Alcoholics Anonymous – Page 74.2
[627] Alcoholics Anonymous – Page 15.3
[628] Alcoholics Anonymous – Page 15.3
[629] Alcoholics Anonymous – Page 79.1-2
[630] Alcoholics Anonymous – Page 77.2
[631] Alcoholics Anonymous – Page 78.2
[632] Alcoholics Anonymous – Page 78.3
[633] Alcoholics Anonymous – Pages 78.4 – 79.2
[634] Alcoholics Anonymous – Pages 78.4 – 79.2
[635] Alcoholics Anonymous – Page 83.1
[636] Alcoholics Anonymous – Page 85.3
[637] Twelve Steps and Twelve Traditions – Page 87.3 – British Edition
[638] Twelve Steps and Twelve Traditions – Page 88.1 – British Edition
[639] Alcoholics Anonymous – Page 85.2
[640] Alcoholics Anonymous – Page 14.2
[641] Came to Believe… – Page(s) – 118.8
[642] As Bill Sees It – Page 144.1-4
[643] Daily Reflections Page 235.2
[644] Alcoholics Anonymous – Page 67.1
[645] Twelve Steps and Twelve Traditions – Page 89.2 – British Edition

[646] Experience, Strength, & Hope – Page(s) 366.2,3
[647] Experience, Strength, & Hope – Page(s) 12.1
[648] Alcoholics Anonymous – Pages 83.4 – 84.2
[649] Twelve Steps and Twelve Traditions – Page 90.1 – British Edition
[650] Experience, Strength, & Hope – Page(s) 431.4
[651] Pass It On—Bill Wilson and the AA Message – Page 128.2
[652] Alcoholics Anonymous – Page 85.2
[653] Experience, Strength, & Hope – Page(s) 325.2
[654] Experience, Strength, & Hope – Page(s) 410.2
[655] Twelve Steps and Twelve Traditions – Page 8.4 – British Edition
[656] Came to Believe... – Page(s) – 116.5 – 6
[657] The Language of the Heart – Page 328.5
[658] The Language of the Heart – Page 329.1 – 329.5
[659] Experience, Strength, & Hope – Page(s) 410.1
[660] Experience, Strength, & Hope – Page(s) 390.4,5
[661] Experience, Strength, & Hope – Page(s) 399.5, 400.1
[662] Came to Believe... – Page(s) – 65.2
[663] Came to Believe... – Page(s) – 95.5,6, 96.1 – 3, 6,7, 97.2,3
[664] Alcoholics Anonymous – Page 8.3
[665] Alcoholics Anonymous – Page 60.2
[666] As Bill Sees It – Page 31.1
[667] Twelve Steps and Twelve Traditions – Page 8.6 – British Edition
[668] Alcoholics Anonymous Page – 60.1
[669] DR. BOB and the Good Oldtimers – Page 256.3
[670] The Language of the Heart – Page 300.2
[671] Jeremiah 9:23
[672] Alcoholics Anonymous – Page 85.2
[673] As Bill Sees It – Page 159.2-3
[674] As Bill Sees It – Page 267.2
[675] Language of the Heart – Page 235.4
[676] As Bill Sees It – Page 216.1-2
[677] Experience, Strength, & Hope – Page(s) 326.3
[678] Experience, Strength, & Hope – Page(s) 332.1
[679] Alcoholics Anonymous – Page 553.1 – 4th Edition
[680] As Bill Sees It – Page 30.1-3
[681] Alcoholics Anonymous – Page 553.1-2 – 4th Edition
[682] Alcoholics Anonymous – Page 16.3
[683] Alcoholics Anonymous – Page 25.2
[684] Alcoholics Anonymous – Page 25.3
[685] Alcoholics Anonymous – Page 48.1
[686] Alcoholics Anonymous – Page 510.1 – 4th Edition
[687] Alcoholics Anonymous – Page 511.1 – 4th Edition
[688] Alcoholics Anonymous – Page 511.2 – 4th Edition
[689] Alcoholics Anonymous – Page 28.2
[690] Alcoholics Anonymous – Page xiii.1
[691] Alcoholics Anonymous – Page 518.2 – 4th Edition
[692] Alcoholics Anonymous – Page 559.3 – 4th Edition
[693] DR. BOB and the Good Oldtimers – Page 119.2
[694] Best of the Grapevine – Page(s) – 128.3,5
[695] Best of the Grapevine – Page(s) – 171.2
[696] Experience, Strength, & Hope – Page(s) 69.1
[697] Alcoholics Anonymous – Page 541.3 – 4th Edition
[698] Alcoholics Anonymous – Page 275.2 – 4th Edition
[699] Twelve Steps and Twelve Traditions – Page 72– British Edition

700 Alcoholics Anonymous – Page 85.2
701 Alcoholics Anonymous – Page 29.2
702 Alcoholics Anonymous – Page 275.2 – 4th Edition
703 Experience, Strength, & Hope – Page(s) 315.5
704 Alcoholics Anonymous – Page 85.2
705 DR. BOB and the Good Oldtimers – Page 290.4
706 Alcoholics Anonymous – Page 541.2 – 4th Edition
707 Alcoholics Anonymous – Page 542.2 – 4th Edition
708 Best of the Grapevine – Page(s) – 12.8 – 13.5
709 Alcoholics Anonymous – Page 429.1 – 4th Edition
710 Daily Reflections – Page 72
711 Language of the Heart – Page 255.3
712 The Language of the Heart – Page 315.1-5, 316.6, 317.1
713 The Language of the Heart – Page 334.3
714 The Language of the Heart – Page 319.2
715 The Language of the Heart – Page 348.1
716 Daily Reflections Page 245.2
717 Daily Reflections Page 260.3
718 Twelve Steps and Twelve Traditions – British Edition – Page 9.3
719 Came to Believe... – Page(s) – 17.6
720 Alcoholics Anonymous – Page 60.1,2
721 Twelve Steps and Twelve Traditions – British Edition – Page 93.3
722 Best of the Grapevine – Page(s) – 184.2
723 Experience, Strength, & Hope – Page(s) 32.3
724 Experience, Strength, & Hope – Page(s) 218.2,3
725 Experience, Strength, & Hope – Page(s) 341.4 – 342.2
726 Best of the Grapevine – Page(s) – 18.3
727 Best of the Grapevine – Page(s) – 19.6
728 Best of the Grapevine – Page(s) – 20.2
729 Alcoholics Anonymous – Page 59.4.10
730 Alcoholics Anonymous – Page 59.4
731 Twelve Steps and Twelve Traditions – Page 90.1 – British Edition
732 Twelve Steps and Twelve Traditions – Page 112.1 – British Edition
733 Alcoholics Anonymous – Page 84.3
734 As Bill Sees It – Page 98.1
735 Alcoholics Anonymous – Page 84.4 – 85.2
736 Language of the Heart – Page 238.8
737 Twelve Steps and Twelve Traditions – Page 49.1 – British Edition
738 Alcoholics Anonymous – Page 265.1 – 4th Edition
739 Alcoholics Anonymous – Page 64.2
740 Language of the Heart – Page 239.6 – 240.1
741 Language of the Heart – Page 239.6 – 240.1
742 Twelve Steps and Twelve Traditions – Page 118.3 – British Edition
743 Alcoholics Anonymous – Page 60.5
744 Alcoholics Anonymous – Page 58.3
745 Alcoholics Anonymous – Page 66.1
746 Alcoholics Anonymous – Page 381.5 – 4th Edition
747 Twelve Steps and Twelve Traditions – Page 51.4 – 52.1 – British Edition
748 Daily Reflections Page 250.2
749 Twelve Steps and Twelve Traditions – Page 117.2 – British Edition
750 As Bill Sees It – Page 234.3
751 Alcoholics Anonymous – Page 64.2
752 The Language of the Heart – Page 321.5, 322.1-3
753 Twelve Steps and Twelve Traditions – Page 91.2 – British Edition

[754] Twelve Steps and Twelve Traditions – Page 91 – British Edition
[755] Twelve Steps and Twelve Traditions – Page 92.2,3 – British Edition
[756] Experience, Strength, & Hope – Page(s) 255.2
[757] Experience, Strength, & Hope – Page(s) 330.3
[758] Alcoholics Anonymous – Page 417.2 – 4th Edition
[759] Twelve Steps and Twelve Traditions – Page 92.3 – British Edition
[760] Twelve Steps and Twelve Traditions – Page 92.3,4 – 93.1 – British Edition
[761] Twelve Steps and Twelve Traditions – Page 94.4 – 95.1 – British Edition
[762] Living Sober – Page(s) 38.5,6
[763] Experience, Strength, & Hope – Page(s) 23.1
[764] Living Sober – Page(s) 38.8,9, 39.2,4,5,9
[765] Twelve Steps and Twelve Traditions – Page 93.1 – British Edition
[766] Twelve Steps and Twelve Traditions – Page 93.2 – British Edition
[767] Living Sober – Page(s) 40.8
[768] Twelve Steps and Twelve Traditions – Page 90.1 – British Edition
[769] As Bill Sees It – Page 58.1
[770] Twelve Steps and Twelve Traditions – Page 92.3 – British Edition
[771] *Re-written as a formula from the "Big Book" of* Alcoholics Anonymous *Page 84.3 the numbers and format are ours.*
[772] Alcoholics Anonymous – Page 84.4
[773] Alcoholics Anonymous – Page 67.4
[774] Alcoholics Anonymous – Page 68.3
[775] As Bill Sees It – Page 184.3
[776] Twelve Steps and Twelve Traditions – Page 93.3 – British Edition
[777] As Bill Sees It – Page 39.3
[778] Alcoholics Anonymous – Page 133.1
[779] Alcoholics Anonymous – Page 133.1
[780] Twelve Steps and Twelve Traditions – Page 91 – British Edition
[781] Twelve Steps and Twelve Traditions – Page 91.2 – British Edition
[782] Alcoholics Anonymous – Page 61.2
[783] Experience, Strength, & Hope – Page(s) 410.3,4
[784] Twelve Steps and Twelve Traditions – Page 97.2 – British Edition
[785] Experience, Strength, & Hope – Page(s) 431.2
[786] The Language of the Heart – Page 324.5
[787] Twelve Steps and Twelve Traditions – Page 97.2 – British Edition
[788] Twelve Steps and Twelve Traditions – Page 95.5 – 96.1 – British Edition
[789] Twelve Steps and Twelve Traditions – Page 96.2 – British Edition
[790] Alcoholics Anonymous – Page 86
[791] Came to Believe… – Page(s) – 26.4
[792] Alcoholics Anonymous – Page 529.3 – 4th Edition
[793] Alcoholics Anonymous – Page 86.2
[794] Alcoholics Anonymous – Page 84.3
[795] Alcoholics Anonymous – Page 84.4
[796] As Bill Sees It – Page 168.1
[797] Came to Believe… – Page(s) – 94.8 – 95.1
[798] Came to Believe… – Page(s) – 95.3
[799] Twelve Steps and Twelve Traditions – Page 91.2 – British Edition
[800] Alcoholics Anonymous – Page 59.3.5
[801] Alcoholics Anonymous – Page 72.2
[802] As Bill Sees It – Page 253.3
[803] Experience, Strength, & Hope – Page(s) 430.2
[804] Twelve Steps and Twelve Traditions – Page 79.1 – British Edition
[805] Experience, Strength, & Hope – Page(s) 424.3
[806] Daily Reflections – Page 70

807 Twelve Steps and Twelve Traditions – Page 95.2 – British Edition
808 DR. BOB and the Good Oldtimers – Page 105.1
809 Twelve Steps and Twelve Traditions – Page 98.1 – British Edition – 1999
810 Twelve Steps and Twelve Traditions – Page 98.1 – British Edition – 1999
811 Twelve Steps and Twelve Traditions – Page 100.2 – British Edition – 1999
812 Twelve Steps and Twelve Traditions – Page 112.1 – British Edition – 1999
813 The Language of the Heart – Page 240.8
814 Twelve Steps and Twelve Traditions – Page 98.2 – British Edition – 1999
815 Twelve Steps and Twelve Traditions – Page 98.1 – British Edition – 1999
816 Came to Believe... – Page(s) – 26.4
817 Alcoholics Anonymous – Page 64.4
818 Twelve Steps and Twelve Traditions – Page 99.3 - 100.1 – British Edition – 1999
819 As Bill Sees It – Page 294.1-3
820 Came to Believe... – Page(s) – 26.5
821 As Bill Sees It – Page 171.2
822 Twelve Steps and Twelve Traditions – Page 118.2 – British Edition – 1999
823 Came to Believe... – Page(s) – 100.2
824 The Language of the Heart – Page 240.3-8
825 Alcoholics Anonymous – Page 251.1 – 4th Edition
826 Came to Believe... – Page(s) – 47.4
827 Twelve Steps and Twelve Traditions – Page 77.1 – British Edition – 1999
828 The Language of the Heart – Page 240.9 – 241.4
829 Alcoholics Anonymous – Page 44.3
830 Alcoholics Anonymous – Page 53.3
831 Alcoholics Anonymous – Page 387.2 – 4th Edition
832 Alcoholics Anonymous – Page 35.4
833 The Language of the Heart – Page 242.2
834 Came to Believe... – Page(s) – 3.1
835 As Bill Sees It – Page 38.2
836 The Language of the Heart – Page 242.3-4
837 Experience, Strength, & Hope – Page(s) 236.1
838 Alcoholics Anonymous – Page 86.3 – 87.2
839 Alcoholics Anonymous – Page 87.3 – 88.2
840 A New Pair of Glasses – 28.4
841 Best of the Grapevine – Page(s) – 16.5
842 Twelve Steps and Twelve Traditions – Page 106.2 – British Edition – 1999
843 Pass It On—Bill Wilson and the AA Message – Page 172.7
844 Experience, Strength, & Hope – Page(s) 56.1
845 Alcoholics Anonymous – Page 86.2
846 As a Man Thinketh – James Allen
847 Alcoholics Anonymous – Page 527.2 – 4th Edition
848 Alcoholics Anonymous – Page 47.1
849 Came to Believe... – Page(s) – 103.2
850 Alcoholics Anonymous – Page 55.4
851 Alcoholics Anonymous – Page 60.2
852 Daily Reflections – Page 247.2
853 Twelve Steps and Twelve Traditions – Page 104.2 – British Edition – 1999
854 The Language of the Heart – Page 273.4
855 Twelve Steps and Twelve Traditions – Page 107.2 – British Edition – 1999
856 Twelve Steps and Twelve Traditions – Page 99.2 – British Edition – 1999
857 Best of the Grapevine – Page(s) – 196.1 – 3
858 Alcoholics Anonymous – Page 499.3 – 4th Edition
859 Alcoholics Anonymous – Page 49.1
860 Alcoholics Anonymous – Page 85.4 – 86.1

861 Twelve Steps and Twelve Traditions – Pages 130-3 – British Edition – 1999
862 Pass It On—Bill Wilson and the AA Message – Page 252.3
863 Experience, Strength, & Hope – Page(s) 430.3, 431.1
864 Came to Believe… – Page(s) – 111.2 – 5, 7
865 Experience, Strength, & Hope – Page(s) 153.2
866 The Language of the Heart – Page 270.4
867 Alcoholics Anonymous – Page 63.2
868 Alcoholics Anonymous – Page 76.2
869 Twelve Steps and Twelve Traditions – Pages 101-102 – British Edition – 1999
870 Language of the Heart – Page 258.8
871 Alcoholics Anonymous – Page 87.6
872 As Bill Sees It – Page 95.1
873 Daily Reflections Page 248.2
874 Alcoholics Anonymous – Page 88.1
875 Alcoholics Anonymous – Page 85.2
876 Twelve Steps and Twelve Traditions – Pages 105.2 – British Edition – 1999
877 Alcoholics Anonymous – Page 55.4
878 Alcoholics Anonymous – Page 86.4 -87.1
879 As Bill Sees It – Page 221.3
880 As Bill Sees It – Page 247.3
881 The Language of the Heart – Page 245.8 – 256.1
882 Experience, Strength, & Hope – Page(s) 286.4 – 287.1
883 DR. BOB and the Good Oldtimers – Page 261.1
884 Alcoholics Anonymous – Page 49.3
885 Twelve Steps and Twelve Traditions – Page 108.1 – British Edition – 1999
886 Twelve Steps and Twelve Traditions – Page 108.2 – British Edition – 1999
887 Alcoholics Anonymous – Page 87.3
888 Came to Believe… – Page(s) – 100.4 – 5
889 Best of the Grapevine – Page(s) – 171.6
890 DR. BOB and the Good Oldtimers – Page 178.4
891 Alcoholics Anonymous – Page 55.4
892 Alcoholics Anonymous – Page 55.5
893 Experience, Strength, & Hope – Page(s) 287.3
894 Alcoholics Anonymous – Page 29.3
895 Alcoholics Anonymous – Page 419.3 – 4th Edition
896 Alcoholics Anonymous – Page 55.4
897 Twelve Steps and Twelve Traditions – Pages 104.1 – British Edition – 1999
898 The Language of the Heart – Page 241.5 – 242.1
899 DR. BOB and the Good Oldtimers – Page 306.1
900 DR. BOB and the Good Oldtimers – Page 311.4
901 DR. BOB and the Good Oldtimers – Page 307.1 – 3, 307.5 – 308.2
902 DR. BOB and the Good Oldtimers – Page 308.6 – 309.1
903 DR. BOB and the Good Oldtimers – Page 309.5,7 – 310.1
904 Came to Believe… – Page(s) – 99.3
905 DR. BOB and the Good Oldtimers – Page 314.5
906 DR. BOB and the Good Oldtimers – Page 314.6
907 DR. BOB and the Good Oldtimers – Page 313.1
908 Experience, Strength, & Hope – Page(s) 127.5
909 Experience, Strength, & Hope – Page(s) 431.2
910 Alcoholics Anonymous – Page 60.1
911 Alcoholics Anonymous – Page 60.1
912 Twelve Steps and Twelve Traditions – Page 9.3 – British Edition
913 Twelve Steps and Twelve Traditions – Page 109.1 – British Edition
914 Alcoholics Anonymous – Page 60.1

[915] Twelve Steps and Twelve Traditions – Page 109.2 – British Edition
[916] Language of the Heart – Page 233.1
[917] Twelve Steps and Twelve Traditions – Page 9.3 – British Edition
[918] As Bill Sees It – Page 171.1
[919] Language of the Heart – Page 99.1
[920] Twelve Steps and Twelve Traditions – Page 110.1 – British Edition
[921] Came to Believe... – Page(s) – 65.2
[922] Alcoholics Anonymous – Page 374.1 – 4th Edition
[923] Came to Believe... – Page(s) – 48.2
[924] Alcoholics Anonymous – Page 84.2
[925] Pass It On—Bill Wilson and the AA Message – Page 120.7 – 121.1
[926] Pass It On—Bill Wilson and the AA Message – Page 121.3,4
[927] Pass It On—Bill Wilson and the AA Message – Page 124.2,4 – 125.2
[928] Came to Believe... – Page(s) – 66.3
[929] Pass It On—Bill Wilson and the AA Message – Page 127.4
[930] Came to Believe... – Page(s) – 35.1
[931] Alcoholics Anonymous – Page 567.1 – 4th Edition
[932] Alcoholics Anonymous – Page 567.4 – 4th Edition
[933] Alcoholics Anonymous – Page 568.2 – 4th Edition
[934] Language of the Heart – Page 251.2
[935] Alcoholics Anonymous – Page 14.7 – 15.1
[936] Language of the Heart – Page 98.4
[937] Language of the Heart – Page 98.4
[938] Language of the Heart – Page 98.5
[939] Twelve Steps and Twelve Traditions – British Edition – Page 110.2
[940] The Language of the Heart – Page 245.4
[941] Experience, Strength, & Hope – Page(s) 133.1,2
[942] Experience, Strength, & Hope – Page(s) 133.3 – 134.4
[943] Experience, Strength, & Hope – Page(s) 375.3,4
[944] Twelve Steps and Twelve Traditions – Page 112.3 – British Edition
[945] Twelve Steps and Twelve Traditions – Page 116.2 – British Edition
[946] Alcoholics Anonymous – Page xxii
[947] Alcoholics Anonymous – Page 14.6
[948] Language of the Heart – Page 246.3
[949] Twelve Steps and Twelve Traditions – Page 130.1 – British Edition
[950] Alcoholics Anonymous – Page 124.3
[951] Alcoholics Anonymous – Page 124.3
[952] Experience, Strength, & Hope – Page(s) 430.1
[953] Alcoholics Anonymous – Page 89.2
[954] Alcoholics Anonymous – Page 345.2
[955] Alcoholics Anonymous – Page 58.3
[956] Alcoholics Anonymous – Page 164.3
[957] Language of the Heart – Page 204.2
[958] Twelve Steps and Twelve Traditions – Page 113.1 – British Edition
[959] Experience, Strength, & Hope – Page(s) 266.3
[960] Experience, Strength, & Hope – Page(s) 12.1
[961] The Carl Rogers Reader, from Client-Centred Therapy—1951
[962] Alcoholics Anonymous – Page 133.1
[963] DR. BOB and the Good Oldtimers – Page 83.4
[964] DR. BOB and the Good Oldtimers – Page 92.1
[965] Experience, Strength, & Hope – Page(s) 236.1
[966] Experience, Strength, & Hope – Page(s) 244.3 – 245.1
[967] DR. BOB and the Good Oldtimers – Page 70.3
[968] DR. BOB and the Good Oldtimers – Page 234.4,5

969 Experience, Strength, & Hope – Page(s) 39.6 – 40.1
970 DR. BOB and the Good Oldtimers – Page 225.7 – 226.3
971 As Bill Sees It – Page 29.1-2
972 Alcoholics Anonymous Comes of Age – Page 67.6 – 68.1
973 As Bill Sees It – Page 242.1
974 Alcoholics Anonymous – Page 58.2
975 Alcoholics Anonymous – Page 58.2
976 Alcoholics Anonymous – Page 274.3 – 4th Edition
977 Alcoholics Anonymous – Page 449.3 – 4th Edition
978 Alcoholics Anonymous – Page 480.4 – 4th Edition
979 DR. BOB and the Good Oldtimers – Page 209.8
980 DR. BOB and the Good Oldtimers – Page 211.6
981 Experience, Strength, & Hope – Page(s) 81.4, 82.1
982 Alcoholics Anonymous – Page 58.2
983 Pass It On—Bill Wilson and the AA Message – Page 199.2
984 Alcoholics Anonymous – Page 261.2 – 4th Edition
985 Alcoholics Anonymous – Page 261.5 – 4th Edition
986 Alcoholics Anonymous – Page 262.1 – 4th Edition
987 Twelve Steps and Twelve Traditions – Page 24.1 – British Edition
988 Pass It On—Bill Wilson and the AA Message – Page 251.4
989 DR. BOB and the Good Oldtimers – Page 52.4,5
990 DR. BOB and the Good Oldtimers – Page 204.3
991 DR. BOB and the Good Oldtimers – Page 99.2
992 DR. BOB and the Good Oldtimers – Page 99.2
993 Alcoholics Anonymous – Page 58.3
994 Living Sober – Page(s) 26.5,6
995 The Language of the Heart – Page 264.2
996 Alcoholics Anonymous – Page 98
997 Alcoholics Anonymous – Page 542.2 – 4th Edition
998 DR. BOB and the Good Oldtimers – Page 243.3
999 DR. BOB and the Good Oldtimers – Page 134.3
1000 DR. BOB and the Good Oldtimers – Page 136.5
1001 DR. BOB and the Good Oldtimers – Page 246.3,4
1002 As Bill Sees It – Page 3.1
1003 As Bill Sees It – Page 158.1
1004 Language of the Heart – Page 247.5
1005 As Bill Sees It – Page 183.2
1006 As Bill Sees It – Page 183.3
1007 Pass It On—Bill Wilson and the AA Message – Page 250.1
1008 Alcoholics Anonymous – Page 253.3 – 4th Edition
1009 DR. BOB and the Good Oldtimers – Page 69.8
1010 Alcoholics Anonymous – Page 89
1011 Alcoholics Anonymous – Page 15.2
1012 DR. BOB and the Good Oldtimers – Page 77.1
1013 Came to Believe… – Page(s) – 46.6
1014 Alcoholics Anonymous – Page 491.2 – 4th Edition
1015 As Bill Sees It – Page 246.3-4
1016 The Language of the Heart – Page 8.5
1017 DR. BOB and the Good Oldtimers – Page 260.1
1018 Language of the Heart – Page 240.2
1019 Twelve Steps and Twelve Traditions – Page 116.3,4 – British Edition
1020 DR. BOB and the Good Oldtimers – Page 338.4
1021 Came to Believe… – Page(s) – 95.2
1022 Came to Believe… – Page(s) – 112.3

[1023] Alcoholics Anonymous – Pages xxvi-xxvii
[1024] Alcoholics Anonymous – Pages xx
[1025] Alcoholics Anonymous – Pages 562 – 4th Edition
[1026] Twelve Steps and Twelve Traditions – Page 113.2 – British Edition
[1027] DR. BOB and the Good Oldtimers – Page 190.6 – 191.1
[1028] DR. BOB and the Good Oldtimers – Page 192.8
[1029] Experience, Strength, & Hope – Page(s) 88.3
[1030] The Home Group: Heartbeat of AA – Page 23.3
[1031] Experience, Strength, & Hope – Page(s) 377.2
[1032] Experience, Strength, & Hope – Page(s) 341.4 – 342.2
[1033] Twelve Steps and Twelve Traditions – Page 113.3 – British Edition
[1034] Alcoholics Anonymous – Page 62.2
[1035] Alcoholics Anonymous – Page 58.3
[1036] Alcoholics Anonymous – Page 62.2
[1037] Alcoholics Anonymous – Page 15.3
[1038] Alcoholics Anonymous – Page 262.3 – 4th Edition
[1039] DR. BOB and the Good Oldtimers – Page 181.4
[1040] DR. BOB and the Good Oldtimers – Page 263.4
[1041] Alcoholics Anonymous – Page 262.6 – 4th Edition
[1042] DR. BOB and the Good Oldtimers – Page 113.6 – 114.1
[1043] DR. BOB and the Good Oldtimers – Page 334.1 – 2
[1044] Best of the Grapevine – Page(s) – 139.2
[1045] Alcoholics Anonymous – Page 58.2
[1046] Twelve Steps and Twelve Traditions – Page 113.3 – British Edition
[1047] Twelve Steps and Twelve Traditions – Page 114.1 – British Edition
[1048] Alcoholics Anonymous – Page 405.1 – 4th Edition
[1049] DR. BOB and the Good Oldtimers – Page 141.2
[1050] Alcoholics Anonymous – Page 419.3 – 4th Edition
[1051] DR. BOB and the Good Oldtimers – Page 141.2
[1052] Twelve Steps and Twelve Traditions – Page 117.4, 118.2 – British Edition
[1053] Came to Believe… – Page(s) – 103.4
[1054] As Bill Sees It – Page 94.1-3
[1055] Twelve Steps and Twelve Traditions – Page 119.3 – 120.1 – British Edition
[1056] DR. BOB and the Good Oldtimers – Page 250.3
[1057] Alcoholics Anonymous – Page 521.1 – 4th Edition
[1058] Alcoholics Anonymous – Page 14.7
[1059] James 2:15-17—The New English Bible—Oxford/Cambridge Edition
[1060] Alcoholics Anonymous – Page 276.4 – 4th Edition
[1061] Alcoholics Anonymous – Page 19.2
[1062] Alcoholics Anonymous – Page 133.1
[1063] Alcoholics Anonymous – Page 83.2
[1064] Alcoholics Anonymous – Page xx
[1065] Experience, Strength, & Hope – Page(s) 219.2
[1066] DR. BOB and the Good Oldtimers – Page 262.1,2
[1067] Experience, Strength, & Hope – Page(s) 289.2
[1068] As Bill Sees It – Page 169.1-2
[1069] Experience, Strength, & Hope – Page(s) 221.1
[1070] Best of the Grapevine – Page(s) – 180.5 – 181.1
[1071] Twelve Steps and Twelve Traditions – Page 9.3 – British Edition
[1072] Twelve Steps and Twelve Traditions – Page 95.3 – British Edition
[1073] Twelve Steps and Twelve Traditions – Pages 129.2 – British Edition
[1074] Experience, Strength, & Hope – Page(s) 296.4
[1075] Best of the Grapevine – Page(s) – 183.3
[1076] Alcoholics Anonymous – Page 77.1

[1077] Alcoholics Anonymous – Page 17.3
[1078] Came to Believe... – Page(s) – 99.5
[1079] Twelve Steps and Twelve Traditions – Page 15.2 – British Edition
[1080] Twelve Steps and Twelve Traditions – Page 15.3 – British Edition
[1081] Twelve Steps and Twelve Traditions – Page 16.4 – British Edition
[1082] Language of the Heart – Page 302.2
[1083] Pass It On—Bill Wilson and the AA Message – Page 128.1
[1084] Alcoholics Anonymous – Page 60.5
[1085] DR. BOB and the Good Oldtimers – Page 105.1
[1086] Alcoholics Anonymous – Page 60.1
[1087] Alcoholics Anonymous – Page 77.1
[1088] Came to Believe... – Page 64.6
[1089] Alcoholics Anonymous – Page 68.3
[1090] Alcoholics Anonymous – Page 88.1
[1091] Best of the Grapevine – Page(s) – 129.2,3, 130.1
[1092] Best of the Grapevine – Page(s) – 131.2 – 5
[1093] Best of the Grapevine – Page(s) – 132.2 – 133.1
[1094] Best of the Grapevine – Page(s) – 142.2
[1095] The Language of the Heart – Page 320.4
[1096] DR. BOB and the Good Oldtimers – Page 264.3 – 265.1
[1097] Alcoholics Anonymous – Page 565.4 – 4th Edition
[1098] As Bill Sees It – Page 241.1
[1099] The Language of the Heart – Page 14.5
[1100] DR. BOB and the Good Oldtimers – Page 265.4
[1101] Alcoholics Anonymous – Page 565.5 – 566.1 – 4th Edition
[1102] Alcoholics Anonymous – Page 253.3 – 4th Edition
[1103] Pass It On—Bill Wilson and the AA Message – Page 149.5 – 7
[1104] DR. BOB and the Good Oldtimers – Page 145.8 – 146.1
[1105] The Language of the Heart – Page 13.1
[1106] As Bill Sees It – Page 198.2
[1107] The Language of the Heart – Page 17.7
[1108] The Language of the Heart – Page 264.3
[1109] Experience, Strength, & Hope – Page(s) 202.2
[1110] The Language of the Heart – Page 261.3-4
[1111] Twelve Steps and Twelve Traditions – Page 68.2 – British Edition
[1112] The Home Group: Heartbeat of AA – Page 62.3
[1113] The Home Group: Heartbeat of AA – Page 64.3
[1114] The Home Group: Heartbeat of AA – Page 23.3
[1115] DR. BOB and the Good Oldtimers – Page 240.4
[1116] Alcoholics Anonymous – Page 450.2 – 4th Edition
[1117] Alcoholics Anonymous – Page 534.3 – 4th Edition
[1118] Experience, Strength, & Hope – Page(s) 253.1
[1119] Alcoholics Anonymous – Page 17.2
[1120] As Bill Sees It – Page 234.2-3
[1121] DR. BOB and the Good Oldtimers – Page 248.2
[1122] Alcoholics Anonymous – Page 17.3
[1123] DR. BOB and the Good Oldtimers – Page 241.6
[1124] The Language of the Heart – Page 294.3
[1125] The Home Group: Heartbeat of AA – Page 24.1-3
[1126] The Home Group: Heartbeat of AA – Page 26.4
[1127] DR. BOB and the Good Oldtimers – Page 84.5

Also available from ℋ𝒫Publishing:

Meditation CDs	USA	UK
– Prayer of St Francis of Assisi	$ 16.95	£ 7.95
– Forgiveness Meditation – (available soon)	$ 16.95	£ 7.95
– Life's an Ocean – (available soon)	$ 16.95	£ 7.95

Books		
– Deep Soul Cleansing (text) Hardcover	$ 43.95	£ 22.50
– Deep Soul Cleansing (text) Paperback	$ 26.95	£ 13.95
– Deep Soul Cleansing – Workbook Paperback	$ 44.50	£ 22.95
– Maintaining the Promises – Daily Hardcover	$ 55.95	£ 27.95
– Maintaining the Promises – Daily Paperback	$ 32.95	£ 19.50
– 366 Daily Prayers – Paperback	$ 24.95	£ 12.50
– Four Column Inventory Forms Only Paperback	$ 28.95	£ 14.50

Write for more information about upcoming Retreats and/or workshops or send your order to:

United Kingdom

ℋ𝒫Retreats

63 Shepherds Court
LONDON England
W12-8PW
44+ 208-740-8567
www.hpretreats.org

United States

ℋ𝒫Publishing

1701 The Greensway
Building 1425
Jacksonville Beach FL 32250
1+ 904-543-0608
www.hppublishing.com

Orders are best made via the internet do to our busy travel schedule.

CPSIA information can be obtained
at www.ICGtesting.com
Printed in the USA
BVHW040206170522
637221BV00006B/19